MW00629134

Port Republic:
The History of a
Shenandoah Valley River Town

Port Republic: The History of a Shenandoah Valley River Town

By

George Elliott May

Copyright © 2002 Society of Port Republic
Preservationists, Inc.

All rights reserved. No part of this book may be reproduced, stored in a retrieval system, or transmitted, in any
form or by any means, electronic, mechanical, photocopy-
ing, recording, or otherwise, without the written permission of the Society of Port Republic Preservationists, Inc.

Lot's Wife Publishing
P.O. Box 1844
Staunton, VA 24402

Library of Congress Catalog Card Number 2002113569
ISBN 0971937036

Contents

George E. May

Foreword

George Elliott May was born in Port Republic in 1869. He was raised and always lived there, and died in 1960 at the age of ninety. He was one of ten children, four of whom stayed in Port. My father was his youngest brother.

My sister Catherine May Adams recalls that every time she visited Uncle George in Port, he would be sitting on the front porch reading a book. George had a great love of books. He read constantly throughout his life, and he had an extensive library. My cousin Claybrook Elder recalls George having a complete set of the original publication of the Official Records of the Civil War. When George became old and began to lose his sight, he would ask his daughter, Virginia May Merrill, to go to a certain bookshelf, to remove a certain book and turn to a certain page, and to begin reading at a certain place. She would, and after a sentence or so, George would recite the next few pages. My father always said George had a wonderful mind. He obviously remembered a great deal of detail from his reading. My cousin Bobby May recalls Uncle George visiting his parents: "George always wore a white shirt, tie and cane, and brought me a lot of books. He would sit on the front porch and tell tales; he was full of tales, usually about the War Between the States and about Port Republic."

George was descended from the Adam May family of Port Republic. Adam May filed his bond to marry Elisabeth Bott on February 11, 1791, in the Augusta County Court. His descendants have lived in and around Port ever since then, and some remain today. However, George and his two brothers, who died in the 1950s, were the last of Adam's descendents named May to be full time-residents of Port. This family does not appear to be related to the Brock's Gap Mays of Rockingham County. No positive relationship has been proven despite the evidence that the two families appear to have come from Pennsylvania at about the same time, knew each other, used almost exactly the same names for their children, and may have acted as God-parents for the other family. George's father, James Henry May, was a Confederate soldier and active veteran, having served initially in Co. B, 10th Va. Inf., and later in the 6th Va. Cav., where he was shot in the groin, taken prisoner, and confined in Fort Delaware. This must be the basis for George's intense interest in the War Between the States.

George's primary occupation was woodworker and mill builder, but he was very interested in local history and spent much of his life researching and collecting information about Port, its history, and inhabitants. He drafted a manuscript of what he called "A History of Port Republic." The dates in the manuscript I have indicate his last revision was done in 1933. His attitudes and views reflect his Confederate heritage and the opinions of that era, and provide an interesting insight into the times after "The War." His daughter Virginia, now deceased, was very interested in getting this history published, both as a remembrance of her father and as being of interest to the community. I am very grateful to the Society of Port Republic Preservationists for undertaking this publication, and I hope this history will help the community preserve its old memories.

Harrison May

Notes from the Editor

In publishing this work, no attempt was made to "modernize" either the style or the period. May's handwritten scripts and notes were scoured to ensure the manuscript was accurately transcribed. Occasionally editor's notes are added for the sake of clarity.

A reader must remember that the writer's references to what he considers the "present time" actually refers to the period between 1920 and 1934. Terms that are considered politically incorrect in the twenty-first century were quite acceptable then. May refers to "colored people," which then was a term of respect. His references to "Negroes" are direct quotations from documents of the era.

To a modern reader, the author's style of writing may seem at times archaic or verbose, yet it reflects the style of his times. His writing appears subjective, often editorial; his opinions should not be considered the viewpoints of the Society. Nevertheless, both the subject and style of writing provide insight to the character of the writer, himself, as well as to the character of the community he loved.

For several decades George May dug into books, libraries, attics, and trunks, searching for details that would tell the story of Port Republic. He conducted many hours of interviews with the elder residents and endless correspondence with anyone suspected of having first-source material. His huge collection of documents, notes, letters, and photographs represents the "preservation" of much of this little town's history. Several writers and historians have used this information in recent publications.

Among the boxes of papers, research materials, and

notes was found an autobiographical sketch in May's handwriting. In it, he says:

Have written many articles, some controversial, for newspapers in the State. Have had extended correspondence with British Army officers on the American Civil War. Have prepared and read to schools papers on subjects as wide apart as the "Battle of Port Republic" and "What to Read".

I collected, for many years, materials for a history of this town, and not finding any one who would do the writing I did it myself and now have in manuscript "A History of Port Republic and Environs" which I shall have published at a more convenient time. I spared myself no pains, time, or money to collect every bit of information on the subject I had read or heard of, buying, borrowing, copying, or having copied as I found I must.[1]

Anita Cummins

[1]George E. May's sketch is written on hotel stationery from the (Fireproof) Selwyn Hotel in Charlotte, N.C., which advertises "rooms without bath $1.50, rooms with bath $2.00, $2.50, $3.00."

Acknowledgments

The Society expresses its gratitude to the late Virginia May Merrill, the daughter of George May who entrusted the Society with his manuscripts and research materials, along with a generous trust fund which helped make this publication possible.

We thank Harrison May, George May's nephew, who supported this publication and permitted the use of the most recent draft of the manuscript. We appreciate as well that he served as our "special consultant."

We are indebted as well to Miss Mattie Meyerhoeffer, deceased, who first made and circulated photocopies of an early draft of the manuscript; although it was incomplete and unedited, it has provided helpful information. We appreciate the work of Lois Emswiler who first transcribed that draft to computer disks.

We are very appreciative of the patience and expertise of our publishing consultants, Lot's Wife Publishing of Staunton, Virginia, particularly Barbara Corse, Sue Simmons, Nancy Sorrells, and Dorothy A. Boyd-Rush. Thanks also go to Steve Zapton, Art Director and Design Consultant for the project and Cheryl Lyon for her work on the cover graphics and the map. Most importantly, this project could not have occurred without the endless hours of patient editing and research of Anita Cummins.

All photographs are from the files of the Society of Port Republic Preservationists, housed in the Port Republic Museum, and are not to be reproduced without express permission of the Society.

The Society of Port Republic Preservationists, Inc.

Chapter 1

Port Republic: Where the Shenandoah River Begins

When East Rockingham, in all her pristine beauty, looked up and smiled into the surprised and delighted eyes of the Knights of the Golden Horseshoe as they gazed down upon her from the summit of the Blue Ridge, she knew that no longer would the feet of the Red Man alone press the verdant turf on her many hills and in her numerous dales. At the foot of the mountains rolled the "Daughter of the Stars," the south fork of the Shenandoah River, whose head lay a score of miles to the southwest. Between North and South Rivers, at whose confluence begins the stream famed in song and history, lay the site of the town with which this story has to do.

The northern and southern Indians used the Valley of Virginia as their most convenient route to get at each other in their numerous wars. The Delawares of the north would leap like famished wolves from the southwest end of it upon the Catawbas, and would kill and scalp and carry off captives and goods to their distant home. Sometimes before reaching home and safety they would be overtaken by the pursuing Catawbas and every one of them would be destroyed. Many of their battles occurred in the Shenandoah Valley. In these fights no mercy was shown, few lives were spared, and these for future torture.

When Governor Spotswood came to the Shenandoah Valley in 1716, it was, in all probability, inhabited by the

Shawnee Indians. If not inhabited by them as a whole, they had their principal villages on the east side of the Allegheny Mountains, not far from the present town of Winchester. Some of their tribes were settled on the Ohio River; others about the forks of the Delaware. They were a fierce and warlike people. Holding all other men in contempt as warriors, they boasted of their many bloody exploits, claiming that they had killed ten times as many of the white intruders as any other tribe of their red brothers did.

The Tuscaroras had their villages near present Martinsburg, W.Va., and there may have been some Cherokees south of James River.

The Senedos were on the North Fork of the Shenandoah River in what is now Shenandoah County. They were exterminated in 1732 by Southern Indians. Very small units of other tribes may have been scattered through the Valley.

The Indians frequently came to what is now East Rockingham to fish and hunt. War, hunting, and fishing were their principal pursuits.

Vast quantities of chipped flint and imperfect arrowheads are found on the left bank of North River where Mill Creek flows into it, and at the home of John F. Wagner opposite to Port Republic on the right bank of South River. This abundance indicates that the Indians manufactured their implements of war in this vicinity. No flint of the kind used in making these weapons is found in this part of the country. There is no doubt but that it was carried here by the Indians who, after a successful hunt, settled down to the manufacturing of arrowheads, spearheads, and tomahawks necessary to their existence. The flint is usually found in caves in the form of nodules. These are pure flint at their centers. When disengaged of their stony exteriors, they were heated, and by dropping cold water upon them, flakes suitable for the purposes of the Indians split off.

2

Here, then, they warred; and in their more pacific visits, when they came to hunt and fish and to manufacture arms, they also wooed and mated. An Indian maiden sat upon the grassy bank of the Shenandoah River iridescent with dreams of her future life. The sycamore murmured above her and the weeping willow sighed at her back. A tall lithe brave sought and found her.

The larger animals of the Valley whose flesh was used as food were the buffalo, elk, deer, and bear. There were many fur-bearing animals, including the beaver and otter. Huckleberries, grapes, and persimmons grew abundantly. There were many kinds of nuts, such as chestnuts, chinquapins, acorns, and walnuts. Turkeys, geese, ducks, partridges, and other wild fowls fit for food were plentiful in season. The rivers teemed with fish.

It is reasonably clear to the writer that the site of present Port Republic was included in Jacob Stover's "Upper Patent" of 5,000 acres, confirmed to him by deed bearing the date of Dec. 15, 1733, or in the grant of 60,000 acres which adjoined Stover's patent on the south and were obtained by John Tayloe, Thomas Lee, and William Beverley, Oct 28, 1734, which adjoined Stover's patent on the south. Stover had obtained a grant for 10,000 acres of land on the Shenandoah River from the Virginia Colonial Council June 17, 1730. The condition imposed was that he should import a certain number of families to settle on his grant within two years. He selected two tracts of land each containing 5,000 acres. The deed of 1733 confirming the upper grant to him recites that he had met the conditions imposed by importing and settling on the grant 100 persons. The deed gives the names of 101 persons. The family names and numbers of each were: Miller 15; Mire 29; Sowder 23; Hain 18; Funk 16. At this distance of time, the metes and bounds are not certain. Those who have studied these patents have arrived at dif-

3

ferent conclusions. A letter of inquiry to Charles E. Kemper of Staunton, a tireless investigator of colonial Virginia patents, elicited the following information:

Port Republic is in Stover's upper grant. The line went up South River to a point nearly opposite to Weyers Cave, thence in a north line taking in Madison Hall to the Muddy Mill Creek, thence up Mill creek to about the Pirkey Graveyard on the Keezletown Road about half-mile from my birthplace, now the Herring place. The north line stopped about a quarter of a mile above it, crossing Mill Creek on the Keezletown Road. Stover's mill was on Mill Creek close to old Alexander Kyger's old mill place.

Jacob Stover died near the end of 1740, involved in financial difficulties. His son Jacob Jr., with Henry Downs and Jacob Castle, gave bonds for administering the estate on March 22, 1741. Probably it was at this time that Downs decided to buy the tract of land lying between North and South Rivers at their confluence. Mr. Kemper continues:

Henry Downs had a survey recorded of the land you wrote to know about. This appears in Survey Book No. 1, County Surveyor's Office, Augusta County, Va.
Probably the patent did not issue because this land was included in the Stover patent.
But in 1745 or 1746 Henry Downs built a mill on South River in or near Port Republic, which shows that he was then settled here. He was a native of Orange County, Va.

In Thomas Lewis's "Journal" it appears that the surveyors of the Fairfax line rendezvoused at Captain Downs' place in Orange County. But there is no doubt that the Captain had his home at that time in present Port Republic.

That Mr. Kemper is right in locating the southern boundary of Stover's upper patent at Weyers Cave (now

Grand Caverns) is proven by the fact that this locality (and it alone) has all the topographical features mentioned in the patent. The line ran "to the foot of a Naked Mountain at the upper end of a Large Island in the River." Cave Hill (Weyers Cave) admirably fills the description of "a Naked Mountain", and is on the left bank of South River. The "Large Island" referred to in the patent is, in all likelihood, the "Big Island" in South River below Weyers Cave mentioned in a deed for land made by Charles W. Carthrae to George W. Kemper, Feb. 10, 1822.

Some writers believe that Jones' Island in the Shenandoah River about a mile below its forks is the southern limit of Stover's upper patent. But there is no "Naked Mountain" or other kind on or near the banks of the river at this island. From Jones' Island to where Mill Creek flows into North River is about two miles. This creek was in Stover's upper patent and he built a mill on it not far from its mouth. It is described as "Stover's Mill Creek" in a crown patent for 200 acres lying on the creek made to William Downs, March 5, 1747.

In the length of the Shenandoah River no more beautiful spot could have been found for a pioneer to build his cabin and settle for life than the one Captain Downs chose. On his trips exploring the Valley he was not overly careful of the religious susceptibilities of the inhabitants of his native county, for he was presented by the Grand Jury of Orange County on Nov. 27, 1740, "for Sabbath-breaking by travelling with loaded horses to Sharrendo."

Adam Miller and William Purce were ordered by the county court of Augusta in 1745, to "view and mark a way from the top of the Blew (Blue) Ridge at the head of Swift Run Gap to Capt. Downs place." This is one of the oldest roads in East Rockingham, and there is no doubt that it was the first road to run to the site of future Port Republic. It is on the east side of Shenandoah River and known as the Swift Run Gap Road. It is now sometimes called the Mountain Road. This road figured largely in the strategies of General Thomas J. "Stonewall" Jackson and Union General James Shields in Jackson's Shenandoah Valley Campaign.

At an early period in the history of the town, a road from Staunton connected with the one from Swift Run Gap, the two making a continuous road for forty miles or more. Most likely, a path led from the home of Captain Downs to Madison Gap in the Blue Ridge Mountains, now called Brown's Gap, but the main trail across the Valley led past the Peaked Mountain and on to the gap. Mr. Kemper says that the Cross Keys and Port Republic Road was established in 1746.

Chapter 2

Colonial Settlers

Christopher Francisco, Sr., of Lancaster County, Pennsylvania, bought 3,100 acres of land of Jacob Stover, the deed bearing date of June 25, 1740. This tract of land was on the Shenandoah River and about two miles below its head.

William Downs obtained a grant of 200 acres of land on "the north side of Shanando River" from George II in 1747. This tract included the mouth of Mill Creek, but lay mostly on the western side of that stream. One of the considerations of the grant was the "Importation of three persons to dwell within this our said Colony and Dominion whose names are John Blower, Mary Blower, and Jane Blower." Upstream, this tract of land cornered "at a black oak near the land of William Lamb." Henry Null acquired this property in 1751. It has remained in the possession of the Null family to the present time.

Between the Null property and the Shenandoah, at a somewhat later time, tracts of land were owned by John Pirkey, John Weaver, Richard Austin, John Miltenbargar, George W. Burton, and a Mr. Yount. On the bluff opposite Port Republic, Robert Scott patented a tract of land in 1756. This property passed into the possession of William Lewis at a later date.

John Madison was appointed Clerk of Augusta County by a "commission under the hand and seal of Thomas Nelson, Secretary of Virginia" on Oct. 30, 1745. He was the first to fill the position and at the time of his appointment

Madison Hall

he was living in a cabin on the north branch of Christian's Creek, about six miles south of Staunton and not far from the present village of Barterbrook. In this cabin was born his distinguished son, the Rt. Rev. James Madison, D.D., Aug. 27, 1749.

In 1751, John Madison moved to a tract of land lying at the southwest end of the town of Port Republic and there, on elevated ground affording a fine view of the surrounding country, built his residence, which he named Madison Hall. The loghouse in which he kept the county records was torn down not many years ago. No marker was placed to indicate the spot where it had stood.

John Madison was a man of courage and affairs. The management of his large estate, the care of his young family, the duties of his office, while often fretted with alarms of Indians, were enough to wear down an iron constitution and weaken the strongest will.

His home was in an exposed locality and rather invited an attack from hostile Indians. To offset this danger, he built a fort in 1755, naming it Fort Drummond, as a protection for his loved ones and neighbors against Indian forays.

The Indians of the Valley had been uniformly friendly with the white settlers up to the beginning of the French and Indian War, 1754-1763. Indian confederates of the

French from west of the Allegheny Mountains visited their red brothers in the Valley and had many powwows with them. According to Samuel Kercheval:

In the year 1753, emissaries from the Western Indians, came among the Valley Indians, inviting them to cross the Allegheny Mountains, and in the spring of the year 1754, the Indians suddenly and unexpectedly moved off, and entirely left the Valley.

That this movement of the Indians was made under the influence of the French, there is but little doubt.[1]

The French were preparing for war, and had drawn many northern and western tribes into alliance with them.

This ominous abandonment of their homes should have awakened the most lively apprehension in the minds of the settlers. But not until the defeat of General Braddock, did the Indians fall upon the settlers with fury and flame, with tomahawk and scalping knife, and with the more modern arms unwisely put in their hands by both the French and English. Scarooyadi, a Delaware chief, speaking to the Governor of Pennsylvania about Braddock and his army said, "They are unfit to fight in the woods. Let us go ourselves — we that came out of this ground."

So John Madison built himself a fort. It stood at the east corner of the front yard of Madison Hall, and some of its foundation stones may yet be seen. As illustrative of these times of hardships and alarms, the following extract from President Madison's biography, containing part of a letter written by John Madison, Aug. 19, 1755, to his cousin Col. James Madison of Orange County, is given:

Among the papers of President Madison is a letter addressed to his father in 1753 (1755) by John Madison, the pioneer of the western branch of the family, who had then recently established himself in the transmontane region of Virginia. It presents so lively a picture of the dangers, distresses, and hardships of our ancestors who first occupied that portion of the State, and of the mingled bravery and tenderness, resignation and magnanimity, which they displayed in their trials, that some passages of it are here inserted, as belonging, of right, to the domain of history. From familiarity with danger, the intrepidity of the writer seems sometimes to turn almost to recklessness.

Four families, on their flight from a branch of New River, this minute passed my house, who say that five men were murdered at the house of Ephraim Voss on Roanoke since the death of Col. Patton. 'Tis shocking to think of the calamity of the poor wretches who lived on the Holston and New rivers, who for upwards of a hundred miles have left their habitations, lost their crops and vast numbers of their stock. Could you see, dear friend, the women who escaped crying after their murdered husbands, with their helpless children hanging on them, it could but wound your very soul.

As the Governor has been pleased to appoint Captain Andrew Lewis the Lieutenant of this county, I expect I shall see his instructions at court. Perhaps he may fall upon some measures to put a stop to the inroads of those barbarians, without giving the people below the trouble of marching over; of which I will write you by Mr. Semple.

I am extremely obliged to all my good friends for the guns sent. Pray tell them they shall all be carefully returned, as soon as I can be otherwise provided. I am also much obliged to you for your kind invitation, and much to my good aunt for the concern she expressed to Mr. Johnston for our welfare. But when I consider what a train I have, I cannot think of being so troublesome. Besides, should I lose my all with my life, I think my children had as well go hence, whilst in a state of innocency.

I am with the greatest esteem,
Your affectionate kinsman,
Jno. Madison[2]

In a postscript, after reciting some further outrages of the Indians, he concludes with the following characteristic passage:

I verily believe they (the Indians) are determined on our destruction. However, as they come in small parties, if they will be so kind as to stay till I have finished my fort, may Heaven send me a few of them. Perhaps I may defray all expenses.

Farewell.

That the white settlers were equal, man to man, to the Indians in small parties, may be taken for granted; but of large bodies another story is told: "When large bodies of the red men and white borders were pitted against each other, the former were if anything the more likely to have the advantage.[3]

The settlers were a hardy people. Their exposed situation made them liable to attacks by the Indians. This danger bred in them the habits of caution and vigilance. No one went far from home without taking his trusty rifle with him. Francis Parkman's celebrated description of the Virginian frontiersman vividly depicts his characteristics:

The advancing frontiers of American civilization have always nurtured a class of men of striking and peculiar character. The best examples of this character have, perhaps, been found among the settlers of Western Virginia, and the hardy progeny who have sprung from that generous stock. The Virginian frontiersman was, as occasion called, a farmer, a hunter, and a warrior by turns. The well-beloved rifle was seldom out of his hands; and he never deigned to lay aside the fringed frock, moccasins, and Indian leggins, which formed the appropriate costume of the forest ranger. Concerning the business, pleasures, and refinements of cultivated life, he knew little, and cared nothing; and his manners were usually rough and obtrusive to the last degree. Aloof from mankind, he lived in a world of his own, which, in his view, contained all that was deserving of admiration and praise. He looked upon himself and his compeers as models of prowess and manhood, nay, of all that is elegant and polite; and the forest gallant regarded with peculiar complacency his own half-savage dress, his swaggering gate, and his backwoods jargon. He was willful, headstrong, and quarrelsome; frank, straightforward and generous; brave at the bravest, and utterly intolerant of arbitrary control. His self-confidence mounted to audacity. Eminently capable of heroism, both in action and endurance, he viewed every species of effeminacy with supreme contempt; and, accustomed as he was to entire self-reliance, the mutual dependence of conventional life excited his especial scorn. With all his ignorance, he had a mind by nature quick, vigorous, and penetrating; and all his mode of life, while it developed the daring energy of his character, wrought some of his faculties to a high degree of acuteness. Many of his traits have been reproduced in his offspring. From him have sprung those hardy men whose struggles and sufferings on the bloody ground of Kentucky will always form a striking page in American history; and that band of adventurers before whose headlong charge, in the valley of Chihuahua, neither breastworks, nor batteries, nor fivefold odds could avail for a moment.[4]

Due to the infirmities of old age, John Madison resigned the clerkship of the county court Nov. 17, 1778. His son Richard followed him in that position. Richard Madison died in February 1785.

John Madison's wife was a Miss Strother, of Stafford County. Their distinguished son, James, the future first Episcopal Bishop of Virginia, was educated at William and Mary College, and afterwards studied law. He soon tired of his profession and studied theology, which was more to his liking. He became Professor of Mathematics at William and Mary College in 1773, and its president in 1777. He went to England and was inducted into the ministry of the Anglican Church by the Bishop of London. He was elected bishop by the first Convention of the Episcopal Church in Virginia in 1785, and presided at the meetings. Five years later, he was formally consecrated in the Chapel of Lambeth, London, by the Archbishop of Canterbury. The Episcopal Church found itself much weakened at the close of the War of the Revolution. It had been an established church in several of the colonies and was much hated for that reason. It took men such as Bishop Madison to reinstate it in the estimation of the people. The University of Pennsylvania conferred the degree of Doctor of Divinity upon him in 1785. He had a son and a daughter, James C. of Roanoke County, and Mrs. Robert G. Scott of Richmond. Madison died in 1812.

Not far from the home of John Madison, down the Shenandoah River, lived Gabriel Jones, the lawyer, and Thomas Lewis, the surveyor. These three men had married sisters.[5] The place where Jones lived is known as Bogota; Lewis's home is now called Lynnwood.

Gabriel Jones was of Welsh descent and was born near Williamsburg, May 17, 1724. He was educated in London, studied law and was admitted to the bar. Returning to Virginia, the County Court of Augusta, at the April term, 1746, recommended him, on the declination of the office of prosecuting attorney by John Nicholas, "as a fit person to transact his majesty's affairs in this county." He received the appointment and was qualified at the following court. When the new county of Rockingham was organized in 1778, he was appointed deputy attorney. He resigned in 1795 and was followed in office by David Holmes. Mr. Jones bought the Bogota farm from the Franciscos in 1751. He died there in October, 1806.

Thomas Lewis, eldest son of John Lewis, the pioneer, was commissioned Surveyor of Augusta County by "William Dawson, president, and the master of the College of Wm & Mary," Oct. 30, 1745. He was appointed the first surveyor of Rockingham County, April 27, 1778. He was born in 1718, settled at Lynnwood in 1754, and died in 1790. The house in which he lived at Lynnwood is still standing.

How many persons lived in the neighborhood of the Madisons, there is very little information at hand to show. However, Joseph and Thomas Hanna were living on or near the present Augusta County line at LeRoy in 1784 or 1788, and well into the next century. When Rockingham was cut off from Augusta in 1777, the Act directs that the line separating the two counties shall run by Benjamin Yardley's plantation so as to strike the North River below James Byrd's house, etc. The Yardley plantation became the Mohler homestead near LeRoy. The names of some other persons who owned land in the vicinity in those early days are James Craig, James Beard, and Robert Craig in the Mt. Meridian section; Mathias Doubt, John Machall, James Raines, Henry Mace, and Adam May east of South River and in Brown's Gap. Robert Scott obtained a patent for land on the far side of North River, Aug. 16, 1756.

At the coming of the Carthreas, the dimness somewhat lifts from the scene, and the names of a number of the settlers who located in the vicinity near the end of the eighteenth century emerge.[6]

John Carthrea, Jr., married Sophia Lewis, Sept. 24, 1792. His father resided at Madison Hall, and whether John Jr. made his home at his father's or lived elsewhere, is not certain. It would appear, for reasons given later, that John Carthrea, Sr. married a Miss Brown, of Brown's Cove, which is just across the Blue Ridge Mountains from Port Republic.

On March 26, 1781, Daniel Fisher bought 140 acres lying on North River a short distance from where it unites with South River, of John Carthrea, Sr., for which he paid $1575.00. The lower corner of this tract was on the bank of the river "opposite to Henry Downies Mill," which definitely locates Captain Downs' mill on the north bank of the river. The upstream corner of this tract was opposite the land of Robert Scott, also on the north side of the river. It

Lynnwood: Shows an 18th century addition to the original Thomas Lewis home.

was patented by Patrick Frazer, June 20, 1749, and included Belle View, the home of the late J. Jefferson Nicholas.[7]

On Sept. 6, 1798, the Commonwealth of Virginia conveyed to John Whitmore by patent 225 acres lying "Between the South Branch of Shenandoah & South Mountain." This tract was in the present Grottoes section.[8]

Chapter Two Endnotes

[1]Samuel Kercheval, *History of the Valley of Virginia*, 3rd edition, (Woodstock, Va.: J.H. Graybill, 1902), 65.
[2]William C. Rives, *History of the Life and Times of James Madison*, vol. 1, (Boston: Little, Brown and Co., 1899), 5-7.
[3]Theodore Roosevelt, *The Winning of the West*, Presidential edition, (New York: G.P. Putnam's Sons, 1889), 126-127.
[4]Francis Parksman, *The Conspiracy of Pontiac*, 2 vols., (Boston: Brown, Little, and Co., 1880), 81-82.
[5]Jones and Lewis married Margaret and Jane Strother, respectively.
[6]It is important to note that Carthrea's name appears in various official documents spelled Carthrea, Carthrae, McCarthrey, Carthrey.
[7] Rockingham County, Virginia, Deed Book 0:73. Most of the deed books cited in this book can be found in the Rockingham County burnt records.
[8]Deed Book, 0000:314.

Chapter 3

The Frontier Town
Takes Shape

In a deed conveying a small tract of land to John Dundore
by John Carthrea, Jr., and his wife Sophia, April 2, 1816,
it is recited that the property is a part of a larger tract
deeded to him by his father, John Carthrea, Sr., Feb. 24, 1801.
This larger tract included the site of Port Republic.

Viewing the beautiful and extensive open stretch of
land, having few if any inequalities of surface, lying between North and South Rivers at the head of the South Fork
of the Shenandoah River, with a tableland in the rear quickly
rising to the height of about twenty feet. Viewing this property, John Carthrea, Jr., foresaw a prosperous town rising
from this ground, and decided to lay the foundations for
its beginning at once. What success attended his efforts the
following paragraph, taken from an Act of the Assembly
passed Jan. 14, 1802 shows:

Be it enacted by the general assembly, that twenty-three acres
of land, the property of John McCarthrey, junior, lying between
the north and south branches of the south fork of Shenandoah
river in the county of Rockingham, shall be, and they are
hereby vested in George Gilmer, Benjamin Lewis, Matthias
Aman, John Givens, and Henry Pirkey, gentlemen trustees, to
be by them, or a majority of them, laid off into lots of half an
acre each, with convenient streets, and established a town by
the name of Port Republic.

A note on a copy of the original plat of the town informs:

Pursuant to an Act of the General Assembly of Virginia entitled an Act for Establishing Towns passed the 14th of Jan. 1802 We the trustees therein named or a majority of them accordingly met on the 29th day of August 1805 on the land mentioned in the said Act and being assisted by George Huston, a surveyor, did lay off said twenty acres of land the property of John Carthrea Jr. into lots of half an acre each with convenient streets and is represented in the plat and numbered. Given from under our hands Benjamin Lewis, John Givens, Henry Pirkey, Mathias Amon.

The original town was composed of twenty-eight half-acre lots. It lay parallel to South River and its lower end rested on the bank of North River. The side of the town lying along South River was bounded by Southeast Alley, and the other side by Northwest Alley. At a later date, the county road, crossing North River Bridge into the town, forked at the end of the bridge, and, the left fork, hugging the bank, crossed South River at The Point, and connected with the Browns Gap Pike and Swift Run Gap Road. Two lots lay between this road and the first cross alley. The streets and alleys are named and described in the following note taken from the plat:

Main Street course S. 63 W. and 60 feet wide. N.W. Alley 20 feet wide. S.E. Alley 20 feet wide. Pleasant Alley 14 feet wide. Water Street 50 feet wide. Comfortable Alley 14 feet wide. Chestnut Street 50 feet wide. Agreeable Alley 14 feet wide. High Street 50 feet wide. Upper Alley 14 feet wide.

According to a United States Government survey in 1930, the elevation of the town is 1062.98 feet.

John Carthrea, Sr., almost doubled the size of the town by having twenty-four lots surveyed and added to it. This section of the town is called the Carthrea Addition. This

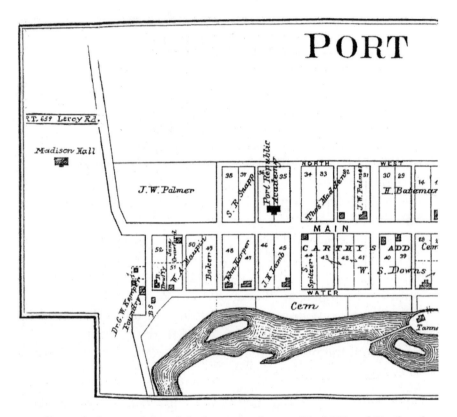

Shows the layout of the original town as chartered in 1802 and Carthrae's Addition the next year; lots are labeled with owners or uses in the year 1885. Based on a map from Lake's Atlas, 1885.

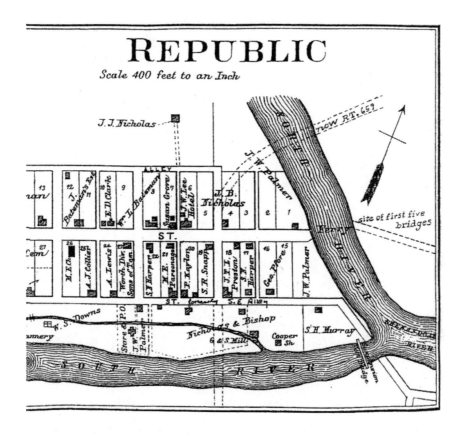

REPUBLIC

Scale 400 feet to an Inch

addition was made at an early date, for Mr. Carthrea was selling lots situated in it the following January after the original town was laid out.

There is little doubt but what Southeast Alley was at that time, or shortly after became, a section of a county road. It certainly soon lost its original name, was widened, and by common, if tacit consent, the name of Water Street was transferred to it. Verbally and in legal papers, it has been called by this name for over a century. So a suitable name should be given to the original Water Street.[1] When that paragon of chivalry, Gen. Turner Ashby, was killed near Harrisonburg in the War Between the States, he was brought to Port Republic and laid out in a large house standing on the corner of this street and Southeast Alley. Old Water Street could have no better name than Ashby Street.

In 1928, P.B.F. Good, the county surveyor, surveyed several lots in the town for the writer, and it was found that Chestnut Street is between two and three feet wider than it is marked on the plat of the town. Measurements were made from old established points on both sides of it, but for some unknown reason it is wider than the other cross streets.

There are two old abandoned graveyards in the town. One lies just above the milldam on South River, and the other is on the east side of Main Street about midway of its length. Neither ever had a name. In this writing they will be referred to as Riverside Graveyard and Central Graveyard respectively.

The lots of the original town were to be sold at public auction. Improvements to the extent of "a dwelling house 16′ x 16′ at the least, with a brick or stone chimney to be fit for habitation within ten years from Nov. 29 last past," that is Nov. 29, 1805.

The names of some of the purchasers of lots were preserved from oblivion when a number of deeds were saved from the torch Gen. David Hunter had applied to them near Port Republic, June 4, 1864.

On Dec. 17, 1805, the trustees of the town deeded to:

Jacob Christ, lot No.__. It was bounded on one end by Northwest Alley. There is nothing further in what remains of the deed to identify it. Lot No. 12 also was deeded to him.
John Carthrea, Jr., lot No. 13. Lot No. 27 is mentioned in the remaining fragment of this deed.
James Patterson, lots Nos. 10, 24, and one the number of which is burned off the deed. He paid $200 for No. 10.
Hugh Connell, lot No. 15.
Robert Branham, lot No. 22. Cost $200.
Margaret Bowyer, lot No. 16.
Tobias McGahey, lot No. 14. Paid $151 for it.
Robert Hughs, lot No. 23. Paid $200 for it.
William Beard, lot No.__. Cost $1000. The deed is fragmentary.
John McCullock, lots Nos. 7 and 8. Paid $170 for lot No. 8.
Julius Foster, lot No. 5. Cost $200.
John Brockenbrough, lot No.__ Cost $400. The deed is partly burnt and the number is destroyed.
Robert Henderson, lot No. 2. Cost $250.
John Carthrea, Jr., lot No.__. Cost $1000. It adjoined Pleasant Alley on one side. Deed burned in part and many lacunae in what remains. But as Robert Henderson bought lot No. 2, and Margaret Bowyer bought lot No. 16, the lot Carthrea bought was either No. 3 or No. 17. These four lots adjoined Pleasant Alley.
Joseph Graham, lot No.__. Comfortable Alley and Northwest Alley are mentioned as partly bounding it. It was lot No. 6.
John Boyd, lot No. 4. Cost $200.
George Ruteledge, lot No.__. Cost $500. Number lost[2]

Lots in Carthrea's Addition were being sold at this time. John Carthrea, Jr., on Sept. 17, 1805, deeded to William Harper a half-acre lot, price $150. The number of the lot is not given in the deed, but it is known that it was No. 47. Perhaps the lots in the Addition had not yet been numbered.[3] On the same day, Mr. Carthrea deeded a half-acre lot to Holland Furgason, for which he paid $150.[4] Thomas Givens received a deed for lots No. 45 and 46, dated Jan. 21, 1806, from Carthrea.

Small parcels of land lying just without the limits of the town were sold, as a half acre situated between Water Street and the mill race, which was deeded to Phillip Dold; and a smaller parcel, containing seven poles and nine feet, lying on South river, which was deeded to William Mills; in both cases the purchasers paying $150 for the land, and the deeds bearing the date Sept. 17, 1805.[5]

The town now entered on its first boom. Hither came the Harpers, the Kempers, and Crawfords; the Browns, the Trouts, and Mays; the Ryans, the McCanns and O'Brians; and many others who became permanent residents.

These men were strong of brain and brawn; optimistic and venturesome; industrious, frugal, persevering; with good will towards one another, and determined to succeed in their several undertakings. They built comfortable houses, the most of them were of hewn logs, and necessary outbuildings. Their garden spots were of the richest soil, and produced a variety of vegetables and fruits in season. Each family had a cow and raised hogs; had a flock of chickens, and some had ducks and geese. They worked hard, ate heartily, and slept soundly. They had abundant good spirits and enjoyed life. They met on a common footing — they were free and equal. They were given to thought and were fine conversationalists. Few books were in the neighborhood, but these were well thumbed. The Bible was found in every home and was much read and studied. These men were "mighty in the Scriptures," which being in the classic English of Shakespeare, quickened their literary taste. Some of them used tobacco and all enjoyed a drink of whiskey. They were truthful, honest, and hospitable. Their likes are not found among us today. So here they lived, labored, loved, married, and died, leaving sons and daughters to perpetuate their names and families.

At the beginning of the eighteenth century William Lewis was in possession of the Robert Scott estate lying on North River opposite Port Republic, and between the farm of Robert Hooke and the Shenandoah River. February 18, 1802, Mr. Lewis conveyed by deed to Gideon Morgan, of Albemarle County, the right to take water across his land for a mill on the west bank of the Shenandoah River a few hundred yards below its head. Vestiges of the race dug to convey water to the mill may yet be seen, but it seems that the mill was never built.[6]

A sawmill, however, was built a few years later in partnership by Morgan and Lewis on the north bank of North River near the town of New Haven. Its mudsills could be seen as late as 1900.[7]

New Haven was established a town by an Act of Assembly in January, 1804, on the land of William Lewis and Gidon Morgan. Edwin Nicholas, Asher Waterman, George Huston, George Gilmore, Mathias Amon, Benjamin Lewis, Henry Pirkey, and Henry J. Gambill were appointed as trustees. The principal street of the town was named Washington Street. There were more town lots in Port Republic. But the town did not prosper. The writer can remember but five houses strung along Washington Street.

Chapter Three Endnotes

[1]The original Water Street is now Port Republic Road, Route 659. What is now called Water Street was originally Southeast Alley.
[2]Deed Book 1:21-39.
[3]Deed Book, 000:293.

[4]Ibid., 292.
[5]Deed Book, 000:289, 294.
[6]Even those vestiges can hardly be seen since the recent flood of 1985.
[7]Lyman Chalkley, *Chronicles of The Scotch-Irish Settlement in Virginia Extracted From the Original Court Records of Augusta County, 1745-1800*, vol. 2, (Rosslyn, Va.: Commonwealth Printers, 1912), 247.

Chapter 4

The Death of a Boy
and His Dog

There were Carthreas living in the town and neighborhood until near the middle of the past century.
When the writer was a child he heard old persons
tell of the death of Lowrie Carthrea and his dog. It seems
that one of the Carthreas married a Miss Brown, of Brown's
Cove, which lies east of Port Republic near the top of the
Blue Ridge. Lowrie was their son and he had a dog of which
he was passionately fond.

One of Lowrie's maternal uncles frequently visited at
his father's home and showed a strong liking for Lowrie
and his dog. This uncle was subject to sudden attacks of
insanity. At his home, he spent much of his time hunting
deer, bears, and other game. He understood well the habits
of deer and how to conceal himself at a deer stand and lie
in wait till the unsuspecting animal came within easy rifle
shot when its death was certain.

Just above the present town of Grottoes, there was a
spot in South River where the water was very deep, which
was a watering place on a deer run. It was called the Blue
Hole, and was well known as the best deer stand in the
vicinity. To this place the uncle took the boy and dog on a
chance of killing a deer. Perhaps the feel of a deadly weapon
in his hands, or the thought of smoking blood and the
groans of a dying animal upset him; certain it is that insanity lowered upon him, and while his mind was thus dark-

25

ened he cut off the heads of the boy and dog, and placing the bodies side by side on the ground, he put the head of the boy to the carcass of the dog and the dog's head to the corpse of the boy.

When Wilson C. Harper, at present the oldest inhabitant of the town, was a young man, he stayed overnight at the home of Jefferson Brown, of Brown's Cove, who told him the sad story in all its harrowing details.

The Carthreas had a private graveyard near the north end of their home, Madison Hall, in which their dead were buried in a single row. Grapevines are now growing on the spot.

Chapter 5

Early Residents and Their Homes

From the foundation of the town to the War of 1812, the people were engaged in building their homes and establishing their businesses.

There is at hand an old account book that was certainly the property of Reuben Wallace and James Burgess. They were partners in business. The top of the first page is torn off, but the index shows that it carried the name of Reuben Wallace. What remains of the page gives the amount of money he subscribed to the partnership, which is the same amount subscribed by James Burgess, whose name and the amount he subscribed are on the opposite page.

Entries begin in 1802 and continue to 1806. What is called "an old account" with William Smith on page 150, is dated March 18, 1798. The names of so many persons who lived in Harrisonburg in its early days appear on the pages of this book, as to indicate that town as the seat of their business. Wallace and Burgess bought 591 acres of land of Asher Watermann, Sept. 23, 1806, and on November 21, of the same year, Burgess conveyed to "Joseph Flick in trust to secure a debt due John Graham," a certain house and lot in Harrisonburg.[1]

James Burgess was one of the trustees of the Methodist Church at Port Republic to which group a parcel of land was deeded in 1793, for the purpose of a graveyard and a site for a church building. He married Mary Beard, March 20, 1794, and he and his wife and daughter were members of the Port Republic church in 1812 and 1813. So he was a man of standing and influence in the neighborhood. He was enterprising and engaged in various businesses. The place of his establishment here was at Sandy Hook, lying on South River a quarter of a mile above the town.

The deed for this property was made to Burgess by John Carthrea, Sr., and Mary his wife, and is dated Oct. 13, 1809. As a sample of the mutilated condition of many of the deeds in the Burnt Records division of the County Clerk's Office, apart from the historic character of Sandy Hook itself, the deed is given:

xxxxx That for the sum of One hundr xx Dollars xxxxx tract piece or parcel of land lying on the north west si xxx South river and opposite Mrs. Macalls house contain xxxxx estimation four acres be the same more or less and xxxx as follows. Beginning at a small sycamore on the edge xxxx river opposite the fork made in the river by Mrs. xxxxx Island above John Carthrea Jr. mills dam and run xxxxx by a straight line across the corn field to two sycam xxxx are partly dead on the edge of the river above the enxxxx of a gully and thence down the several windings and xxxxx ders of the river to the place of Beginning and also the xxxx and free privilege of raising a mill at the enxxxx the sd Gully afored to the height of four feet above the xxxx of the water as it now stands at low water en xxxx backing or damming the water in the South xxxx the sd. river as the said dam xxxx m xxxx and her son owning the land th xxxx of the river with all and singular the xxxx names therein or thereto belonging to xxxx farm tract piece or parcel of land un xxxxx Burgess and his heirs and assigns forever a xxxx use intent or purpose."[2]

The Mrs. Macall mentioned in the above instrument was very likely the widow of John Macall, who was a large landowner in East Rockingham. If so, then the "son" in the above deed was named Edward for John Macall had a son by that name who was sixteen years old in 1792. Mrs. Jane Macall, widow, was a member of the Methodist Church at Port Republic in 1812. Margaret Macall, married, also belonged to this church at that date and may have been the wife of Edward. It is on record in the County Surveyor's Office in Harrisonburg that there was an abutment for a milldam on the Macall land on the east side of South River, which land is now owned by the heirs of John I. Harnsberger.

Mr. Burgess built his dam, a flour mill, an oil mill, and perhaps a sawmill; a blacksmith shop, and a cabinetmaking shop, and did business on a large scale.

It seems that Mr. Burgess was located here and engaged in business before he bought the Sandy Hook property. In an account he had with John Carthrea in 1808, the latter is charged with ten different items, from "work Done to waste gates," to "paying Retshard Osten," who lived in the neighborhood. The credits given Mr. Carthrea are such as to indicate that they were doing business in the same locality; as, "By 1 pece scantling 14 feet 4 by 5."

The names of the residents of the town and of persons living at some distance from it who had business dealing with Mr. Burgess from 1808-1815 are:

1808   Edward Day, John Dalton, Gideon Morgan, John
        Carthrea
1809   John Clark, William Beard, George Gilmore, George
        Meford, Charles Lewis, James Rankin
1810   Jacob Morse, John Craig, Lewis Sawreles,
        John Smith, Cata Delkut
1811   Felty Miller, Patrick Lambert, Peter Fitch,
        John Macall, Reuben Scantling, George
        Compton, John Givens, Burzael Brown, Euen Reece,
        Josiah Emmit

1812   John Rust, Henry Mace, James Johnston,
        Patrick Murray
1813   Jesse Ellis, Thomas Givens, Thomas Clifton, Elijah
        Craig, Andrew Decker, Henry Pirkey, Jacob Rust, Sr.
1814   William Clark, John Dundore, Samuel Caldwell, Jacob
        Rust, Jr., James Murray, William Craig, Jacob Apley,
        James Kennerly, Sr., John McGuire, Matthew Bustle,
        William Douglas, Maj. Wm. Beard, Sarah Owens,
        James Hooke, Gabriel Cross, John Meltebarger, Thos.
        Rice, Saml. Harry, Abram Fisher, Chas. Patrick, James
        Harris
1815   Samuel Harris, William Harper, William Hinchy,
        Joshua Cattleton, Stephen Harnsberger, Thomas
        Hanna, Major Galliday, Michael Whitmore, John
        Hanna, John Huston, South River James Craig, George
        Sauffley, George Moss, Mrs. Boyer, Jacob Kyger,
        Samuel Evans, Joseph Graham, Robert Mills, Jacob
        Harshberger, Chrisley Hawk, William Ellerson, Morris
        Hinchy, Jacob Grider, Henry Tutwiler, Benjamin Cash,
        Alex. Givens, John Murray, Henry Eutsler, Widow
        Hanna, Daniel Protzman, Wm. Tingley, Adam
        Trobaugh, Jacob Yost

A number of persons whose names appear in the above list have descendants still living in or near the town, while others are remembered for various reasons.

Gideon Morgan was the founder of New Haven; John Carthrea was the most influential man in the neighborhood; John Clark owned lot No. 31; William Beard lived at Mt. Meridian; George Gilmore lived a few miles down the river; Charles Lewis lived in the town; James Rankin lived in or near the town; Patrick Lambert worked at Sandy Hook; Peter Fitch owned a farm a mile up North River; John Macall was a large landowner nearby; George Compton owned land nearby; John Givens lived in the neighborhood; Euen

Reece owned land in Browns Gap; Josiah Emmit lived in or near the town.

Henry Mace, a large landowner, obtained several grants of land from the State, one of which bearing the date of Nov. 16, 1789, was signed by Gov. Henry Lee. Mr. Mace built a large substantial house, which is still standing, about half-way between Port Republic and Mt. Vernon Furnace. Besides being a farmer, he was a blacksmith and a Baptist preacher. He was the first to cross the Blue Ridge through Brown's Gap with horses and wagon, cutting a road through the brush and trees. He made the trip to Richmond for flour.

James Johnston and his brother John lived on what was later known as the Yellow House lot; Patrick Murray lived at LeRoy; Thomas Givens owned two lots in the town; Thomas Clifton lived near Brown's Gap; Henry Pirkey lived in the Cross Keys neighborhood; William Clark lived in the town, most likely; John Dundore lived in the town; James Murray, of LeRoy; Wm. Craig of Mt. Meridian; James Kennerly, Sr. lived in the town, probably; Sarah Owens lived in the town; James Hooke lived in the Cross Keys section; John Miltebarger, a nearby landowner; Abram Fisher, large landowner of the neighborhood; James Harris lived in or near the town; William Harper, of the town; Stephen Harnsberger lived at "Cherry Grove", across South River from Port Republic; Thomas Hanna lived near LeRoy; Major Galliday lived in the town; John Hanna of LeRoy; John Huston of the Cross Keys section; George Sauffley of the Mill Creek section; Mrs. Boyer probably lived in the town; Jacob Kyger lived north of North River; Samuel Evans lived in the town; Joseph Graham of the town; Jacob Harshberger near North River; Henry Tutwiler, of the Mill Creek section; Benjamin Cash lived near the Augusta County line; Alex. Givens of Mt. Meridian; John Murray, of LeRoy; Daniel Protzman lived in the town, most likely; Wm. Tingley probably in the town; Adam Trobough owned lots in the town;

31

and Jacob Yost lived on his farm half a mile down the Shenandoah River.

Mr. Burgess used the English monetary system throughout his book. Accounts fill the first 157 pages. Beginning at page 158 there follow seven pages used as a daybook. The remainder of the book is unused. The accounts are singularly free of charges for whiskey.

The next oldest daybook at hand belonged to Joseph Trout, saddler. He came to Port Republic in 1818 and the first entry in his daybook is dated the 24th of the following December.

Those persons who had business relations with Mr. Trout from 1818-1820, and whose names are not included in Mr. Burgess's book are:

1818   Dct. Kemper, Widdow Roberts, Mr Whitmore, Thos Johnston, Musto Chambers, Wm Cohenouwr

1819   Mr Ohara, Samuel Galaday, Mathias Wheelbarger, Nicholas Kinney, Wm Carthrae, Parker Welch, Benj Lewis, Thomas Frame, Sirkle, Samuel Lewis, Campbell, Whitsell, Bittle, Mr Bingham, Mr Stover, Adam Arebawk, Wm. Wheste, Mr Parsons, Mr May, S Holbrook, Wm Lewis, Doct Chambers, Adam Fisher, Bigerton, Benjamin Huston, Jonathan Rush, Wm Hall, Joshsia Catling, old Mr Baley, Thomas Clark, James Cross, Enoch Allen, Smith Eddins, Martin Garber, Valentine Cash, John Patterson, Frederick Foster, David Staufer

1820   Thomas Holt, Andrew Hudlow, Abraham Boon, Daniel Hoot, Smith Batman, Jacob Spitzer, Adam May jr, Christian Delkert, Joseph Miller, James Eddings, Joseph Earman, T Brown, Gregar, William Bateman, Mr Lare, Samuel Fitch, John S Snow, William Seals, Joseph Smith, McCallester, Mr Weller, Samuel Crawford, John Roberts

The given names of several persons in the above list are lacking, and a few of the surnames are variously spelt, as Hoot, Holt, Batman, Bateman, etc.

The persons whose names are in the two preceding lists are fairly representative of those who built the town and established it on enduring foundations, and of those who patronized its shops, stores, and factories.

In the third decade of its existence, an era of prosperity dawned upon Port Republic, the like of which it had not known before. It continued for a score of years, since which nothing comparable has been experienced. The possibilities were dazzling, and with clear heads and firm hands, these early residents labored for the realization of their expectations. The Shenandoah River had been made navigable for flat-bottomed boats, the various business ventures were in a flourishing condition, and Port Republic bode fair to become the chief town near the headwaters of the river.

There were eight public roads leading to the town. The last to be built was surveyed in September 1868 by Henry B. Harnsberger and Edward S. Kemper. Harnsberger had been County Surveyor and Kemper was yet to be. This road connected Port Republic and Harrisonburg and shortened the distance by public road between the two towns to ten and one-half miles. To call attention to the undertaking in a spectacular way, rockets were sent up one night in Harrisonburg to make light so the surveyors could see to get the bearings of the course. The places of entrance into the town of some of the roads have been changed in recent times. The more important roads are macadamized, and it is hoped that all of them will be in the not distant future. Automobiles and motor trucks necessitate good roads. Trucks come to the town from all points.

Home names

The Old World custom of giving a name to one's home is still strong in Virginia. In Port Republic and environs are a number of homes with identifying names, the principal of which are the Jacob B. Yost home, Oakhill; Harrison Bateman, Buena Vista; James A. Maupin, Locust Dale; Jacob J. Nicholas, Belle View; M. Amos Scott, River View; John W. Palmer, Green Island; Jacob B. Nicholas, North Bend; Stephen Harnsberger, Jr., Cottage Plains; Daniel P. Shuler, Valley View; John Harper, Dublin; John I. Harnsberger, Cherry Grove; James E. Shuler, Woodside; William L. Nicholas, Madison Hall; Ryland J. Hall, Mayhall; Charles O. Hooke, Valley View; and Capt. Robin Hooke, Riverside.

Some of the above homes are showing the weight of the hand of time; others have been well cared for and are in good state of preservation; while those built in recent times have all the conveniences and comforts of modern country homes.

Chapter Five Endnotes
[1]Deed Book, 000:505.
[2]Deed Book, 1:347. Note that xxxx indicates illegible letters in the original document.

Chapter 6

Farming Valley Soil

Port Republic is fortunate in being surrounded by a fertile agricultural country. Nature has blessed the people with a productive soil, a salubrious climate, and an abundance of pure water. The farmers are usually prosperous and contented. They are thrifty and progressive. Their homes have all the modern conveniences found in town houses and their barns and other out-buildings are well devised for the comfort and easy handling of the stock, the storing of fodder and grain for their feeding, and the housing of machinery.

Many speak and write of life on the farm as if it were an idyllic existence. In a few rare instances it does approach this desirable state for the owners and overseers. For the actual laborers there is much hard work and even drudgery. It will interest many to learn what wages were paid these latter a hundred years ago.

Stephen Harnsberger, a farmer and man of affairs, lived across South River from Sandy Hook. Under the name of Wilson Marshall, a farm hand, Mr. Harnsberger made this note in his account book in 1831:

Memorandum of a agreement - I agree to furnish Wilson Marshall a house and a garden spot also to haul him Ten loads of Firewood and give him $96 out of which sd Wilson to bord himself for one year's labour with this provision however that if sd Wilson does not prove a good & faithful hand I am at liberty to discharge him by paying him at the above rates per year for the time he may have been in my service at which time he is to leave the house & garden. Stephen Harnsberger.

At this rate Mr. Marshall got $8.00 a month, provided he laboured every workday. The account book shows that he was charged 4 cts. a pound for pork, 10 cts. for bacon, 12 ½ cts. for butter, 2 ½ cts. for flour, 50 cts. a bushel for potatoes, and 33 1/3 cts. for corn. At the end of the year he was 89 cts. in debt.

A leaf of the old account book is turned and instead of advancing in time we fall back a year. Under Samuel Lineweaver's name the following was written in 1830: "Memorandum of Bargain, For one years labour I am to pay $80 and find him diet washing & loging - Commencing Novr. 9th."

The account of Mr. Lineweaver shows nothing new except the introduction of the name of a new storekeeper in the town, James W. Eskridge. At the end of the year when settlement in full was made Mr. Lineweaver had $2.25 to his credit.

In 1832 Mr. Harnsberger wrote in his account book that:

William Alexander commenced work for me by the year this 8th day of March, under the following agreement viz I am to pay him $96.00 & find him house and garden spot haul him 12 loads of wood and a cow to milk after I have pasture to let my cows in, for one years Labour at such work as I shall direct upon the plantation.

During the year Mr. Alexander was charged 50 cts. a bushel for corn, the same for wheat and buckwheat; pork cost him at 4 cts., salt pork 8 cts. a pound, and bacon at 10 cts a pound.

At the end of the year Mr. Alexander was in debt to his employer $3.25 ¾ cts. But the matter of being unable to make both ends meet did not dismay Mr. Alexander. He seems to have been a man of grit and muscle, and with a surplus of energy that only hard work could keep down to normal. So it is not surprising that the following was agreed to:

For the ensuing year commencing March 16th 1833, I have agreed to give Wm. Alexander $8 pr. month for whatever time he is in my employt. with the use of the house and garden until after harvest when I wish to pull down the house, and should I not keep him employed I am to make no charge of rent for that time, with the understanding that if I fail to have the house taken down & he continues in it during the year & not in my employ. he is to pay at the rate of $15 a year.

Whatever may have happened to the house, Mr. Alexander worked well into the following year before settlement was made. On July 21, 1833, this note was written: "This day made settlement with Wm. Alexander & find him due me $7.70." Mr. Alexander was still at work for Mr. Harnsberger as late as 1838.

Charles Davis worked several years for Mr. Harnsberger at 33 1/3 cts. a day, beginning in 1832.

Augustus Hopkins began to work for him in 1842. His services were so satisfactory that this note was made in 1843: "Augustus agrees to work for me another year at $85. - term to commence on the 10th day of February inst."

Several notes of interest are found in Mr. Hopkin's accounts. He was absent three days from work "during the big flood" April 1843, and six days during the "camp meeting" in May 1844.

William Miller had made a profound study of the so-called prophetical books of the Old and New Testaments, and from him a message went out to the world that the second advent of Christ would occur in 1844. In the United States, this mighty religious windstorm swept thousands out of the orthodox churches only to find themselves broken and scattered on the enduring rocks of experience and common sense; and later to gather, or rather to separate, into several small sects. Perhaps the fame of the movement leaped all obstructions and had become a topic of conver-

Programme	Programme
Friday Evening, May 10, 1918	Saturday Evening, May 11, 8 o'clock
By Pupils of the Graded and High School	Gold Medal Contest by Pupils of the Grades
Play in Three Acts	"Somebody's Mother"..........Ryland May
	"The White Footed Deer"....Herman Scott
"Down on the Farm"	"The Color Bearer"..........Arthur Scott
	"Scruggin's Black Rose"..Herman Huffman
Gold Medal Contest by Primary Pupils.	"The Boy Hero".............Susie Lowance
	"The Song of the Camp"
	Frances Dinsmore
	"A Leak in the Dike"........Elsie Wagner
"Bob White"...................Leon Kyger	"Selling the Baby".......Frances Wagner
"A Fellow's Mother"......Claude Crawford	"Baby in Church"..........Bernice Good
"A Lesson for Mother"....Margaret Miller	
"The Ballad of the Tempest"	Gold Medal Contest by the Pupils of the
Pauline Alexander	High School.
"Little Blossom"...........Eloise Rodgers	"Marse John"...............John Wagner
	"One Niche the Highest"...Herold Rodgers
	"Cigarette".......... ......Bessie Nicholas
Instrumental Music by Mrs. W. H. Palmer	"The Curfew Heroine"....Virginia Nicholas
	"Grand Ma Keeler Gets Grand Pa Keeler
	Ready for Sunday School"
	Kathleen Groah
	"The Legend of the Organ Builder"
	Virginia May
	Instrumental Music by Mrs. W. H. Palmer.
Drills Refreshments	Drills Marches Refreshments

Program from the Closing Announcement of Port Republic Graded and High School, 1918

sation even here. Such movements are very exciting and it is no wonder that Mr. Hopkins spent a whole week at camp meeting.

March 7, 1833, just one hundred and three years ago at this writing, Mr. Harnsberger gave Charles Davis credit for 400 nails for $2.00. There were no nail-making machines in the State at this time. Nails were usually made by black-smiths out of iron rods manufactured at slitting mills. Some-times they were made by industrious persons at their homes during the winter months.

Thomas Wood worked for Mr. Harnsberger at times. In 1839 he was charged with one Bible at 62 ½ cts., 10 cts. for postage on a letter to Winchester, and 20 cts. postage on a "double letter" to a town not named.

Harrison Bateman, in 1840, was charged, "To 19 ½ lb bacon to take on the river not accounted for when my freight was paid. $2.44."

Working conditions described above may in general have existed on all the farms in the neighborhood. On some farms they may not have been quite so good; certainly on few, if any, were they better.

About one hundred years ago wheat was selling for about the same price it is selling for now. According to Trout's daybook, on Dec. 16, 1828, he sold to Adam May two bushels of potatoes at 66 2/3 cts. a bushel. In 1819 Mr. Trout bought of John Dundore one and one-half bushel of "Deers hair" which cost .37 ½ cts.

Dealings with a few other persons will now be noted. In 1842 Mr. Harnsberger charged George G. Butler "To cash for church $1.00" and May 7, "To 25 cts. paid to parsonage as directed pr self."

George W. Kemper, Jr., was given credit "By subscription to bridge $25.00" in 1854 and charged "To $5.00 his subscription to the preacher," February 1856.

Mr. Harnsberger had an account with Jacob Strayer, a member of the board of overseers of the poor, for food, clothing, etc., advanced to needy persons.

A list of names of representative persons living in the town and within a radius of four or five miles, in rare cases even farther, taken from existing account books of Stephen Harnsberger, follows:

1831   James O'Brian, Thomas Mansfield, Daniel Steel
1832   James Mullens, Jacob May, Jr.
1833   Harrison Austin, Jacob Roach, John Anders
1834   Milchus Jarman
1835   Garland Yarth
1836   A. Clyfton, Thomas Thomas, Wm. A. Maupin, George Sipe
1837   Samuel Allen, Thomas King, George Snyder, John Crawford,

J.M. Stout, Mitchell Crawford, Tyre Maupin, James H. Triplett, Jonathan Kaylor

1838   C.W. Carthrea, James Bateman, Christian Staubus, Amos Scott

1839   Samuel Austin, David Watkins, James Peyton, Wm. D. Smith, Bluford Smith, James Shephard, Henry Price, Daniel Carthrea, Daniel Lutz

1840   Benjamin F. Kemper, Harrison Bateman, Daniel May, Wm. L. Smith, Jacob Sipe, John Huff, George Raynes, Jefferson Randall, Joshua Catland, Hugh Bruffy, John B. Yost, Henry Mace, John L. Moore

1841   Thomas W. Ryan, Robert Ewan, Jacob Haffner, Mr. Teter, Gideon Dunn, Balzer Lutz, Charles B. McCann, George Utzler (Eustler?), Joseph Trout, Jonathan Taylor, Martha Lewis, Maria B. Yost, Jacob Mohler, Oliver T. Mann, Jacob Smith

1842   Ross Rippertoe, Fielding Matheney, Peyton Dawson, Samuel Pearson, George G. Butler, Jonathan Bateman, John Lee, Archibald Huston, John Fisher, Joseph Randall

1843   Biblins Webster, Andrew Campbell

1844   Mrs. V. Talifarro, Jacob May, Leroy Daingerfield, Robert W. Palmer, John Bailey

1845   Abraham Fisher

1846   J.G.H. Raynes

1847   Rev. T.H. Busey, Samuel Grubb

1848   Rev. G.W. Israel

1849   Rev. Tilletson Morgan, James O. White

1850   Rev. Patrick Kelley

1851   James Eddings, John Werner

1852   Zachariah Raines

1853   Thomas E. Brown

1854   I. J. Grove

1855   E. Hughs, John Morgan

1856   Daniel E. May

1857   Peter Sipe, H. M. Harris, W. D. Maiden, Rev. J. W. Wolf, Cain Rogers, James A. Lewis

1858   Peachy Roadcap

1859   Rev. Smith

1860   Hiram Eddings

Chapter 7

Boating: A Commercial Enterprise

Perhaps the most important public business with which Mr. Stephen Harnsberger was connected was as president of the New Shenandoah Company. The General Assembly by an Act of January 23, 1798, had appointed John Koontz, Thomas Harrison, John Waterman, and Frederick Spangler a commission to report upon the feasibility of making the Shenandoah River navigable. On the basis of this report the Potomac Company was incorporated. An Act incorporating a new company to open and extend the navigation of the Shenandoah River and its branches was passed by the General Assembly, Feb. 3, 1814. The reasons given for the passage of this Act follow:

Whereas the extension of the navigation of Shenandoah River will be of public utility, and the Potomac Company, which has failed to complete the said navigation within the time limited by their charter, has, on certain conditions, agreed to relinquish any further claim thereto: And whereas, it may be necessary to cut canals and erect locks and other works on both sides of the river; and the General Assembly, impressed with the importance of the object, are desirous of encouraging so useful an undertaking.

The "importance of the object" was a good and sufficient reason in justification of the undertaking, and for over half a century the Shenandoah River was a beehive of industry. A few extracts from the Act may be of general interest:

I. Be it therefore enacted, That for the purpose of raising a capital sum of one hundred thousand dollars in shares of fifty dollars each, it shall and may be lawful to open books of subscription in Winchester, under the direction of James Singleton, Griffin Taylor, Isaac Hollingsworth, James Ware, Thomas Buck, and David Carlile; in Charlestown, under the direction of George Humphreys, John H. Lewis, Hiram L. Opie, Thomas Griggs and William Tate; in Woodstock, under the direction of William Carson, Robert Gaw, Jacob Rinker, Jacob Ott, and Isaac Bowman; in Harrisonburg, under the direction of Charles Lewis, George Huston, Joseph Graham, Joseph Mauzy, Martin Kite, Robert Grattan and Robert Gray; in Staunton, under the direction of John Wayt, Charles A. Stuart, Alexander Nelson, James Bell, James Cochran, John H. Peyton, John McDowell and David Golladay; and in Martinsburg, under the direction of Joel Ward, William Wilson, Elisha Boyd, Philip Nadenboush and Andrew Waggener.

The charter empowered and required the subscribers, or a majority of them, to elect a president and four directors. Stephen Harnsberger was elected president. The position was not altogether a sinecure, as shown by one officers' report, which is at hand.

In regard to tolls the Act prescribes:

II. It shall be lawful for the said President and Directors, at all times forever hereafter, at Little's Falls on the said river, or any place which the President and Directors or a majority of them may fix upon for that purpose to demand and receive the following tolls or rates, that is to say, for:

Every pipe, or hogshead of wine containing more than sixty-five gallons, ... sixty-six cents
Every hogshead of rum or other spirits, ... fifty-five cents
Every hogshead of tobacco, ... forty-four cents
Every cask of wine containing more than thirty-five and not more than sixty-five gallons, ... thirty-three cents
Every similar cask of rum or other spirits, or of linseed oil, ... twenty-eight cents

Every cask of wine containing not less than twenty or more than
    thirty-five gallons, ... seventeen cents
Every barrel of rum or other spirits, or of linseed oil of similar
    capacity, ... fourteen cents
Every keg or other vessel of wine containing less than
    twenty gallons, ... eight cents
Every similar keg or vessel of rum, or other spirits, or of linseed oil,
    .... six and a quarter cents
Every bushel of wheat, peas, beans or flaxseed, ... two cents
Every bushel of Indian corn or other grain or salt, ... one cent
Every barrel of pork, ... twenty-two cents
Every barrel of beef, ... fifteen cents
Every barrel of flour, ... twelve and a half cents
Every ton of hemp, flax, potash, bar or manufactured iron,
    .... one dollar & ten cents
Every ton of pig iron or castings, ... forty cents
Every ton of copper, lead, or other ore, other than iron ore,
    .... ninety cents
Every ton of stone or iron ore, ... twenty cents
Every hundred bushels of lime, ... fifty-five cents
Every chaldron of coals, ... twenty cents
Every hundred pipe staves, ... ten cents
Every hundred hogshead staves, or pipe or hogshead
    heading, ... six and a half cents
Every hundred barrel staves or barrel heading, ... four cents
Every hundred cubic feet of plank or scantling, ... forty cents
Every hundred cubic feet of other timber, .. twenty-two cents
Every gross hundred weight of all other commodities
    and packages, ... six cents
Every empty boat or vessel, which has not commodities on
board to yield so much, except an empty boat or vessel returning, whose load has already paid at the aforesaid place
the sum fixed, in which case she is to pass toll free, one dollar
& ten cents, which tolls may be discharged in dollars and cents
or other coin made current by law.

This Act was slightly amended by the Legislature March
19, 1860, but no changes were made in the tolls.

Men of ability and power faced what was in that time a Herculean undertaking—to clear the Shenandoah River and its two branches of obstructions; to dig canals and make tow paths; to build dams and banks so that it might be navigable for the boats to be used in its bosom. They accomplished much work, and the foundation was so broad and well laid that even after our dreadful civil estrangement with our Northern brothers there was a revival of the business for a few years. But the Valley had been so ravaged by the enemy, even farm implements were destroyed, that the surrounding country could no longer feed the business with freight and shipment.

In a printed, but undated, report of the president and directors of the company, mention was made of the work already done to make the river navigable and safe, and attention was called to what remained to be done. The work was let to contractors, and no divisional sections of the river were made for the contracts. The contractors did this themselves, and remembering the divisions of ancient Gaul, they divided the river into three parts, upper, middle and lower. The report says that Mr. Lewis worked the part from Port Republic to the White House, which is near the river between Luray and New Market; Captain Gatewood that from the White House to Flint Run; and Major Galloday from Flint Run to Harper's Ferry. Some estimation of the undertaking, says the report, may be formed from the fact that in the upper section there were, besides fluke walls, 148 dams, in the middle 147, and in the lower 66, besides those built along the canals from Little's Fall downstream.[1]

When the transportation of the products of the farms, mills, shops, the furnace and forge, etc., was at its height, The Point (the point of land at the head of the Shenandoah River) was the scene of much activity. Here were gathered the multifarious products of the surrounding country for shipment to points as far as Georgetown. Depending on the nature of the consignments, some were placed in the warehouse, some under sheds, and such as inclement weather would not damage were left exposed.

Here, too, was heard the ringing of the hammer, the thud of the mallet, and swish of the saw, as the boat-builders, with much good cheer, laboured at their appointed tasks. It seems that, in some cases at least, patterns were used to build the boats by, and that they were built on both sides of the river. Stephen Harnsberger charges Jacob May, Oct. 30, 1844, "To hauling 1 boat pattern over the big river $.75." In another account book Mr. Harnsberger, on May 28, 1847, charges John Holbrook, "To hauling Boat pattern to the point $.63." On February 14, 1848, he gives Henry Mace credit for one boat pattern at $12.00. While it is doubtless true that no blueprints were used here in the boat-building business at that time and that some of the builders may

Victorian paddleboat on North River at Port

have needed a pattern for a guide, nothing is more certain than that some of the workmen were master-builders and that nothing more than length and breadth needed to be given for them to build a first-class boat. Perhaps "pattern" meant the lumber used in building a boat.

The lumber used in the boat-building business gave employment to wood-cutters, teamsters, and sawmill operators; the necessary nails, to coalburners and blacksmiths; and the farmers found it profitable to grow flax for the corking.

The staple products of the neighborhood sent to market via the Shenandoah River were iron, lumber, and flour. Mr. Harnsberger did considerable hauling of flour to the boats. On May 29, 1838, he charges Selah Holbrook, "To hauling 50 barrels flour to River, $1.50." Altogether he mentions about twelve flour mills of the neighborhood in his account books. A number of persons were regularly engaged in the business of hauling produce to the markets.[2]

Chapter Seven Endnotes

[1]There were a total of 351 dams between Port Republic and Harpers Ferry.

[2]The chapter, "Zachariah Raines, the Commodore of the Shenandoah," provides a good deal of information about boating. See Index for more information.

Chapter 8

The Flourishing of Industry

From its foundation down to the Civil War, Port Republic was a self-sufficient town. Goods, sufficient to supply the needs of the people of the town and neighborhood, were manufactured in its shops, mills, and factories. There were tanneries, harness shops, saddle makers, shoemakers, cabinet-makers, foundries, sawmills, flour mills, woolen mills, machine shops, contractors and builders; and whatever else was necessary to meet the wants and supply the comforts of the people.

Henry Howe included a brief description of the town in his Historical Collection of Virginia, "Port Republic, 12 miles s. of the C.H., at the junction of the North and South Rivers, contains a church and about 35 dwellings."[1]

Another able and enterprising historian of the State, writing about 1832, described the town:

Port Republic, P.V. 121 ms. from R. and 143 N.W. by W. of W. situated at the junction of the North and south Rivers, branches of the Shenandoah, 2 ms. below the Augusta line, 2 ½ from Weyer's Cave, 12 ms. S. of Harrisonburg, 20 E. of Staunton, and 32 north of Charlottesville. It contains 30 dwelling houses, 1 house of public worship, free for all denominations, 1 common school, 1 house of entertainment, 2 mercantile stores, 1 manufacturing flour mill, 3 saw mills, 2 tan yards, 1 tilt hammer shop, with carriage manufactory flour mill, 2 other smith shops, 1 tin plate worker, 3 boot and shop factories, 1 saddler, 1 cabinet maker, 1 turner and chair maker, 1 hatter, and 2 tailors. The Shenandoah is navigable for flat boats from Port Republic to the District of Columbia, running at all times (except at very dry seasons) with from 60 to 120 barrels of flour on each boat. Both branches of the river furnish manufactories of any common extent. Population 160 persons: of whom 1 is a physician."[2]

Early in the history of the town and probably before it was laid out, a dam was built across South River and a race was dug which conveyed water almost half the length of the town to several industrial plants. These plants were built and owned by John Carthrea. In this group there were a sawmill, flour mill, woolen mill, foundry, and machine shop. In the account book of Dr. George W. Kemper, Sr., is found an account with the factory (Holbrook, Kemper and Ramsburg) running from May, 1859 to November, 1861. At this time John W. Holbrook lived in the house provided by the factory for its superintendent. Shields, Preston & Co., of Lexington, owned these properties in later years. They did a thriving business and gave employment to a number of persons. A. B. Tanquary was the superintendent. It was a sad day for the people when Gen. David Hunter burned these and other properties in the town in 1864.

John W. Lee, John Harper, and Zan Fulton formed a partnership, rebuilt the foundry and operated it for a short time. One Mr. Moffat, of Baltimore, was the moulder. Mr. Harper, who furnished the ready cash to meet the obligations of the company thought he was not getting a fair return on his money so he retired from the concern. The business was discontinued.

George Wesley May rented the sawmill and flour mill of Shields, Preston & Co. Old ledgers and account books show that he loomed large as a businessman of the town. He seems to have been in active control of the two mills for about fifteen years before the Civil War, and for a number of years when they were rebuilt after the war.

The town has at all times been peculiarly fortunate in having able and ingenious mechanics. These designers and fashioners of tools and machinery, artificers in woods and metals, producers of useful goods and articles of comfort and luxury, have been the brainy men of the town. To become rich by buying calico at five cents a yard and selling it at ten or fifteen cents, requires no great mental capacity. But it did require an unusual amount of brains for a mechanic of a few generations ago to solve the many problems that presented themselves at different times in his work. He had no trade paper or magazine to help, nor books to guide in the deep things pertaining to his trade. Intelligent and respectable mechanics are the backbone of any town or neighborhood. Without them related industries and crafts, tradesmen, and professional men cannot exist. Some employers think that they provide bread for their workers. All should know that it is an economic truth that without the workers the employers would soon be hungry.

The prince of these mechanics was Selah Holbrook. He lived on South River just above Port Republic. His home was named "Sandy Hook."[3] Here he built a sawmill, a flour mill, and a foundry; a machine shop, a blacksmith shop, and a woolen mill. The last named was one of the woolen mills burned by Hunter when he passed through Port Republic. Of course he burned the other mills and shops. After the war was over Mr. Holbrook rebuilt his blacksmith shop and flour mill.

It is said that Mr. Holbrook was the inventor of the notched sickle used on the McCormick reaper, and that a negro gave the idea of driving it with eccentric. William M. Groah, of the town, said that his father, Michael Groah, worked for Cyrus H. McCormick at Vesuvius, and was the inventor of this sickle. However this may be, it is certain that Mr. Holbrook made a number of these sickles in his shop.

This shop was destroyed by the flood of 1877 and was never rebuilt. Charles L. Kemper shipped the rock on which the anvil stood to the New Orleans Exposition 1884-1885.

The part played by Selah Holbrook and his son John H. Holbrook in making the McCormick reaper a success was an important one.

The steel sickles demanded fine workmanship and in 1842, John McCown, whose tilt-hammer shop had produced the knife for the first McCormick machine in 1831, was found unreliable because of his fondness for liquor. McCormick was compelled to make the cutters at Walnut Grove. This proved impracticable after trial, and for the next year his knives were fashioned by Selah Holbrook at Port Republic, forty-five miles away, and Cyrus brought them home on horseback.[4]

Robert McCormick, father of Cyrus, was also the inventor and manufacturer of a reaper. Cyrus sold the right to manufacture his machine to several persons in different parts of the country. All those engaged in the manufacture of the reaper had trouble to get first class sickles. That the making of them called for the most careful and expert workmanship is shown by the few who were trusted with their production.

Jabez Parker at Richmond had his sickles fashioned by an edged-tool maker; Robert McCormick relied upon John McCown's blacksmith shop or Selah Holbrook's tilt-hammer foundry for this same careful work, and Henry Bear sent from Missouri to the Brown Factory (at Cincinnati) for his knives. It was customary for Cyrus McCormick to forward a model machine or patterns for the guidance of these manufacturers, but he was never sure that they would be faithfully copied.[5]

Hutchinson gives John McCown the credit of making the sickle for McCormick's first machine in 1831 but the matter remains open to debate. Herbert A. Keller, an historian of merit, author of *Rockbridge County, Virginia, in 1835: A Study of Ante-Bellum Society*, is custodian of the voluminous data gathered by the McCormick family from every known source in the last thirty years. He is librarian of the McCormick Historical Association in Chicago, and has always been interested in John H. Holbrook, and at one time endeavored to find out what he could about him.

Mr. Keller contributes the following interesting and illuminating paper on this subject:

The central portion of the Valley of Virginia is rich in iron ore, therefore iron furnaces were numerous in the period before the War between the States. These furnaces, using charcoal for fuel, produced an excellent grade of iron in many instances. Much of it was in the form of pig, but they also turned out respectable quantities of bar-iron and castings. Blacksmiths who could work the iron into the primitive tools and utensils of the time were scattered here and there throughout the region and performed an important service for the communities in which they lived. Two of these men, John McCowan located on South River near Riverside, in Rockbridge County, and John Holbrook, who lived at Port Republic in Rockingham County, possessed an especial reputation and men brought them work to do from far and near. The renown achieved by these men grew out of two things: the fact that they had facilities for making fine steel and the quality of their product. Each of them had a tilt-hammer operated by water power-a machine equivalent to the later steam-hammer. With the aid of a forge and the tilt-hammer they were able to undertake a type of work which other blacksmiths could not handle.

When Cyrus Hall McCormick invented his reaper at Walnut Grove Farm in Rockbridge County in 1831, he went to John McCowan who lived only a few miles distant and he had him make, according to specifications furnished by Cyrus, a straight sickle or cutting knife, made of fine steel. John McCowan continued to make excellent sickles for Cyrus McCormick's reapers from that time until construction of ma-

51

chines at Walnut Grove was discontinued at the end of the season of 1847. In 1841, Cyrus, feeling the need of additional assistance, had engaged John Holbrook and Selah, his father, to construct sickles for his reapers.

The Holbrooks originally came from Massachusetts; Ezra, the first of the family in Virginia, settling in the Valley shortly after the close of the American Revolution. Ezra had a son, Selah, who was born in 1793 and died in 1874. John Holbrook, son of Selah, was born about 1820. Tradition has it that Ezra lived in Rockbridge County and Selah was born there. Selah later moved to Port Republic in Rockingham County, where he established the Holbrook Iron Foundry. His son, John, made it famous throughout Virginia. The arrangement of McCormick with the Holbrooks continued from 1841 to 1847 and was mutually satisfactory, the sickles made by the latter proving of fine quality.

John Holbrook's reputation in constructing sickles for McCormick brought him additional business as he was employed as early as 1843 to make sickles for Jabez Parker of Richmond and for Col. Tutwiler of Fluvanna County, each of whom had obtained licenses from C.H. McCormick to make and sell McCormick reapers in certain counties east of the Blue Ridge, located respectively in Tidewater and Southside, Virginia. In the fifties, John Holbrook, in addition to his iron business, operated a woolen factory and a grain mill. Until the outbreak of the War Holbrook prospered at Port Republic, although he experienced several serious reverses because of floods. In common with the fate of other patriotic southerners, the War ruined his business. Holbrook attempted to revive it several times thereafter, but the combination of depressed economic conditions, floods, new mechanical technique and old age proved too great a handicap, and he was never able to regain his former economic status.

The extensive iron establishment created by John Holbrook has long since disappeared-washed away by floods. Only an iron ring imbedded in stone, located on the banks of a stream near Port Republic and now almost covered with sand, remains to show the site of his former extensive foundry. At the New Orleans Exposition of 1885, a huge stone anvil block used as the base for the anvil in the tilt-hammer process, was a prominent feature of the Virginia State Exhibit accompanied by a legend to the effect that it was used in making early McCormick reaper sickles. Following the close of the Exposition, through the courtesy of Mr. C.D. Harnsberger, this old stone anvil block was acquired by the children of Cyrus McCormick, and now reposes in the court yard of the McCormick Works at Chicago, a mute memento of the industry of John Holbrook and his father and the early manufacture of the McCormick reaper.

The above paper, together with the letter of Mr. Holbrook given below, contain about all the information now available on this interesting and historic site, and the part Selah Holbrook and his son, John, had in making the McCormick machine the greatest of reapers.

June 10th 1884
Glenora (Spotsylvania County, Va.)
Mr. C.H. McCormick
Dear Sir
Yours of 25th is to hand which has been carefully looked over I surely do sympathize with you in your bereavement, but we must all have such to bear the best we can just about two years since My Dear Wife Departed this life but My Dear friend we must not consider them lost only gone before, we must try to meet them in a better world than this. I am sorry I did not write to your Dear Father or get to see him long before, he staid at My Fathers several months when he was getting up his Reaper we were both then comparatively young men we were all very attached to each other whilst with us we all enjoyed his company besides he was great benefit to us and we to him were the only ones in this State to help him through with his Reaper, he had tried many on his sickles in which they all failed They were then made all in one piece much harder to make than those made in sections he sold to one Col. Tutwiler the rite all south of James River after finding the Sickles could be made at the same time recomending me

to Mr. Tutwiler to have work don he at once wrote for me to get them up for him which I did so I went to Tutwilers built and started all them for him with great success. I then went to Richmond & was about contracting with a firm to make sickles for them but Tutwiler came after me as he was full of orders.....to fill them. After that time went back to my Fathers old place started business for myself got into the milling & wool Factory business then the war the cruel war came on then the enemy burnt me out. I had slaves lost of course after that was washed out so my Lathes have not been any good to me since Since that time hae not been able to do much for the want of something to do with. That was the reason why I worte to your Dear Old Father for some Position My friends in Rockingham often told me I ought to go and see or write to the Dear Old Gentleman C Sprinkle one of your agents at Harrisonburg told me to write to him. The anvil Rock was from the old tilthammer Shop we made the sickles at my Fathers Shop at Port Republic.

I believe I have given you all information about my acquaintance with your Father. Should you ever come to this State I would like for you to come to see me. We made sickles for several other companies to hoom your Father sold cont(ra)cts one in Clark one in Richmond your machine is a more labour saving than the those but much heavier draft and I think they would cut more wheat in the same length of time I put them on James River at that time they cut 20 acres in heavy wheat, in one day if you should have any thing here after for me to do I can Refer you to many as to my qualifications & character but my Age will not permit me to do much hard labour but am more active than most of men who has don so much hard work as I have I am near 64 yhears of age never will be able to set the River on fire with my work. I hope you will excuse bad writing & spelling am a nervous. Believe me as ever your

True friend,
(signed) John H. Holbrook

"Sandy Hook" is no more. The bank of the river is covered with trees, the sycamore, walnut, and willow, the cedar, locust and elm. Sand, still accumulating, covers the scene leaving exposed only the foundation stones of the blacksmith hearth. A brooding heaviness hovers over the locality, broken only by the call of the partridge, the whirring flight of the pheasant, and the passing of the leaping rabbit. Black bass play in the purling stream and wild ducks flutter on its rippling boson. This place, once a center of industry, is now a small pasture field.

The Dundore tannery has long been a landmark of the town.[6] John Carthrea, Jr. conveyed the site to John Dundore, April 2, 1816. During his lifetime, the tannery was one of the leading enterprises of East Rockingham. He had an addition built to the fine old house across the street from the tannery which he used as an office. In the body of the deed the use to be made of the land is mentioned as a tanyard "erected, or to be erected, on this Ground".

Two tanyards had been built before this one of Dundore's. One of them had stopped work or was about to suspend operations. One was built on lot No. 51, which lies near the south end of the town; the other was on the Galliday property and was located just across the mill race at the foot of Chestnut Street.

Jonathan Rush bought a lot near the southeast end of the town, paying therefor the sum of $100, which lot was deeded to him July 14, 1815. On this lot (present Dinsmore property) Mr. Rush built a tannery which he operated successfully for almost a score of years.

On Sept. 25, 1834, Mr. Rush and his wife Margaret signed a deed conveying this property to Selah Holbrook for the consideration of $620. The deed is interesting in that it locates the lots of others in that section of the town. The property is described in the deed as "one certain Lot of Land in that part of the Town of Port Republic which was added by John Carthrea, Sr., and being the same which was conveyed to said Rush in part by Daniel Protzman & in part by said John Carthrea, Sr. containing a half acre; also one Lot containing about one fourth of an acre near the first described; the first described being the Lot of which the Tan Yard of the said Rush is situated."[7]

The quarter-acre lot above mentioned was deeded to Mr. Rush by Richard Swift Emmit, July 14, 1815. The lot was bounded "on the south side by the street called Water Street thence running back 41 yards joining R. S. Emmit's lott and on the west bound by Adam Troughbroughs lott and on the east by an alley between sd lott and Jonathan Rushes Lott."[8]

William M. Groah's home is on this lot, and Luther Sipe lives on the Troughbough lot.

The half of lot No. 50 which Daniel Protzman and Mary his wife deeded to Mr. Rush, was conveyed by John Carthrea, Sr., to George Wolf, and by Benjamin Lewis as trustee for Mr. Wolf to Joseph Graham, and by him to Mr. Protzman.[9]

Mr. Rush moved to McGaheysville where he reentered the tanning business.

Major Frederick and Samuel Galliday owned land on both sides of Carthrea's mill race at the foot of Chestnut Street before 1816. They, too, were engaged in the tanning business and operated a tannery on this property.

When Dundore's tannery began to turn out a good grade of well finished leather, there came to the town shoemakers, saddlers, and harness makers. Of these, theses most actively engaged at their several trades were Joseph Trout, Thomas W. Ryan, James O'Brian, Thomas E. Brown, Charles B. McCann, and Willis Jackson.

Trout's book still exists in a fair state of preservation with an occasional page missing. On its first page is written, "Port Republic Joseph Trout December 13th 1818." One item charged in this old daybook, on Nov. 13, 1819 is of much interest. It is, "Doct Kemper Dr To 1 pair saddle bags $6.00." As doctors filled their prescriptions at this time, one can imagine the immense amount of medicine carried in their bags. Many horseback riders in those days used saddlebags. M. Whitmore is charged $4.50 for a pair, Aug. 3, 1820; Thomas Frame is charged in the following month "to making six pair" for $8.00, and four more pair for $5.33 1/3. Mr. Frame must have furnished the leather for these bags.

An itemized account, amounting to $25.57 ½ due by John H. Austin to Thomas E. Brown, harness-maker and saddler, beginning Sept. 20, 1849, and running to Jan. 26, 1851, is still in existence. The penmanship is excellent. Most of these older citizens who could write at all, usually wrote with good hands. However, Mr. Brown "made his mark" when his signature was needed. He was the father of Abner, William, and Andrew Jackson. The two latter were Confederate soldiers with enviable records. William was shot in the heel, which never entirely healed; Andy, as many of his friends called him, served through the war in Stuart's cavalry without receiving a scratch and was killed in his old age at Mt. Crawford by an automobile.

For 190 years there has been a flour mill at Port Republic. The mills in the town and vicinity were usually named for the owners: Downs, Carthrea, Burgess, Mohler, Scott, Raynes, Lewis, Holbrook, Whitmore, Dunn, Chester, and Harper.

Captain Henry Downs built the first flour mill in or near Port Republic in 1746. John Carthrea built the next one before the beginning of the nineteenth century, so far as the writer knows.

Stephen Harnsberger mentions the following: Mohler's Mill, 1833; Holbrook's Mill, 1835; Lewis's Mill, 1836; Kemper's Mill, 1840; Dunn's Mill, 1840; Miller's Mill, 1841; Whitmore's Mill, 1842, Raynes's Mill, 1846; Mt. Vernon Mill, 1856; Walker's Mill, 1857; and Johnston's Mill.

The records of Dr. George W. Kemper, Sr., mention Jacob Pirkey 1842, as a mill owner and probably ____ Stultz 1858, and ____ Pifer 1861, were proprietors of mills. Frederick Smith, 1847 was the miller for William Harper's mill, a mile below town on the west side of the river. Amos Scott built a mill at Scott's Ford, upstream on North River.

After Hunter had destroyed the mills in 1864, flour was brought in from sections that the hands of the ravager had not reached, or an inferior grade manufactured in an improvised mill was used.

The writer remembers, when a mere child, seeing at the site of the destroyed mill, what appeared to be heaps of shot. When he came up to these heaps the "shot" were found to be rather oblong, of little weight and very brittle. He was told later that he had come upon piles of burnt wheat.

Within the memory of the writer the last functioning mill has been in the possession of several companies. The water power and all pertaining thereto was bought of J.T.L. Preston by Jacob J. Nicholas in 1889. Mr. Nicholas built a modern flour mill on the original site and so well did he build, that the mill has been in continuous operation since. In 1899 he sold this property to John J. Fulton and others, who in turn sold it to the Port Republic Milling Co. in 1903. In 1915 it was again sold, this time at public auction on the premises, and was bought by The Coiner Milling Co., and is now under the active control of L.V. Walker.[10]

The Port Republic Foundry is one of the leading industries of the town. "Bud" Hinkle bought the water power and the site of the plant of Dr. George W. Kemper, Jr., about 1878. He gave the contract for necessary buildings to James H. May and when the plant was ready for operation, Mr. Hinkle turned it over to his brother-in-law, John King.

The story of the building of a stable on the foundry premises by Mr. King is amusing. He hired John K. Morris to build it. Either because of the lack of lumber or ground space the stable was made just long enough for a horse to stand in, as was thought. It so happened that the horse Mr. King owned was of unusual length and it was found that the stall was not long enough to get head, body, and tail in at the same time. The predicament was surmounted by cutting a hole in the end of the stable large enough for the horse's head to go through and building a hood over it on the outside with a feeding trough attached below.

The foundry is a valuable property and was purchased by William M. Groah and George W. Cash in 1888. In 1900 Mr. Groah bought the interest of Mr. Cash, and a year later sold a half interest to Hugh Connell. At the death of the latter, Mr. Groah repurchased his share. Until 1903 an engine was used to furnish the motive power; since then water power has been used.

In 1906 John F. Wagner installed woodworking machin-

Port Republic Milling Company: included are John Bennington, C.H. Mundy, Bob Meyerhoeffer, J.O. Stickley, C.H. Mundy, and Marvin Wampler

ery in the shop and power building of the foundry, and manufactured chairs, church and lodge furniture, did repair work, etc., until 1911. In this year he entered the building business and became a contractor and builder on a large scale.

The Port Republic Electric Light Company was organized in 1916 and the foundry's water power was used to drive the electrical machinery. The company transferred its charter and machinery for a price to the Shenandoah River Company in 1926. As these two businesses were carried on in his buildings, Mr. Groah was more or less interested in them.

Groah began work at the early age of eight years in McCormick's Foundry which was located near Steele's Tavern in Rockbridge County. His uncle, Joseph McCormick, a nephew of Cyrus McCormick, the inventor of the reaper, was in charge of the foundry at this time. When he sold the property to Frank Lyle, Mr. Groah worked for him until 1888, in which year he came to Port Republic

Mr. Groah has always taken interest in forwarding all public and private enterprises of the town. He served on the Building Committees of the Town Hall, the Methodist Parsonage and Church, and was an active and efficient member of the local School Board for sixteen years.

There is evidence at hand to show that there have been at least five wagonwrights in the town since 1860. The muster roll of a militia company for that year contains the name of John H. Licklighter, who was a wagon maker and had a shop on lot No. 50. James H. May was an expert with a broadax and at times hewed axle trees for Mr. Licklighter. William S. Downs, in an account with him, charged him $15.00 for "a day's hauling" on May 21, 1863. In 1866, he charged him to the "amt. Paid Jim May" which shows that Mr. May was still working for Mr. Licklighter as late as 1866.

About the middle of the nineteenth century, Luncefield Lee began to operate a wagon-making shop on the site of the present store building of John F. Miller.[11] The Lees came to the Valley from eastern Virginia and settled in the neighborhood of McGaheysville. Mr. Lee lived a few years in that section and then removed to Port Republic. In his preparation for the manufacturing of wagons, he installed the necessary machinery which was driven by horsepower. Altogether he had, for that time, the most up-to-date wagon factory in East Rockingham.

Myers and Drumheller built wagons here in 1878. That same year, John F. Long came to Port Republic. He ran a wagon-making shop and pump factory. He stayed here but one year.

Thomas Madden came to the town in 1873. He bought the Sigler property consisting of lots Nos. 32, 33 and 34. A dwelling house was on lot No. 32 and had a wagon-making shop built on lot No. 34. He sold half of this to Joseph H. Lamb who employed James H. May to build a blacksmith shop on it. The two shops complemented each other.

In looking through the daybooks and account books of pre-Civil War days, the curious are struck with the articles charged by employers to the accounts of their employees, articles known not to have been made or handled by the employers. For instance, coffee and sugar, staple articles sold at all grocery stores, were often charged to the accounts of men at work in the mills and on the farms. The explanation seems to be that an order for a certain amount would be given on the grocer or storekeeper who sold the articles, which were itemized and charged to him who gave the order. At stated times, at least once a year, the accounts were made out and presented for payment. The articles were then charged in the account of the employee who had received the order.

Orders, duebills, and notes were more extensively used than they are now. Money was scarce and everyone's paper seemed to be good. But the papers of a constable of that time, some of which are at hand, show that it sometimes fell to him to make collections.

It is interesting to speculate on the relationship between heads of industries and stores.

The account books of Stephen Harnsberger, Sr., barely help to solve the puzzle.

In October 1831, Jacob May is given credit for "1 chair at Mr. Perry's 50 cts." Whether Mr. Perry was a storekeeper, a manufacturer of chairs or whether Mr. May left the chair in his hands to be delivered to Mr. Harnsberger is not clear.

The account book shows that on the following Feb. 6, Charles B. McCann was still running a boot and shoe factory, Thomas W. Ryan also was in the boot and shoe business in 1841 and James O'Brian in 1839.

A Mr. Mann was in the tailoring business this same year and Samuel Grubb in 1847. John W. Lee may have been in the same business at this time.

Isaac J. Grove was a cabinetmaker and George W. Eutsler a cabinet-maker and chair-maker.

Industrially, Port Republic does not measure up to what it was three-quarters of a century ago. Perhaps, in the chapter, "Lost Opportunities," the reason may be found.

Horses and wagon loaded with Oliver plows; the Groah Foundry in the background

Chapter Eight Endnotes

[1]Henry Howe, *Historical Collections of Virginia*, (Charleston, S.C.: Babcock and Co., 1845), 460.

[2]Joseph Martin, *Gazetteer and History of Virginia*, (Charlottesville, Va.: Mosely & Tompkins), 434.

[3]This is the name usually applied to this area on the "upper race" in Port Republic.

[4]William T. Hutchinson, *Cyrus Hall McCormick*, (New York: The Century Company), 301.

[5]Ibid., 305

[6]It is no longer standing, but its site is visible.

[7]Deed Book, 11:530.

[8]Deed Book, 2:522.

[9]Deed Book, 0000:399.

[10]This mill operated until 1940.

[11]John F. Miller's store was located on lot No. 20.

Chapter 9

Lost Opportunities

I t is painful to reflect on the short-sightedness of the business men of the neighborhood who slammed the door shut in the face of progress, when it so graciously knocked at our very door, offering opportunities of advancement and improvement that may not again come our way in another lifetime. How mournful to contemplate the spectacle of what we are when we visualize what we might have been had these misguided men decided otherwise than they did.

When the Shenandoah Valley Railroad was being built, and it was found that Port Republic was about midway between Roanoke and Hagerstown, the two towns to be connected by rail, an effort was made by the railroad company to purchase land on which to build the railroad shops. The effort was a flat failure. No land could be bought for the purpose. Perhaps with a few honorable exceptions, the farmers and other employers of labor feared a rise in wages and that they would no longer have men competing for the few driblets of work they were compelled to hire others to do if the railroad built its shops here. The shops were built at Milnes, now Shenandoah City.

A little later a certain Mr. DeFord came to the neighborhood and looked over the situation. He decided that Port Republic was the best location in the Valley for the tannery he intended to build. He, too, could not buy land for his purpose. The farmers and others were not to be insulted by being requested to sell the land on which to build a "foreign" industrial plant, that would, in the nature of things, give employment to laboring men as well as to others. Failing to obtain land here for his tannery, Mr. De Ford built at Luray.

Later still August Wolfe tried to negotiate the purchase of a piece of land to build thereon shops and foundries in which to manufacture flour mill machinery. It is almost unbelievable, but he, too, was turned away and later built his factory at Chambersburg, Pa.

Port Republic is admirably situated and should become the leading industrial town between Lexington and Riverton, in the Shenandoah Valley. Had it not been for the narrow idea of those who preceded us that a dollar in hand is worth all the dollars any fool ever dreamed about, it would long ago have become such.

With a few notable exceptions, it is a disheartening fact that since the Civil War to the present time, men with limited vision, lacking energy and incapable of leading in any progressive movement, have been at the head of our public and business affairs. It is no business feat worthy of praise for a man in business, by hook or crook, to prevent the coming of a possible competitor. The desire for unreasonable profits is driving those who have automobiles to Harrisonburg and other towns to do their buying. Without the infusion of new blood, Port Republic may yet fall prey to the approaching cornfields.

The Methodist Episcopal Church of Port Republic

The Port Republic Methodist Episcopal Church, from its organization to the present time, has been decidedly the strongest and most influential church in the town and neighborhood.[1] This denomination was founded by the Rev. John Wesley, an Episcopal clergyman. He did not become a member of the society he fathered. He lived and died in the Church of England. The Methodist Societies in America were organized as a separate body at the Christmas Conference held in Baltimore, December 1784.

Rev. Robert Williams, born in England, was the first to plant Methodism in Virginia. He landed at Norfolk in the year 1772 and at once opened his mission. Standing on the steps in front of the Court House door, he began to sing, and when a crowd had gathered he preached the first Methodist sermon ever delivered in Virginia.

Brunswick Circuit, the first in the Old Dominion, was formed in 1774. The conference held at Leesburg, 1778, was the first ever held in the States.

Rockingham was constituted a circuit in 1788 under Philip Bruce as Presiding Elder. Philip Bruce came of Huguenot ancestry. He was born in the vicinity of King's Mountain, N.C., Dec. 25, 1755. The first of his family to unite with the Methodist Church, he entered upon the labors of preaching with animation, and the flame of his enthusiasm burned brightly for more than fifty years. In the annals of

Methodism in Virginia, his name is deservedly placed with the greatest. He died among his kindred in Tennessee May 10, 1827.

William Phoebus was the first preacher appointed to serve Rockingham Circuit. He labored valiantly, but in the following year had only seventy-nine members scattered over an extensive territory. He died in 1831.

The mists of time conceal the date when the Methodist Episcopal Church was organized at Port Republic. There is little doubt but there were some Methodists in the neighborhood in the 1780's, if not earlier. Asbury was here very likely in 1781 for he wrote of his itinerary under the date of Thursday, July 21, 1781:

Last evening I rode a mile and a half to see some of the greatest natural curiosities my eyes ever beheld: they were two caves, about two hundred yards from each other; their entrances were, as in similar cases, narrow and descending, gradually widening towards the interior, and opening into lofty chambers, supported, to appearance by basaltic pillars. In one of these I sung, "Still out of the deepest abyss."

The sound was wonderful. There were stalactites resembling the pipes of an organ, which, when our old guide, father Ellsworth, struck with a stick, emitted melodious sound with variations according to their size; walls like our old churches; resemblance to the towers adjoining their belfries; and the natural gallery, which we ascended with difficulty: all to me was new, solemn, and awfully grand. There were parts which we did not explore; so deep, so damp, and near night. I came away filled with wonder, with humble praise, and adoration.[2]

Bishop Francis Asbury preached here on Sunday, Feb. 26, 1809. He was attended by Bishop William McKendree and others. On the preceding Friday they passed Charlottesville, "within sight of fair Monticello, the seat of

Thomas Jefferson, we rested at Daniel Maupin's, his father and mother are gone to rest. We crossed the ridge at Brown's Gap, and came to Port Republic, and lodged with Doctor William Douglass. Sabbath, 26, I preached upon Acts 11: 21. We found it dangerous riding through the snow to Harrisonburg on Monday."[3]

Through necessity Asbury's entries in his "Journal" had to be brief, yet we can only regret that he did not write more fully on this occasion. It is probable that Dr. Douglass was the preacher in charge here at the time of Asbury's visit, and that he held the degree of Doctor of Divinity. As one of the early ministers in Rockingham County who made marriage returns, his name is written in 1807: Rev. William Douglass. John Carthrea and his wife, Mary, on Oct. 30, 1807, deeded a lot in Carthrea's Addition to Dr. Douglass. It cost $400.

The early Methodist preachers were emotion-mongers. Of striking personalities, they were fluent exhorters; with piercing eyes, a vast knowledge of human nature, and with an air of solemn mystery, they roused their audiences to a sensuous feeling, to the very delights of animal magnetism. When one of them stood up to preach, the gathered people were awed into deep silence. The preaching was aimed at their hearts and not at their heads. With practiced hands, these men struck the keys to their emotions as surely as an expert pianist touches the keys of his instrument. God was described to them as a literal person, and heaven was said to be above the clouds, filled with singing and shouting brethren who had gone hence, and flaming hell but a short distance beneath their feet. "Hark!" "Hush!" "Watch!" were words sometimes shouted to the assemblage. The effect was magical. Tremors ran through their bodies, and when the preacher rose to his highest and loudest descriptions of the agonies suffered by lost souls, the people screamed, some fell to the floor, while others sang and prayed.

𝔐ethodist 𝔈piscopal 𝔠hurch, 𝔖outh

(THE CHURCH WITH THE LIGHTED WINDOW)

Port Republic, Virginia.

𝔚. 𝔉. 𝔏owance, 𝔓astor

Special Evangelistic Services

Each Evening at 8.00 P. M., During.......Aug. 7 to 20th.

Keep This Time Sacred in Soul Winning

JESUS WAITS   TIME FLIES   DEATH URGES

God's Time is Now.   Come—Bring One

(*Over*)

Announcement of the Methodist Episcopal Church, South, c. 1915

The following is extracted from Abbott's description of one of his meetings:

I sang, prayed, began to exhort, and God laid to his helping hand, and came down in his Spirit's power as in ancient days: some fell to the floor, others ran out of the house, many cried aloud for mercy, and others were shouting praises to the God of Hosts with hearts full of love divine. Seeing the people set on the joists upstairs, I was afraid they would fall through, this caused me to withhold: I quitted the pulpit.[4]

Knowing nothing of psychology, these men had no other explanation for these phenomena than that they were caused by the operation of the Holy Ghost. Any explanation of them must take into consideration the fact that they have occurred under all forms of religion, whether believed to be true, or known to be false. Concentrated attention, reinforced by strong religious emotions, and fear of the unknown, produced powerful impressions upon their nervous systems; the effects of which manifested themselves in various ways, according to the constitution of the individual. Some wept, or found relief in hysterical laughter; others sang, prayed, or shouted; many became unconscious; and in those "struck" the hardest, a complete catalepsy was produced.

Methodism soon overleaped the Blue Ridge and found a congenial home among the pioneers of East Rockingham. It waxed strong and many sheep were added to the fold. In all probability, the Methodists had so increased in numbers in the early 1780's as to impel them to organize a church. Here as elsewhere, no doubt, they held open-air meetings when the weather was suitable, and at private homes upon notice. That the church was organized and in pressing need of a piece of land for a church site and a graveyard at an early date, the following deed plainly shows:

This Indenture made this 28th day of October 1793 between John Carthrea and Molly his wife of Rockingham County and State of Virginia of the one part and John Hicks, James Kennerly, Philip Kennerly, James Burgess, and John Walsh of the county and State aforesaid of the other part, Witnesseth, that the said John Carthrea and Molly his wife for and in consideration of the sum of five shillings to them in hand paid the receipt whereof is hereby acknowledged and have granted bargained sold conveyed and confirmed and by these presents do give grant bargain and sell convey and confirm unto the said Trustees above mentioned a certain lot of land situated lying and being in the aforesaid County and State close by the said John Carthrea house, Beginning at a sycamore at the mouth of the lain being a south west course, and thence North 67 East 38 poles thence South 35 Degrees East four and one third poles to two sycamores standing on the brink of the river, and with the same to the beginning 2s an acre be the same more or less. Together with all and singular the rights members privileges powers profits immunities hereditaments and appurtenances whatsoever to the same belonging or in anywise appertaining and also all the estate, right title, interest property claim and demand whatsoever belonging to him the said John Carthrea and Molly his wife, either in law or equity of in or to the aforesaid lott of land hereby granted or any part of parcel thereof to have and to hold the above mentioned lot of land premises and every part thereof with the hereditaments and appurtenances hereby granted or intended to be granted, unto the aforesaid trustees and their successors trustees for the time to hold to them the said Trustees their successors as aforesaid in trust. Nevertheless and to the intent and purpose that the same shall be and ensure, and shall be adjudged continued deemed and taken to be and ensure to the only purpose use and benefit and behalf of the Methodist Episcopal Church to hold and perform the worship of Almighty God upon and to bury their dead, at all times hereafter forever, as they may see meet, and for no other use interest or purpose whatsoever. Nevertheless, and it is hereby intended that as often as any of the trustees aforesaid or of the trustees for the time being shall die or cease to be member or members of the said Methodist Episcopal Church then the remaining part of the trustees for the time being or their successors as soon as conveniently may be made and shall choose another trustee or trustees in order to keep up the Number of Trustees forever who shall stand and act in behalf of the said Church as Trustees aforesaid. Nevertheless upon special truth and confidence and to the intent, that they shall account allow all such person or persons at all times who shall be appointed at the yearly Conference of the aforesaid Church in America to preach and expound Gods holy word therein provided always that the said person or persons so appointed preach no other doctrine than which is contained in the Rev. John Wesley's notes on the holy Scripture and his volume of sermons and enforce the discipline as laid down and contained in the form of Discipline comprehending the principles rules and doctrines of the aforesaid Church, and the said John Carthrea and Molly his wife for themselves their heirs executors administrators and assigns do hereby further covenant grant for and agree to warrant forever defend all and singular the afore mentioned lot or parcel of ground for the use and purpose aforesaid John Hicks, James Kennerly, Philip Kennerly, James Burgess, and John Walsh, Trustees as aforesaid and their successors for the claim or claims of all manner of person or persons whatsoever who now claim or may hereafter claim the same or any part or parcel thereof In witness whereof we have hereunto set our hands and seals this 18th day of February and year of our Lord one thousand-seven-hundred-and-ninety-three.

        John Carthrea   Seal
        Molly Carthrea   Seal

The alert reader has, presumably noted the discrepancy in the dates in this deed. It was presented in open court, October, 1793, and admitted to record. S. McWilliams was clerk of the court at the time. The copy herein used was made by H.J. Gambill, who succeeded Mr. McWilliams in 1817.

If the deed was made on the 28th of October, it could not have been signed on the 18th of February of the same year. It seems reasonable to suppose that the latter date is wrong, for the copyist could hardly have made a mistake in writing the first date at the beginning of the document. This date left three days, in which the deed could be offered for record before the adjournment of the court.

The above deed is convincing proof that the Methodist Episcopal Church of this place had been organized and had appointed five trustees to hold property in trust for it before the date of the deed; and certainly no man ever deeded real estate to trustees of a non-existent institution.

Bishop Asbury's presence in the neighborhood doubtless so increased the number of church members that a house for religious purposes was an imperative need in 1793. In all probability the church was built the following year. James Burgess had it reshingled in 1812, which shows that it had been built so long before then, that time and weather had caused the roof to deteriorate.

The efforts of the writer to get information concerning the above trustees has met with small success.

Philip Kennerly was a native of Augusta County and was born Oct. 18, 1769. He was converted at an early age, and entered the Baltimore Conference in 1804. After serving three years as a traveling preacher, he located and moved to Logan County, Ky. His interest in the propagation of his faith did not cease and he was re-admitted into the traveling fraternity in 1821. He was received by the Kentucky Conference, but scarcely had he entered upon his work when he was seized by a mortal disease and died Oct 5, 1821.

James Burgess married Mary Beard March 20, 1794. He was class leader at Harrisonburg in 1802. In that year, Bishop Asbury visited the town in company with Enoch George and Nicholas Snethen. The ensuing meetings flamed into a revival that continued for nine days. The Rev. Joseph Travis was present and was an eyewitness of the scenes he so vividly described. Of Mr. Burgess he wrote:

I can never forget the night I attended my class, when the leader sang and prayed, unfolded his class-paper, burst into a flood of tears, and with a half-choked utterance said: 'Brethern, go home, I cannot meet you in class tonight.' He picked up his hat and walked out; in slow procession the rest of us followed. On my way home, passing by the stable of the leader, I heard a groan, the sound being that of a human being. I approached, and it being a moonlight night, on looking in I saw the leader, James Burgess, upon his knees begging God to have mercy upon the Church. Oh, that we had more such leaders in this day as he then was.[5]

James Kennerly married the widow Harpine. He had business dealings with James Burgess at Sandy Hook as late as 1814.

John Hicks lived, most likely, in that part of Rockingham County that is now Central District. He was a member of Capt. Charles McClain's militia company No. 5,

West District, in 1792. It seems that he was a silversmith and had as an apprentice one James Brown.

Rev. John Walsh was a Methodist preacher and was much sought, about the beginning of the nineteenth century, by couples desiring to have the nuptial knot securely tied. Rev. Walsh was a school teacher in a Methodist school at Harrisonburg in 1794.

Below are given several pages taken from an old book recording the class-meetings held in the Methodist Episcopal Church at Port Republic. On the inside of the front cover of the book is written "1812 & 1813" and the letters J.E.L. are written below the figures. The book is homemade, of unruled paper and limp sheepskin cover. It contains the following information.

Class Paper for the Morning
Josiah Emmit Leader
Little Children Love one another. Remember Every Friday preceding the Quarterly Meeting Is to be observed as Days of Fasting and Prayer for the prosperity of Zion.

Christofer Fry P E
John Gill Watt A P
Ezra Grove   P C

No.	State 1	State 2	Names & Meeting Days	Station	July 5	12	19	26
	1	2			5	12	19	26
		b	Josiah Emmit	m	p	p	p	p
		b	James Burgess	m	p	p	p	p
		b	Mary Burgess	m	p	a	p	p
		b	Abigail Roberts	w	p	p	p	s
5		b	Lilpha Roberts	s	a	p	p	a
		b	Mary Roberts	s	p	p	p	a
		b	Azuba Robert	s	p	p	a	a
		b	Patsey Robert	s	p	a	p	a
		b	John Roberts	s	p	p	p	a
10		b	Curtis Roberts	s	p	a	e	a

	b	Sarah Fitch	m	p	a	a	a
	b	Richard S. Emmit		a	p	p	p
	s	Jane Burgess	s	p	p	p	a
	s	Margaret Makall	m	p	a	a	p
15	b	Amena Smith	m	a	a	p	p
	b	Samuel Tingley	m	p	p	p	p
	b	Jane Tingley	m	p	p	p	p
	b	Jane Makall	w	p	p	p	a
	b	Ann Arnold	w	p	p	p	p
20	b	Sarah Owens	w	a	p	a	a
	b	Mary Owens	s	p	p	p	p
	b	Samuel Evans	m	p	p	p	p
	b	Juliet Ann Evans	m	p	p	a	p
	b	Michal Trainer	m				
		Henry Moss					
		Polly Moss					

The aforementioned is a complete list of those marked present or absent for the month of July 1812. The last two names have no markings and are in another handwriting.

On the extreme left the names are counted in fives. The next column has but one letter in it, s, and is opposite the name of Jane Burgess. Its signification is unknown to the writer. This column does not appear in any of the other lists. The column of Bs is understood to mean "baptized."

The first column on the right has the m's, s's, and w's which are taken to mean "married", "single", and "widowed" respectively. The remaining four columns containing the p's and a's denote who were present and who were absent. In the last column but one, opposite the name of Curtis Roberts is an E the meaning of which is not plain; it may mean "excused" or "expelled".

The names in the succeeding lists and not found in the one above are: Catharine Emmit, M; William D. Clark, M; Rachel Clark, M; Sally Carroll, Henry F. Carroll, Tracey Catline, Richard Ferguson, M; Rachel Decker, S; Mary Moss,

Daniel Protsman, M; Mary Protsman, M; Stephen Harnsberger, M; Elizabeth Harnsberger, M; Sarah Cash, S; Morris Hinchey, M; Mary Hinchey, M; Mary Ann Hinchey, S; Betty Rolley, S; James Rankin, Bertha Rankin, and Edward Mooney.

No meetings are recorded after August 1813. Exactly half of the book was not used which indicates that the meetings were discontinued. Whether the war, then in progress, was the cause is problematical.

Rev. Christopher Fry, of Winchester, was a model Presiding Elder and an able preacher. He traveled extensively and was fatally hurt in an accident.

It was reported at the Conference in Baltimore, March 15, 1843, that the Rev. John Gill Watt had died.

So far as known there is but one more of these interesting books in existence. It is for the years 1833-1840 inclusive. All for the years between 1813-1833 are misplaced or lost.

The title of this book is:

Balt. Con. Rockingham District, Port Republic Circuit
Port Republic 1834
C.B. Tippett, W.H. Enos, Preachers
J. A. Henning for 1833, J. Spriggs

A tract of four pages being "The General Rules of the United Methodist Societies" is attached to the inside of the front cover of the book. These rules were read at every Quarterly Conference. A little over one hundred years ago the following persons belonged to the Morning Class:

Minerva Holt m	Ann Alexander m
Stephen Hernsberger m	Sally Palmer m
Moses Alexander s	Robert Pettus s Run off
Agnes Palmer s	Fontaine Layton s
Daniel Burk s Probationer 18 Aug	

Jane Harper s
Joseph Trout m
Oliver T. Mann m
Charles W. Carthrea m
Nancy Hamilton s
Walter Covington s
  removed Jan 17, 1833
James O'Brian m
Margaret Scott m
Eliza J. Holbrook s
Tobias R.M.G. Bolinger s
  withdrawn by certificate
Mary A. Palmer m
  Removed to Staunton
  Jan 19, 1834
Catharine Graham w
George Snyder m on certificate
Benjamin F. Lewis s Defunct
H.B. Harnsberger, on probation
J.M.C. Harnsberger, on probation

John Trobough m
D. P. Teel, dismissed
Virginia A. Lewis s
Harriet Mann m
Elizabeth Carthrea m
Amos Scott m Backed transferred
  Aug. 1833
Amanda J. Harnsberger s
Phebe Fort m
Mary Alexander s
James Q. Palmer m
Christina Spitzer m
Clinger T. Mann
Mary Ann Trout s
Samuel Orbison s
Franklin Kemper s Expunged
Margaret Catland s
John F. Lewis New member
Mary Utzler s on trial Feb 2

Rev. Charles B. Tippett was born in Prince George County, Md., in 1801. He began to preach in 1819, and was admitted on trial in 1820. In 1832 and in 1844, he was elected delegate to the ensuing General Conference. At the latter conference, he was elected assistant book-agent for New York. He died in Hookstown, Md., in 1867.

Rev. William H. Enos was born at Salem, Mass., in 1800. Left an orphan, he went to Virginia about 1816. He was a man of parts and taught in a private family when he came to Virginia. Converted in Montgomery County, he entered conference in 1829 and continued in the work until 1849. He died Oct. 6, 1855.

Rev. John A. Henning was received in 1827, and located in 1850. He was a man of talent, but unfortunately he was eccentric. This caused several misunderstandings, one of

Methodist Episcopal Congregation in front of its second church building

which culminated in a trial. He was charged with maladministration, tried at the Conference of 1848, and was acquitted.

Rev. Joseph Spriggs was received on trial by the conference in 1824. He adhered to the Church South in 1851 and served in the Virginia Conference.

The names of new members, and the notes opposite their names for the succeeding years, are given, together with the notes:

1834
David H. Martin, s   transferred from Augusta, Oct. 1834
Catharine Miller, w   by letter from Winchester
Mary Shutler, m   transferred from Providence
1835
Jacob Davey, s   upon certificate, removed
Clarissa Hamilton, s
Phebe Fort, m   removed
Mary Triplett, m   on certificate
William Baker, m   removed
1836
Harriet Mann, m   transferred to afternoon class
William Baker, m transferred from Harrisonburg
James M. Stout, m
Sarah Pickering, s
Jane Snyder, m by certificate Dec. 2, 1836

1837

Charles W. Carthrea, m   removed Sept. 8, 1837, to Mo.
Elizabeth Carthrea, m   "   "   "
Eliza J. Holbrook, s dropped Sept. 1837
Benjamin F. Lewis, s withdrawn
David M. Martin, s   departed this life
James M. Stout, m   withdrawn, dropped
George Mozings, s   trans.
1838
Mary Triplett, m   moved to Augusta
Jacob Snyder, s   removed
George Mozings, m   under censure and removed
Agnes Herendon, m
Catharine Dundore, m
1839
Mary A. Trout, s   removed to Luray
B.H. Crever, s
Mary Welsh, m
Mary Ewing, w
Martha Burton, s
Eliza Lewis, s
Caroline Lewis, s
John Herrington, m on trial, moved
Margaret Huff, m   transferred
Elizabeth R. Trout, s   transferred
Robert McClune, m   by certificate
Susanne McClune, m   "   "
Francis C. Browne
1840
Clarissa Hamilton, s   removed
John Snyder, s
John S. Moore, m   removed, reproach
Malinda Dunn, s
Samuel Spitzer, m
William Moore, s
Cassandra McClune, m   certificate
Elizabeth Rutherford
Martha S. Trout,   on probation
Mary J. Eddins,   on probation

Ann M. Eddins, on probation
Elizabeth Ewan, on probation
Elizabeth Alexander, on probation, on trial

In a number of instances there are no letters to indicate whether certain persons were married or single.

Considering the following notes and that human nature was the same then as now, those "morning classes" were composed of exceptionally good material.

There are a number of notes written lengthwise the pages stating when and where conferences were held, the condition of the weather, and much other interesting matter. Some of the notes are not dated, or if they are the writer cannot determine which date applies, as in some instances they are put down in a very confusing manner.

The first one for the winter of 1833 is, "Four Days Meeting Mud & Snow good time W.H.E." The initials are those of the Rev. W.H. Enos, pastor in charge. This circuit was so large that two preachers were usually assigned to it, but this year there were four laboring in the circuit. Rev. J.A. Henning was Mr. Enos's assistant. For March 1, 1835 is found, "Bro. Henning present, the morning very cold." On the 15th, "No class by reason of high water," and the 22nd, "Five present owing to inclement weather." January 10, 1836, this, "Bro. Week's day" to preach most likely. The 17th, "Few present Inclement." The 24th, "Bro. Coffin not well-his c day." July 3, "Quart. Meeting Spring Creek-Pray. Mtg. In Brick Ch."

This note shows that the Methodists were holding some meetings in the Brick Church at this time and were preparing to abandon the Old Meetinghouse. It was near this time that Joseph Martin wrote, there was "1 house of public worship, free for all denominations" in the town. The Lutherans, Presbyterians, Episcopalians, and Methodists held meetings in this building. June 5, this was noted, "No Class Rain and high waters." The Old Meetinghouse was on a low bank of South River, and "high waters" would prevent the holding of meetings in it. There are two slips of paper waxed to the page for 1837. One informs:

1838 Janr. 1st Members names carried forward -
    Since the commencement of this Conference year.

Deaths	1
Removed	2
Dropped & withdrawn	4
Standing members	<u>25</u>
	32

Across the left of the above is written "Dear Somebody," meaning the unnamed dead one, no doubt. On the other piece of paper is written, "Norval Wilson P. Elder John C. Lyon P. in charge W. McR. Ward jr Preacher."

It seems that the Old Meetinghouse was not well equipped with suitable stoves or fireplaces for the purpose of heating the building, or else fuel was lacking at times, as the following notes for the year 1838 appear to show. February 4, "The day very cold no persons present at the hour." April 15, "Weather Inclement 24 absent." December 9, "The class was met. Bro. Young failed to attend." The 23rd, "the day very cold Bro. Lyon present." Nothing but cold weather could damp the ardor and chill the enthusiasm of these early Methodists. As a general rule the early history of sectaries shows their contempt for creature comforts in their meetinghouses. Some were so extreme as to consider it sinful to be comfortable while worshipping. Without heat in cold weather, and with no backs to the benches, which were so high that the feet of the children were several inches above the floor, none but a valiant "soldier of the cross" could endure the discomfort.

The following is a description of the first Methodist Meetinghouse built in America. "On Sam's Creek, Strawbridge built a log chapel. It was twenty-two feet square, without windows, door or floor, and, though long occupied, was never finished."[6]

The following year is found:

For 1839 Samuel Brison P.E. Wheler in Charge Levi Monroe assistant.
May 23—Rules read by Br. Wheeler after Sermon.
August 18—Bro. Harnsberger (illegible) Class led by Bro. Crever.
April 25, 1840—Bro. Eskridges first sermon to day.
December 13—Deep snow clear shine & pliant (pleasant?) weather.
The 20th —Day for preaching (no one to preach) cold clear day.

The previous entries are all the information in this Class Book. In these notes the names of several preachers are mentioned.

Rev. R. Carl Maxwell says, "In 1834 Daniel Burk was transferred from the Port Republic Methodist Episcopal Church to the Methodist Episcopal Church at Naked Creek."[7]

Rev. Mr. Weeks was here in 1836. Salathiel Weeks, an elder, was at a conference held in Greenbrier County in 1792. The writer does not know whether he was here forty-four years later.

Rev. Mr. Coffin is also mentioned as being here in 1836. If he was the Rev. William H. Coffin, he was received into the conference in 1829, and located in 1850.

In 1857 Rev. Norval Wilson was Presiding Elder of the District and Rev. John C. Lyon, pastor in charge of the circuit with Rev. W. McR. Ward as assistant. Rev. Norval Wilson was an able preacher. He was born Dec. 24, 1802, and died Aug 9, 1876.

Rev. Mr. Young was here in 1838. Rev. Charles B. Young and Rev. Jared H. Young were in the Conference at this time.

Which, if either, was here, the writer does not know.

Rev. Samuel Brison, born 1798, was a native of Newtown (now Stephen City), Frederick County. He entered the itinerancy in 1821 and labored for thirty-two years with unabated ardor. The preacher in charge may have been Rev. Thomas Wheeler.

Rev. Levi N. Monroe was born in Prince George County, Md., Aug. 11, 1810. He was admitted on trial in 1836, labored in the Conference eleven years, patiently bore great bodily afflictions for five years, and died in peace Nov. 16, 1853.

The "Bro. Crever" mentioned as leading the class Aug. 18,1839, was, probably, Rev. Benjamin H. Crever.

A note of April 25, 1840, informs, "Bro. Eskridges first sermon to day." Rev. Alfred A. Eskridge was born in Centerville, Fairfax County. For several years he was clerk of the Court of Loudoun County, and resided at Leesburg. He joined the Methodist Church at Leesburg, Rev. Charles B. Tippett being the preacher in charge. The latter preceded

Methodist Church Ladies Aid Society, 1911

him at this appointment by a few years. He lived to the ripe age of nearly ninety-three years. He was superannuated for sixteen years, residing in Harrisonburg and Staunton.

The minutes of four meetings of the trustees of the "Methodist Meetinghouse in Port Republic," as it was called, have come down to the present.

The first meeting was held June 1, 1833. Rev. William H. Enos presided. The following is taken from the record of the meeting:

Selah Holbrook Charles Carthrea Jas. O'Bryan John Huff Being present and Stephen Harnsberger Jas. Altaffer and John Roberts absent. Proceeded to business. We have a deed for a Part of the lot John Carthrea will Give a deed for remainder Selah Holbrook was appointed to provide a deed a debt of Two Dollars upon the house to repairs needed.

Attempts have been made to enclose the lot materials nearly enough provided. Selah Holbrook appointed to Superintend the finishing (fencing?) of the lot. Selah Holbrook was appointed Recording Secretary of the Board of Trustees

S. Holbrook Sectr

W. H. Enos Prestd[8]

It is not clear what lot they had a deed for a part, and John Carthrea would deed the remainder to them. It may have been a lot for a parsonage. It could not have been the Old Brick Church property, for that had been deeded to trustees for religious purposes nine years previous.

In a deed bearing date Sept. 4, 1824, "Dundore & Givens and Alexander R. Givens of the one part, and William Craig, Samuel Linn, and Samuel Lewis of the other part," the parties of the first part convey the half of a certain lot in Port Republic "it being the one half of Lot __ and that part of it which when divided cross wise lies next to Main Street" to the parties of the second part; and Alexander R. Givens, of himself, conveys to the above trustees one half of a lot lying next to the above lot. The number of this lot is blank also. It is further described as the lot "on which the Brick Meetinghouse now stands."

Givens names William Craig, Samuel Linn, Charles Lewis, George Gilmore, and John Carthrea as trustees. In the index of the deed book they are given as trustees of the Presbyterian Church. The property was to be held by them as a place for religious meetings, and when not in use by them it "shall be free for Preachers in regular standing in any other denomination of Christians."[9]

The above church lot was composed of the half each of lots Nos. 27 and 28, and facing on Main Street.

The absence of church records and the destruction of numerous county deed books in whole or in part in the Civil War, casts a shadow, almost impenetrable, over the Old Brick Church. That the Methodists had an interest in it and that it was used by them as early as 1826 the following subscription paper clearly shows:

We the undersigned bind ourselves to pay to Stephen Harnsberger the sums respectively annexed to our names to be applied: under the direction of the Trustees of the two meetinghouses in Port Republic - first to laying a plank floor and making other necessary repairs to the Brick Meetinghouse secondly to enclosing the lot on which said house stands - and thirdly to enclosing the old meetinghouse lot, or so much of the above as the funds raised shall be sufficient to accomplish. Witness our hands this 18th March 1826.

It is regrettable that the subscribers' names are torn off and, probably, lost.

At the second meeting of the Trustees of the Methodist Meetinghouse in Port Republic, held April 14th 1834:

William H. Enos, Preacher in Charge Presd, James O'Bryan, Charles W. Carthrea, John Huff, Selah Holbrook Being present and Stephen Harnsberger, Jas. Altaffer and John Roberts being absent Proceeded to business. Selah Holbrook Presented account for materials for enclosing lot and work for the same and some stove pipe amounting to Twenty Dollars and Twenty-Six cents admitted by the Trustees.

Trustees of Methodist Meetinghouse
To S. Holbrook Dr
March 1st 1831

To 18 Stove pipe at 12-1/2	2.25
March 20 1834	
To 7 ditto at 25	1.75
" Sawing 460 feet plank at 2/3 p 100	1.71
" 80 feet Ditto at 75	.60
" 240 feet Layths at 1.25	3.00
" 3 new Gates and hangings at 2.25	6.75
" 560 feet Plank got of J. Palmer .75	4.20
	$20.26[10]

The third meeting was on July 15, 1846, Rev. Thomas H. Busey presiding. James O'Bryan and John Huff were appointed to advertise and sell the Old Meetinghouse on the following Saturday, the 18th, to the highest bidder. But three days were had to advertise and sell the house.[11]

The fourth and last of these meetings, the records of which are still existing, was held July 25, 1846, Rev. Mr. Busey presiding. The Old Meetinghouse had been sold to Robert W. Palmer for $40. The account which Selah Holbrook had presented at the meeting in 1834 was, twelve years later, "given due consideration" and it was agreed to "Pay Said Holbrook ten Dollars which is considered payment in full payable on the first Day of Jany next." It was further ordered that "ten Dollars of the first payment of the Sale of the Methodist House Shall be appropriated to the repairs of the fence enclosing the Said Meetinghouse lot. James Obryan is appointed to superintend the Same."[12]

Rev. Thomas Busey, born in Washington, D.C., was converted at Harpers Ferry in his eighteenth year. He was admitted in 1837, continued in the Conference until 1855, and, broken in health, died April 19, 1856.

The names of several ministers not given in the preceding list, who served this charge, are found in Stephen Harnsberger's account book and given below.

Rev. George W. Israel was born Oct. 27, 1813, in Howard County, Md. He was pastor here in 1848. He was regarded as an able preacher, had a fine legal mind, and in cases of judicial trial in the Conference, was a powerful advocate. He died Nov 25, 1891.

Rev. Tillotson A. Morgan entered the Conference in 1837 and his ministry embraced fifty-one years of active service. He was one of the ministers at Port Republic in 1849. In 1848 he was one of seven trustees appointed by Bishop James for the Wesleyan Female Institute at Staunton.

Following these were Rev. Patrick Kelley, 1850; Rev. Mr. Baird, 1855; and Rev. Mr. Smith, 1859. Mr. Baird may have been Rev. William S. Baird, by birth a Pennsylvanian; and Mr. Smith was probably Rev. Bennett H. Smith, a Virginian.

In John Dundore's daybook, under the date September 1853, this entry is found: "Preacher Aken to John Dundore Dr to 2000 shingles loaned you to cover parsonage." The shingles are marked returned. This "Preacher Aken" was Rev. James N. Eakin who was born Dec. 26, 1824, and died in his prime at Front Royal, Jan. 18, 1859.

William S. Downs notices four ministers in his daybooks. He gives them the title of "Parson." Rev. Mr. Wolfe, 1858; Rev. Mr. Houck, 1858; Rev. Mr. Hyde, 1864; and Rev. Mr. Rexrode, 1865. The "Parson" Wolfe mentioned by Mr. Downs was probably Rev. John W. Wolfe. Rev. Mr. Houck was the minister who officiated at Mr. Downs' marriage.

Rev. John P. Hyde moved from Port Republic to Winchester where he established a female seminary. Rev. Mr. Rexrode was a local neighborhood preacher who belonged to some other sect.

Found in the account book of Dr. George W. Kemper, Sr., are the names of seven preachers: Rev. Mr. Smith, 1859; Rev. Mr. Leach, 1862; Rev. Mr. Gaver, 1862; Rev. John P. Hyde, 1864; Rev. Mr. Rexrode, 1865; Rev. J. F. Liggett, 1868; and Rev. Mr. Wilson, 1872.

Mr. Smith was, perhaps, Rev. Bennett H. Smith, who was born in Mecklenburg County, Jan. 10, 1824, and died in Baltimore, Md., Dec. 28, 1902. Rev. George V. Leech was born at Nassau, N.Y., October 1835, and died in Washington, D.C., March 24, 1905. Mr. Leach may have been he. Mr. Gaver was, probably, Rev. Hamilton A. Gaver.

Rev. James F. Liggett was born in Greenbrier County, April 13, 1831. He is remembered here as a faithful pastor and a successful revivalist. He died at Churchville, April 1875. Mr. Wilson is still remembered by our oldest residents, but the writer cannot identify him.

Mr. Wysong was serving this charge at the time of the outbreak of the Civil War. Not being in sympathy with the South, he quietly left without informing anyone here of his intention. He may have been Rev. Thomas T. Wysong.

In Central Graveyard sleeps a Methodist preacher whose memory is much loved and respected. The grave is enclosed with an iron fence made by William A. Maupin of iron manufactured by the Mt. Vernon Iron Works. A copy of the inscription on the gravestone is a sufficient eulogy:

In memory of Rev. David Wood, Born in Louisa County, Va, Feb'ry 2, 1808. Converted and Licensed to preach in 1827. Joined the Virginia Conference M. E. Church 1829. Died in Port Republic, Va., March 27th 1851. Twenty-four years he preached the gospel faithfully, energetically & with great success, and many souls in eternity will pronounce him blessed. 'They that sow in tears shall reap in Joy.'

John Carthrea deeded, March 8, 1832, to the following trustees of the "Methodist Episcopal Church in the United States of America," namely John Sibert, Charles W. Carthrea, Stephen Harnsberger, Selah Holbrook, James O'Bryan, Joseph Altaffer, and John Huff, the following described piece of land in Port Republic:

Beginning at a stake corner of a Lot of Land attached to the Old Meeting House, Thence N 35 degrees 2 1/25 poles to a stake in a line of the street of Port Republic, Thence S 115 Degrees W 38 poles to a stake on a line of sd. Street formerly a Sycamore tree, thence with a line of the Lot attached to the old Meeting House, N 67 ½ degrees E 38 poles to the beginning containing about one fourth of an acre, "to be used by said church to its rules, etc. for the benefit of its members"[13]

This deed may be of special interest to those living on the south end of Water Street.

On July 27, 1853, Peter Fitch and Fannie Fitch, his wife, deeded the house and lot being one-half of lot No. 21 facing Water Street, and lot No. 26 to trustees of the Port Republic Methodist Episcopal Church as a parsonage lot, and a lot on which to build a church, respectively. The church building was completed the following year.

The Methodist Episcopal Church in the United States was one of the first major religious bodies to separate on the question of slavery. At the General Conference held in New York in 1844, Bishop James O. Andrew, who had become connected with slavery "by marriage and otherwise," was admonished to free Himself of this impediment to the office of general superintendent of the church, or to "desist from the exercise of this office so long as this impediment remains." The fires of disunion burned brightly, and before the conference adjourned a plan of separation had been adopted. The example was set; the precedent was established; and on this same rock of offense, the civil government of our country split sixteen years later. "It was the unfaithfulness of the American churches, and not the least of the Presbyterian churches, to the plain requirements of duty, which suffered the evil to grow and gather head, until its end came in a deluge of human blood."[14]

Port Republic Circuit did not ally itself to the Southern wing of the disrupted church. Not until after the Civil War, did the Southern Methodists come into the neighborhood. They were rather frowned upon and were not allowed the use of the church. They held meetings in what was later called the George Nicholas store. Benjamin Franklin Kemper, William S. Downs, the Hooke family, and others joined them. The hard times that immediately followed the war, the memory of the wanton destruction of property and the brutal treatment of the people by the Yankees, soon caused the whole circuit to unite with the Southern church. For a short time after this, representatives of the Northern Methodists preached to the colored people in Downs' tanyard.

From the close of the war to 1875, Port Republic Circuit seems to have been a "No man's land." It is doubtful if any church records were kept during that time. The names of several of the ministers who were here in those "troublous" years have been contributed: Rev. Alfred O. Armstrong, Rev. Mr. Bear, Rev. Robert Ross, and Rev. James Mann Haines. The last named died near the end of 1874 and was buried in Central Graveyard. No stone marks his grave.

The Southern Methodists finally came in possession of the church property. William Saufley held a bond against it and when the property was sold he bought it and deeded it to the Southern Methodists.[15]

The first time Port Republic appears in the list of appointments of the Baltimore Conference South is in 1875. It is given then as Port Republic Circuit. The next year (1876) it appears as "Port Republic Mission." After that date it is just "Port Republic." (Per Rev. H. M. Canter, D. D.)

The following is a list of the preachers who have been appointed to this circuit from 1875 to the present:

1875	Port Republic Circuit Geo. B. Allen
1876-77	Port Republic Mission Andrew Robey
1878	Port Republic Jacob F. Hopkins, Gilson Mouzy
1879-80	J.T. Maxwell
1881-84	Silas B. Snapp
1885-87	H.D. Bishop
1888	T.Briley
1889-91	W.W. Watts
1892-94	J.K. Gilbert
1895-96	Quincy A. Wheat
1897-1900	J.H. Smith
1900 through 1904	A.L. Harnsberger
1905 through 1906	J.L. Henderson
1907 through 1908	Geo. R. Mays
1909	T.G. Nevitt
1910	G.D. Moses
1911 through 1912	Thos. A. Burch
1913 through 1914	W.D. Eye
1915 through 1918	W.F. Lowance
1919 through 1920	Wendall Allen
1921	M.L. Fearnow
1922 through 1924	C.M. Pullin
1925 through 1927	W.A. Clark
1928	R. Carl Maxwell
1929 through 1934	W. Aubrey Lynch
1935 through 1938	E.A. Wilcher

An examination of the earlier records of the old Baltimore Conference showed that sometimes over a long period there were no recorded appointments of preachers to any of the churches and circuits of the conference, and in several instances there were no preachers listed for Rockingham Circuit. It seems that the secretaries of those early days did not deem it important to keep accurate records of those who served the churches of the conference.

It appears that the preachers assigned to Rockingham County were divided into two bodies, one serving East and the other West Rockingham. Port Republic was the oldest and most important station in the first section.

The names of those preachers appointed by the Baltimore Conference to serve Rockingham Circuit from 1793-1868 as copied from the records are:

1793-Stephen G. Bozel, Randall Smith
(Rockingham Circuit did not appear or there were no appointments in the minutes from 1794 to 1803).
1804-John Bell, Lewis Sutton
1805-J. Davidson
1806-Jno. Simmons
1807-Adam Burge
1808-M. Lawrance
1809-Robert R. Roberts
1810-J. Charles
1811-I. Pinnell
1812-Tobias Reiley
1813-Hezekiah Harriman
1814-Wm. Monroe
1815 and 1816-Circuit named, no appointments listed in minutes.
1817-Jas. Reiley
1818-Tobias Reiley, Wm. Barnes
1819-No appointments in minutes
1820-Robert Boyd, John Miller
1821-G. Morgan, C.B. Tippett
1822-G. Morgan, Samuel Clarke
1823-Jos. Sewell, Jno. Watson
1824-Wm. Monroe, P.D. Lipscomb

1825-Wm. Monroe, J. Howell
1826-Jas. Watts, Chas. Kalbus
1827-G. Morgan, H.S. Keppler
1828-Wm. Hank, N.B. Mills, Sup.
1829-Wm. Hank, Jon. Cleary, N.B. Mills, Sup.
1830-W. Hank, W.H. Enos
1831-John Rhoads, Wm. Edmunds
1832-John Rhoads, Wm. B. Edwards
1833-W.H. Enos, J.H., Henning, J. Sprigg, Sup.
1834-W.H. Enos, J.H. Henning
1835-Wm. Wicker, Wm. H. Coffin
1836-W.H. Coffin, Wm. Houston
1837-John C. Lyon, Wm. McK. Ward
1838-J.C. Lyon, Jared H. Young
1839-T. Wheeler, L.N. Monroe
1840-A.A. Eskridge, Chas. E. Brown
1841-A.A. Eskridge, J. Stine
1842-B.N. Brown, L. Harnsberger
1844-S. Hildebrand, T. Fulton
1845-1856, no appointments in minutes
1857-E. Welty, J.M. Littell
1858-J.N. Davis, F.A. Mercer
1859-Jas. N. Davis, Wm. F. Ward
1860-F. Hildebrand, George V. Leech
1861-no appointments in minutes *
1862-Appointments for Baltimore City only
1863-D.W. Arnold, W.R. Stringer
1864-J.A.H. Moore
1865-1867-A.P. Boude
1868-To be supplied
*Miss Maude E. Hodges, of the Baltimore Southern Methodist, contributes: "I found, among some old files of the paper here, a list of old appointments and note that in 1861 F. Hildebrand and P.H. Whisner were appointed to Rockingham Circuit."

Rev. Carl Maxwell divides the history of the Port Republic Methodist Church into three parts, each part depending on a church building. He says, "There have been three

Methodist Churches at Port Republic-the first, 1793-1840; the second, 1854-1915; the third, 1915 to the present time.[16]

The Lutherans, Presbyterians, and Episcopalians no longer labor in this field. They now confine themselves to holding funeral services here as occasion may require.

Chapter Ten Endnotes

[1]Congregation has since become the United Methodist Church.

[2]Francis Asbury, *Journal of the Reverend Francis Asbury, Bishop of the Methodist Episcopal Church*, vol. 1, (New York: Lane & Scott, 1852), 428.

[3]Ibid., vol. 3, 300.

[4]John Ffirth, *The Gospels and Labours of the Rev. Benjamin Abbott*, (Harrisonburg, Va.: printed by A. Davisson for James Dilworth, 1820), 134-135.

[5]William W. Bennett, *Memorials of Methodism in Virginia*, (Richmond, Va.: W.W. Bennett, 1871), 399.

[6]James M. Buckley, *History of Methodism in the United States*, vol. 1, (New York: Harper & Brothers. 1898), 142.

[7]*Baltimore Southern Methodist*, Baltimore, Md., (11 April 1929).

[8]Minute Book of the Trustees of the Methodist Episcopal Meetinghouse, (1 June 1833), Rockingham, County, Va. (hereafter known as Minute Book).

[9]Deed Book, 6:452.

[10]Minute Book, (14 April 1834).

[11]Minute Book, (18 April 1834).

[12]Minute Book, (25 April 1846).

[13]Deed Book, 11:531-532.

[14]Robert Ellis Thompson, *History of the Presbyterian Churches in the United States*, The American Church History series, (New York: The Christian Literature Company, 1895), 135.

[15]Deed Book, 33:257, 258.

[16]*Baltimore Southern Methodist*, (11 April 1929).

Chapter 11

Port Republic's Other Churches

The first preaching at Port Republic was by Rev. John Hindman in 1742. He was a native of Londonderry County, Ireland. In the above mentioned year he was sent by Donegal Presbytery, of Chester County, Pennsylvania, to the Shenandoah Valley as a missionary. He preached at the "head of Shenandoah River" which "heads" at Port Republic. There was no Presbyterian connection at this place until 1811.

On Nov. 27, 1755, the vestry of the parish of Augusta County ordered that the Rev. John Jones preach, among other places named, "at Mr. John Madison's." Madison lived at Port Republic at the time.

Due to the ministrations and zealous labors of Rev. George Bourne, a Presbyterian congregation was formed at Port Republic in 1811. He was licensed to preach by Presbytery meeting at New Providence the following year. Later in the year a call for his services was made by the congregation of South River, which was accepted.

His ordination took place at the home of Joseph Barger, of Port Republic, Dec. 26, 1812. Rev. William Wilson, the second pastor of the Stone Church, Augusta, presiding and Rev. John McCue delivering the ordination sermon.

A few years later, Mr. Bourne was dismissed from the ministry on account of his antislavery views.[1]

Occasionally Mormon elders, traveling "two and two,"

as is their custom, pass through the town. The distribution of free religious literature, so far, has been the extent of their endeavors.

The Mormon Church was founded by Joseph Smith, Jr., in 1831. The religion of the Mormons is the only one in the country whose fundamentals are authenticated by signed statements and affidavits, the originals of which are still in existence. This church contributed their own sacred book—the Book of Mormon—to the world.

William C. Thurman was a notable man in the religious history of Rockingham County. Of a pleasing and intellectual appearance, he could not remain unnoticed in any gathering of people. He was well educated and his mind was stored with ancient and Biblical lore. Firmly believing, as he was taught in his childhood, that "the Bible means what it says and says what it means," he was headed for disaster. Disdaining the trite and commonplace, his active mind drove him on to pry into matters that lie in deep shadows. He fearlessly preached what he believed, for he was of the same stuff of which heretics and martyrs are made.

He preached that Christ would return to the earth in 1868, and being disappointed he set the time again for 1875. He had another disappointment for his pains.

His honesty compelled him to make definite statements, and his supreme folly was that he set a time for the end of the world. History shows that the arguments of such dreamers are based on shadows hanging over a pit of impenetrable darkness.

He had no known followers in Port Republic, and his religious connection with the town was only to the extent of debating the Sabbath — Sunday question one night in the Methodist Church with Eld. Benjamin F. Purdham, of the Seventh Day Adventists.

Mr. Thurman was a fluent talker, an able expounder, and a great exegete, but tiresome to listen to. The writer met him in Richmond in 1904 at which time he was an inmate of the almshouse. Doubtless in gratitude for favors extended to him, he gave the writer a copy of a book he had written not long before.

The greatest stir the religious life of the town and neighborhood has ever experienced was during the seven weeks that the Seventh Day Adventists held tent meetings here. Persons from quite a distance made it suit to attend the meetings.

On May 11, 1885 Elder Benjamin F. Purdham of Marksville and Elder A.C. Neff of Quicksburg, both Seventh Day Adventist ministers, came to Port Republic and pitched a large tent on lot No. 49, commonly called the McCann lot, the use of which they had procured from Capt. John Harper. The lot is not far from where the old schoolhouse stood, and Water Street is between it and murmuring South River. It was an ideal location for the purpose because fruit trees on the lot furnished the necessary shade for the season, and the nearby river caused gentle breezes.

They began to hold religious meetings in this tent on Friday night the 15th. Elder Purdham preached the first sermon using Acts 28: 22 as his text; "We desire to hear of thee what thou thinkest; for as concerning this sect, we know that every where it is spoken against."

Twenty-six years old, about six feet tall and straight as an arrow, a large well proportioned head, sandy hair and reddish beard, grayish blue eyes and a strong chin, with a resonant tenor voice and of a pleasing personality, Elder Purdham was a striking figure in the pulpit. Like Paul, to whom the words of the text were addressed by the chief Jews living in Rome when they were called by him for an interview a few days after his arrival in the city as a prisoner, Elder Purdham "expounded and testified the kingdom of God," and showed that minority sects frequently suffer from unmerited reproach. He made a favorable impression on the audience of over one hundred persons, who gave him their undivided attention. The best of order was maintained.

Elders Purdham and Neff were assisted during the meetings by Eld. R.D. Hottel of New Market and Mr. B.F. Stebbins of Luray, and by others. (Mr. Stebbins was one of the discoverers of the famous Luray Caverns.) The meetings continued until July 5.

It is safe to say that during the seven weeks of these tent meetings there was more reading of the Bible by the people of the town and neighborhood then they had ever done previously in the same length of time.

The Adventists continued their work in the town and neighborhood for a number of years, and had many members of intelligence and respectability, and not a few friends.

Their two leading doctrines gave this sect its name. They keep the ancient Bible Sabbath and believe in the imminence of the Second Advent of Christ. To prove that the seventh day is the Sabbath of the Lord they quote Genesis 2: 2, 3: "And on the seventh day God ended his work which he had made; and he rested on the seventh day from all his work which he had made. And God blessed the seventh day, and sanctified it; because that in it he had rested from all his work which God created and made."

That the observance of the seventh day Sabbath is obligatory on all Christians, they stoutly maintain, and point to the fourth commandment of the Decalogue as absolute proof. This commandment is found in Exodus 20: 8-11 and reads:

Remember the Sabbath day, to keep it holy. Six days shalt thou labour, and do all thy work: But the seventh day is the Sabbath of the Lord thy God: in it thou shalt not do any work, thou, nor thy son, nor thy daughter, thy manservant, nor thy maidservant, nor thy cattle, nor thy stranger that is within thy gates: For in six days the Lord made heaven and earth, the sea, and all that in them is, and rested the seventh day: Wherefore the Lord blessed the Sabbath day, and hallowed it.

They further affirm that there is no Bible authority for the keeping of Sunday, and that the first law enforcing its observance on Christians was issued by the Emperor Constantine in A.D. 321, and is thus expressed:

Let all judges and town people, and the occupation of all trades rest on the venerable day of the sun; but let those who are situated in the country, freely and at full liberty attend to the business of agriculture; because it often happens that no other day is so fit for sowing corn and planting vines: least, the critical moment being let slip, men should lose the commodities granted by Heaven. Given the seventh day of March; Crispus and Constantine being consuls, each of them for the second time.[2]

Various arguments were made by members of other churches to neutralize the force of the above, chief of which was the seventh part of time theory. The Adventists answered with crushing logic that the Law of the Sabbath and the Day of the Sabbath cannot be separated. In Mark 2: 28 the dignity of being "Lord also of the Sabbath" was claimed by Christ.

The Adventists also teach the proximity and inevitableness of the Second Coming of Christ. To those who believe in the divine inspiration of the Jewish and Christian Scriptures, their arguments are irrefutable. All the great awe inspiring premonitory signs as set forth in the New Testament by Matthew, Luke, Paul and James of this dread event are before our eyes. It is astounding that the shepherds of the various flocks do not warn and prepare them for this culmination of the plan of salvation in the world. Numerous passages of Scripture show that the world has waxed old, and were they accepted as true statements of a fact, its end could be expected next month, possibly tomorrow. Leaders of the "little flock" should always be in the attitude of "watchful waiting."

It was said by some of the not well informed opponents of the Adventists that they had several times set the date for the end of the world and had put on ascension robes. Learning that this fabrication was widely circulated, and finding nothing in their publications to justify the statement, the writer several years later while at North Danville, addressed a letter of inquiry to Prof. Uriah Smith, editor of *The Review & Herald*, Battle Creek, Mich., and elicited the following information under date of Sept. 1892:

Yours of the 18th is at hand. I would say that the story that any Adventist put on ascension robes in 1844, or at any other time, is a base falsehood. There is <u>not a word of truth in it.</u> Years ago we had a standing offer of $50.00 reward for anyone who would prove an instance of that kind, but the reward was never claimed.

A curious circumstance of the coming to town of the Seventh Day Adventists was related to the writer by a lady in whom he had all confidence. She said that she had never heard of the Adventists before they began to preach here. A short time before they came, she had a dream in which she saw a large white tent on the McCann lot in which religious meetings were being held. <u>These people were preaching the truth;</u> thus far the dream. Later when she began to attend the meetings and found all visible objects as she had seen them in her dream, she concluded that they were also preaching Bible doctrine, and united with this church and was a life-long consistent member.The explanation of this extraordinary incident is left to psychologists.

This account of the churches would not be complete without some notice of the church of the colored people.

Jacob Christ and Lydia, his wife, deeded to Dr. George W. Kemper on June 12, 1824, in consideration of $20, a part of lot No. 12, being the west corner, and containing 1650 square feet. On this spot was built a log house of some size, for a schoolhouse, probably. It is remembered as the oldest free public schoolhouse of the town. It was abandoned as a schoolhouse several years before 1880, when a four-room schoolhouse was built.

It was about this time that the colored people began to hold religious meetings in this building, and it was known as the colored church until it was torn down. The flock was shepherded by a colored man by the name of David Wood. ("Brother Wood" we children of the town called him), who lived on the east side of the Blue Ridge. He was a tall well-proportioned man, wearing a beaver hat and ministerial garb. His skin was so black it glistened. The white people frequently went to hear him preach.

On one occasion the subject of his sermon was "hypocrisy." He warmed up to his subject and grew eloquent. As an illustration of the slim chance a hypocrite has of wearing the crown in the heavenly kingdom, he spoke to the brothers and sisters of the congregation saying, it was just as hard for a hypocrite to get into heaven "as it am for a raccoon to climb a red-hot stovepipe wid de teakittle tied to his tail." Needless to say he received prolonged applause.

Previous to the Civil War, the colored people held their meetings at any suitable place which permitted then to attend. One place was the kitchen of a boarding house in the town. One evening they were assembled and had begun the exercises when in walked Harrison Jones, a black man known to have an arrogant attitude. He was much displeased that he had not been waited for. Striding to the middle of the room he looked around and said, "Knee bend, body bound, fishhook de crook, and determinashun. What did you begin dis meeting for befo' de elder come?"

Another story is told of Sally Grandison's prayer, a model of wifely affection. It was made in the old log church at a revival meeting. After praying for all others she ended with this, "Lord, be with my husband Grandison as he travels down the valley of the shadow of death and crown him Lord of all for Jesus Christ's sake, Amen."

The colored church disbanded or moved elsewhere about fifty years ago. No colored person lived in the town for a score of years.[3]

Chapter Eleven Endnotes

[1]William Henry Foote, D.D., *Sketches of Virginia, Historical and Biographical*, (Philadelphia, Pa.: J.B. Lippincott & Co., 1856), 360-365.
[2]Benjamin E. Andrew, *History of the Sabbath*, (New York: Charles Scribner's Sons, 1917), 342.
[3]*Baltimore Southern Methodist*, (April 11, 1929).

Chapter 12

The Graveyards

Port Republic, Va., Dec. 4, 1932

Glenna and I spent several hours today in going over the two old graveyards in the village. The older and larger one is located on the southeast side of the village and on the lefthand bank of South River. Usually referred to as Riverside Cemetery, this lot is known in the annals of the village as the Meeting House Lot. It was deeded by John Carthrea and Molly, his wife, to trustees of the Baltimore Conference Methodist Episcopal Church in America "for the worship of Almighty God," Feb. 18, 1793.

A Methodist church was built on the up-river end of this lot and was in continuous use until 1846. It is said that Lorenzo Dow (Oct. 16, 1777-Feb. 2, 1834) once preached in

South River swimming hole at Riverside Graveyard; among those pictured are Russ Armentrout and his mother, Aline, Belvia Trobaugh, Edna Sipe, and Maggie Sipe

this building. It was sold to Robert W. Palmer, the highest bidder, on July 18, 1846 for forty dollars.

There is a milldam across South River just below the lot and the smooth water and grassy bank make the graveyard an ideal bathing spot. But, sad to relate, vandals have taken many of the oldest tombstones and used them to secure the ends of springboards on the bank and now some of them are at the bottom of the river or else broken into pieces and scattered along the shore.

This graveyard is honeycombed with graves. Many of the graves never had durable markers.[1] The following inscriptions are copied from gravestones still standing. Arrangement, abbreviations, and punctuation are as they appear on the stones:

Our Mother,
Mary J. Weast
Died Feb. 18, 1899
Aged 76 yrs. 4 mos.
Gone but not forgotten

....

Henry Weast
Died Sept. 15, 1877.
Aged 52 yrs. 3 mos.
8 days

....

Nancy Jane
Daughter of
H.& M. Weast
Died Nov. 16, 1853
Aged 4 yrs. & 11 mos.

....

Our Grandma.
Sarah Roberts
Born Nov. 1792.
Died June 5, 1890
Aged 98 yrs. & 6 mos.

Gone but not forgotten
Harrison Bateman
Died Aug. 23, 1889
Aged 77 yrs. 1 mo. 23 Ds.
At Rest

....

Martha Ann,
Wife of H. Bateman
Died May 4, 1863.
Aged 41 yrs.1 mo. 1 day.

....

In memory of
W.H. Bateman
Born Oct. 25th, 1845.
Died Nov. 7th, 1882
Aged 37 yrs. & 13 Ds.

....

In memory of
Elizabeth Bateman
Born April 1st, 1792
(stone broken here)

Elizabeth Connelly,
Died Dec. 13, 1886
Aged 67 yrs. 3 mo. 5 Ds.
Weep not, she is at rest.
....
Mary Elizabeth
Daughter of
H. & M.A. Bateman
Born June 14, 1847.
Died June 13, 1859
Aged 11 yrs. 11 mos. & 29 ds.
She was lovely , she was fair,
And for a while was given
An angel came and———-
And bore her———to heaven.
....
Nancy Whiteside
Born Sept. 22, 1766.
Departed this life on the
26 June 1845.
....
In memory of
Peter Fitch
Died Sep. 15, 1863
Aged 74 yrs. & 8 mo.
....
In Memory of
Sarah J. Fitch,
Born Sept. 8th 1793:
Died Aug. 24th 1852
Rogers,
Richmond
....
Wm. J. Maupin
Born March 10-1770,
Died Aug. 17-1843
(Aug. 15th is correct date,
acc. to Laura Lamb)

In Memory of
James G. Layton,
10th Va. Inft'y
Killed at the battle
Of Chancellorsville
May 3, 1863.
Aged 27 yrs. 7 mo. & 5 da.
....
F.M. Layton
Died Nov. 21, 1874
Aged 70 yrs.
10 mos. & 22 Ds.
....
Eleanor Layton
Died Apr. 2, 1886.
Aged 72 yrs.
3 mos. & 17 Ds.
....
Amos Scott
Died May 12, 1889
Aged 82 yrs. 7 mos. 21 ds.
Asleep in Jesus.
To live in hearts we
Leave behind us, is not to die.
..
Agnes A. Scott,
Died May 29, 1862.
Aged About 50 years
Asleep in Jesus.
....
Annias D. Scott,
Born Dec. 9, 1835.
Aged About 2 yrs.
Robert W. Palmer,
Died Sept. 2, 1861.
Aged 57 yrs. 11 mos. 2 Ds.

Sarah, Wife of
R.W. Palmer,
Died Mr. 3, 1884.
Aged 73 yrs. 10 mos. & 18 d's
....

William, Son of
R.W. & S.H. Palmer,
Sept. 11, 1862
Aged 31 yrs. 9 mos. 24 Ds.
....

In memory of
Our Dear Father
P.H. Wheeler.
Born March 23, 1816.
Died Dec. 25, 1890
Aged 74 yrs. 9 mos. 2 ds.
....

In memory of
Our Dear Mother
Elizabeth R.
Wife of P.H. Wheeler.
Born Aug. 27, 1820,
Died Sept. 11, 1888
Aged 64 yrs & 14 ds.
....

C.R. Allen
Born Dec. 8, 1833
Died July 16, 1898
Asleep in Jesus
Blessed sleep.
....

Annie Ogheltree,
Died Feb. 14, 1864.
Aged 72 yrs. 6 mo. & 28 ds.
Daniel Murray
Died April 30, 1865
Aged 63 yrs.

Susan B., Wife of
Daniel Murray.
Died June 8, 1839.
Aged 31 yrs.—mo. 29 Da.
.....

John A. Murray
Born Aug. 1, 1824
Died Apr. 11, 1;8 85
Aged 60 yrs. 8 mo. 10 Ds.
Rest in peace.
....

Father
Stephen H. Murray.
Died June 27, 1891.
Aged 61 yrs. 3 mos. 28 Ds.
....

Mother, Virginia M.
Wife of S.H. Murray.
Died April 22, 1892
Aged A55 yrs. 10 mos. 22 Ds.
....

Col. Wm. A. Maupin
Died Feb. 18, 1882,
Aged 66 yrs. 9 mo. 17 Ds.
....

Mary A. Maupin
Died Sep. 3 1889
Aged 74 yrs. 7 mo. 25 Ds.
She was a Christian
True and brave.
Her virtue followed
To the grave.
....

In memory of
Caroline A. Fitch,
Born June 9th 1829
Died June 24th 1851

In memory of
Jacob Cupp
Who was born
Dec'r 14, 1767
In Lancaster Co. Pa.
& Died Jan 12, 1852,
Aged 84 years, & 29 Days.
....
Joseph Trout
Born Oct. 16, 1787
In Newtown Frederick Va.
Died March 26, 1850.
In Port Republic
....
William David Trout
Born Sept. 5, 1824
Departed this life
June 25, 1869
....
Jacob Archibald Trout
Born Nov. 9, 1834,
Died Sep. 12, 1879
....
Wm. L. Leckie
Born May 28, 1806,
Died Sep. 24, 1888
Thy will be done O God.
....
Amanda M.
Wife of Wm. L Leckie,
Died Sept. 6, 1881.
Aged 68 yrs. 5 mo. & 21 days.
Asleep in Jesus blessed sleep.
....
Augusta S., Daughter of
Wm. L. & A. Leckie
Born June 9, 1844,
Died May 22, 1864.
Aged 19 yrs. 11 mo. & 3 ds.

Anna Elizabeth
Daughter of
Wm. L. & A. Leckie
Died May 23, 1862,
Aged 3 yrs 3 mo. & 24 days.
....
Cornelia A. Leckie
Born July 28, 1846
Died Sep.24, 1853
Aged 7 yrs. 1 mo. 26 da.
....
Cornelia C,
Daughter of
F.H., & F.A. Young,
Died Feb. 19. 1862
Aged 7 yrs. 3 mo. 1 day
....
In Memory of
Lucy Ann Foster
Who died March 26
1852 aged 2 years
————————?
....
James Willie,
Son of W.R. & M.C. Foster
Died Nov. 12, 1854,
Aged 2 yrs. & 10 mos.
....
Nicholas Rogers,
Son of
W.R. & M.C. Foster
Died April 28. 1859
Aged 10 mos. & 24 ds.[2]

Another old graveyard in Port Republic is usually re-ferred to as Central Graveyard. In 1833 half of each of the two lots, Nos. 27 and 28, lying on the southeast side of Main Street, were obtained from John Dundore and Alexander Givens for a church site and burying ground. A brick church was built on this half -acre lot, and as it was a union church, it was used by Episcopalians, Presbyterians, Methodists, and probably other denominations from 1833 to 1854.

This information is gleaned from the booklet issued by the Port Republic Mutual Cemetery Co. and the Baltimore Southern Methodist, issue of April 11, 1929, and doubtless needs revisions. Corrections would seem to be the more nec-essary since it will be noticed that some who are buried in this lot died before 1833. Of course the bodies could have been removed from another graveyard.

The following inscriptions are copied from tombstones in this burying ground:

William Lewis,
Died Dec. 29, 1828,
Aged 56 yrs. 1 mo. & 26 ds.
....
Martha Lewis
Died March 16, 1860
Aged 71 yrs. 5 mo. & 21 ds.
...
Katherine A. May
Born June 30, 1839,
Died Aug. 25, 1917.
....
Sarah B.
Wife of George W. May.
Daughter of David &
Nancy Buster
Died March 27, 1856
Aged 28 yrs. 5 mos. 7 das.*

Capt. Geo. W. Eutsler
Age 75 yrs.
Asleep in Jesus *
....
Minerva (Mineran?)
Wife of
Capt. Geo.W. Eutsler
Age 67 yrs.
She was the sunshine
Of our home. *
....
St. Clair G., Son of
Capt. G.W. & Minerva Eutsler
Nov. 9, 1849
Aug. 16, 1889
Gone but not forgotten.*

Monie S.
Wife of G.L. Wagner
& daughter of
G.W. & Minerva Eutsler.
Died Apr. 5, 1889,
Aged 27 yrs. & 3 mo.
A precious one from us has gone;
A voice we loved is stilled;
A place is vacant in our home
Which never can be filled.
(Hess & Weaver) *

....

Harry M.
Son of
G.L. & M.S. Wagner.
Died June 19, 1889,
Aged 2 mo. & 29 Ds. *

......

Snapp, Rev Silas R.
Jan 7, 1834
March 10, 1895 *

....

Sarah V. His Wife
Nov. 16, 1836
June 17, 1920 *

....

Son Leonidus R.
Nov. 8, 1872
Oct. 6, 1902 *

In memory of Rev. David Wood,
Born in Louisa Co., Va. Feb'ry 2, 1808
Converted and licensed To preach 1827.
Joined The Virginia Conference M.E. Church 1829
Died in Port Republic Va. March 27th, 1851

Twenty-four years he preached The Gospel faithfully,
Energetically & with great Success, and many souls
In eternity will pronounce Him blessed.
"They that sow in tears shall reap in Joy."
(A. Gaddess, Maker, Balt.) *

(May the memory of those whose names I have copied
above never perish. George E. May)[3]

Hains, Rev. James Mann - Pastor of the Methodist Episcopal Church, south in Port Republic, Va. 1874-born in Newcastle County, Delaware. 17 Aug. 1820. Died Port Republic, 13 Nov. 1874.

May, Adam - May 1, 1798. June. 14, 1874.
May, Nancy -his wife. Nov. 25, 1800. - Apr. 29, 1845.[4]

The Port Republic Mutual Cemetery Co. was organized April 10, 1897. A committee was appointed to select a location, and four acres of land lying half a mile west of the town, were bought of Michael A. Scott. The members of the Company were: W.C. Harper, J.E. Riddle, W.S. Nicholas, W.J. Downs, F.L. Nicholas, N.T. Wagner, W.L. Dinsmore, T.L. Maupin, J.H. Lamb, D.P. Shuler, S.H. Sipe, C.A. Palmer, J.J. Nicholas, M.A. Scott, C.W. Kemper, N.C. Scott, J.F. Wagner, S.H. Crawn, H.B. Harnsberger, and N.J. Wagner. The trustees, to whom the property was deeded, were: W.L. Scott, S.H. Sipe, and W.S. Nicholas. W.C. Harper was president; J.F. Wagner, vice-president; W.L. Dinsmore, secretary; and D.P. Shuler, treasurer.

The cemetery is on the side of an eminence gently sloping to the southeast. Standing in the elevated end of the cemetery and looking over it, the Blue Ridge is seen in the distance and a country unsurpassed for beauty lying between. Altogether it is a suitable and attractive location. But the cemetery was marred in the laying out of the lots. All are so planned that to use them the graves have to be crosswise of the sloping ground. As the cemetery is entered at the end where it slopes down to a level, the beholder is struck with the odd fact that the side of every grave is presented to the eye, and the pleasing effect of the spot itself and of the many fine monuments is dissipated. Had the foot of the graves been downhill, the full beauty of this "city of the dead" would at once be apparent.

The truth, no doubt, why the graves are located as they are, is a survival of the custom of ancient sun-worshippers who buried the dead with their faces toward the east that they might see the first radiant shafts of their god rising in the east. As they are, the graves are out of course 27 degrees with a line running east; had they been put on a line 63 degrees south of east would have added much to the aspect of the cemetery. The dull sameness of it all is depressing.

110

Chapter Twelve Endnotes

[1]Some bodies were removed to the "new" Port Republic Cemetery when it opened, 1897.

[2]A Society clean-up crew several years ago unearthed a forgotten stone, which read: "Jane Dundore, born March 2d 1783. Departed this life March 19th 1837. He spake, and it was done. The memory of the just is blessed." The "Rogers, Richmond" on Sarah J. Fitch's tombstone indicates the manufacturer.

[3]Asterisks indicate stones that were erroneously listed as being in Riverside Graveyard in an early draft of May's manuscript that was photocopied and circulated for years.

[4]These three graves were inadvertently omitted from May's manuscript, recorded by the Daughters of the American Revolution, and submitted by Harrison May in February, 2002.

Chapter 13

Early Wars

French and Indian War (1754-1763)

Capt. Robert Hooke, Sr., of the Cross Keys neighborhood, was actively engaged in the French and Indian War. His sons, William and James, also were soldiers in that war. Gabriel Jones, who lived on the river about two miles below Port Republic, furnished supplies to troops who served in this war. John Madison built a fort on his property as security for his family and neighbors during this time of unrest.

Dunsmore's War (1774)

Col. William Nalle, who lived in East Rockingham, was captain of a company that was engaged in the battle of Point Pleasant, Oct. 10, 1774. Robert Raines, a private in this company, was probably of the Port Republic section. (This surname is variously spelt as Rains, Reins, Reigns, Raines, and Raynes.)

Revolutionary War (1775-1783)

No list of soldiers of East Rockingham who had active service in the Revolutionary War is available to the writer; but it seems certain that one or more members of the families of the Fishers, Boones, Hustons, Hannas, Beards, Pirkeys, Gilmores, and others more or less identified with the Port Republic neighborhood, fought in this war for the independence of their country. But a positive statement should not be made without supporting facts.

It seems to us at this distance of time from that mighty

struggle, that the Carthreas of the town would be found supporting their country in its war for political freedom. But not so. John Carthrea, on complaint of Gabriel Jones, was indicted by the grand jury for alleged disloyal speech and conduct; was tried by jury; and was sentenced to pay a fine of 1000 pounds and to be jailed for one hour.[1] The son of Gabriel Jones, William Strother Jones, was a captain in the Continental Army during the Revolution.

Several members of the Hooke family were in service in this war and should be included with this section. Also Thomas Lewis, Laurence Raynes, and James Palmer of this neighborhood were engaged in the war. The last named moved to East Rockingham from King William County about 1815.

War of 1812 (1812-1814)

England forced the War of 1812 on the United States. She had not recovered from the mortification of being compelled to declare her revolted American Colonies free and independent States. The War of 1812 was her second effort to subjugate them.

Ignoring international law, she harried our coasts, made war on our commerce on the high seas, and impressed our seamen. She stoutly maintained her right of search and seizure, and transferred many of our able-bodied seamen, whom she did not hesitate to declare were her own subjects, from our vessels to the decks of her warships. At the beginning of the war there were recorded in the State Department at Washington, over six thousand cases of impressed seamen. These were scarcely half of the number of our seamen taken by England and put in her own war vessels and who were, in many cases, forced to fight against their country.

Many facts support the conclusion that East

113

Rockingham was more warlike than West Rockingham. The militiamen of East Rockingham were willing to fight for "Free Trade and Sailors Rights." It is difficult at this time to name with certainty all from Port Republic and its environs who fought in this second war of independence.

Captain Robert Hooke's Company, of the 58th Regiment Virginia Volunteers, entered service, July 8, 1813. Richard S. Emmit, ensign, owned property in the town, and probably made his home here. Jacob Fisher, 4th sergeant, was probably a relative of John Fisher, 4th corporal, who owned the present Hooke farm on North River. John Rust, 1st corporal, and Jacob Rust, 2nd corporal, were familiar figures about the town; and George Baker, 7th corporal, lived not far from it. Of the privates in this company, John Hanna, Thomas Lewis, Adam May, George Reece, David Crickenberger, Benjamin Cash, Henry Sipe, George Middleberger, Abram Rust, and Henry Eutsler, can be classed as of this neighborhood.

Several privates in Capt. Robert Magill's Company may have been from this locality: John Matheney, Patrick Reins, Charles Weaver, Christian Eustler, Richard Rankin, and Bennett Reigns.

In Capt. William Harrison's Company, the following privates were probably from this section: Thomas Beard, John Fisher, Henry Pirkey, Jacob Pirkey, John Roadcap, and Charles Weaver. As Captain Magill's Company entered service in 1813, and Captain Harrison's a year later, Charles Weaver and John Fisher may have served in each of them. Dr. George W. Kemper, Sr., was sent to Norfolk at this time as so many soldiers there were dying of fever.

Mexican War (1846-1848)

Although Port Republic supported James K. Polk for president in 1844, still very little interest was manifested in the Mexican War of 1846-1848 which was brought about by Polk's election.

Alexander R. Givens, of Augusta County, commanded a company that was in service in the Mexican War from Aug. 30, to Nov. 30, 1813. Givens, of Mt. Meridian was a partner of John Dundore in the tannery business.

It is related that when the company was organized Captain George C. Robertson (afterwards well known as Colonel Robertson of the Thirty-second regiment) was designated to command it. But Captain Givens (afterwards Colonel) having returned home after a temporary absence, claimed his right to command as senior captain, and accordingly went with the men to the field.

Colonel Givens, as many persons still living remember, was very soldier-like in his appearance and bearing. But while noted for his kindliness to the poor, he had a masterful spirit and was not likely to fill a subordinate position anywhere with comfort to himself or those above him in office. Tradition says he was under arrest all the time in camp upon the charge of insubordination, and therefore, the muster roll has it "company of infantry" etc. "commanded by Lieutenant Samuel Crawford."[2]

The writer does not definitely know that any Port Republicans said:

> I'll put my knapsack on my back,
> And gun upon my shoulder,
> And travel away to Mexico,
> To be a valiant soldier.
> —from a Mexican War Song

Chapter Thirteen Endnotes

[1]Rockingham County, Judgments and Orders Book, no. 65, (n.d.).
[2]Joseph A. Waddell, *Annals of Augusta County,Virginia*, 2nd edition, (Staunton, Va.: G. Russell Caldwell, 1902), 586.

Chapter 14

The Civil War: Answering the Call to Arms

Various were the causes leading to the Civil War. They are thus epitomized by an able historian:

It was a mistake to refer the great Rebellion, for ultimate source, to ambiguity in the Constitution or to the wickedness of politicians or of the people. It was simply the last resort in an 'irrepressible conflict' of principles - in the struggle for and against the genius of the world's advance. Economic, social, and moral evolution, resulting in two radically different civilizations, had enforced upon each section unfaithfulness to the spirit and even to the letter of its constitutional covenant.[1]

The South, proud and aristocratic, depended on slave labor for the production of those staples of an agricultural country that were salable in the markets of the world for her wealth; the North looked to her craftsmen and inventive mechanics to lead the way to wealth and industrialism. In the race for wealth and the influence that it puts in the hands of its possessors, the South was sadly outdistanced.

When the doctrine of Abolitionism had permeated the North, the constitutional guarantees concerning "persons held to labor" were not regarded by the triumphant Republican Party. A leading historian sets forth the intentions of the party in the following temperate language:

They meant by law and force to keep slavery from getting any growth or outlet whatever. They meant also to nullify, if they could not repeal, the laws whose adoption the constitution commanded for the apprehension and return of runaway slaves, and put the whole system of slavery, so far as they might, within the formal limits of the fundamental law, beyond the recognition or the countenance of federal statute. Their creed and their actions alike were compounded of hostility towards the south; and the challenge of their success was direct and unmistakable. Men of southern mettle could not disregard or decline it.[2]

The North favored the Hamiltonian idea of a strong centralized government and interpreted the Constitution accordingly. Her great historian of the war is very clear on this subject:

History teaches scarcely anything more clearly than that it was the purpose of the framers of the Constitution to render the inhabitants of all States substantially and perpetually one people, living under a common Government, and known to the rest of mankind by a common national designation.[3]

The South believed that the States existed first and thus created the Union; they saw the National government as their agent. The position of the South on the relationship of the several states to the United States is well expressed by an eminent Confederate historian of the war as follows:

The Union was not a consolidated Nationality. It was not a simple republic, with an appendage of provinces. It was not, on the other hand, a mere league of States with no power to reach individuals. It was an association of sovereign States with a common authority qualified to reach individuals within the scope of the powers delegated to it by the States, and employed with subjects sufficient to give it for certain purposes the effect of an American and national identity.[4]

117

The election of Abraham Lincoln caused the seething political cauldron to boil over, and the South withdrew from the Union. The American Flag, the symbol of Hope to the oppressed peoples of the world, disappeared in the South from the Potomac to the Rio Grande, and a Southern Confederacy, with her "stars and bars," was set up in Montgomery, Alabama.

When the clarion call-to-arms rang through the Southland, Port Republic responded with unanimity and enthusiasm. Some of her soldiers lost their lives on hard-fought battlefields; others returned home maimed for life, and many received minor wounds.

In the Blue Ridge section east of the town the anti-slavery sentiment was strong and the martial spirit being equally so in some cases, a few joined the Union Armies.

The names of those of Port Republic and neighborhood who marched forth to fight the battles of the Confederacy and were in Co. B, Tenth Virginia Volunteer Infantry are: William S. Brown, Jacob R. Grove, George B. Kemper, William M. Kemper, William P. Kemper, Andrew Lewis, George R. Lewis, William M. Lewis, James A. Lewis, James H. May, Larkin R. McCauley, J. Leonard Mohler, John P. Roadcap, John Rodgers, J.K. Ryan, Jacob H. Yost and George Sipe.

Robert Shifflette was in Co. C, and George F. Mayhew and David Funkhouser were in Co. G; Abraham Miller belonged to Co. D, and Derrick Byrd was in Chew's Battery, Laurel Brigade.

In the River Rangers, a troop of the Sixth Virginia Cavalry from East Rockingham, those from in and near the town were: C.M. Kemper, Captain A.J. Sigler, Second Lieutenant, Jonathan Bateman, Andrew J. Brown, Edward Brown, John Burket, James Burket, William Burket, Tobias M. Grove, A.L. Harnsberger, William M. Harnsberger, J.B. Huffman, J.N. Humes, Samuel Hinckle, Abraham Scott Hooke, Capt. Co. C,

R.J. Hooke, S.H. Kaylor, William Knuckols, Warfield Lee, G. Wesley May, Wm. H. Harrison Maupin, James W. Murray, George N. Nicholas, Silas C. Nicholas, Albert Phillips, Granville Phillips, Hiram Phillips, Tobias Phillips, A.H. Pirkey, Benjamin Powell, Henry Raines, Jacob Raines, Reuben Raines, Michael A. Scott, William Scott, George Talley, and Fayette H. Weaver.

The writer does not know what organization the following were in: Christopher R. Allen, W.H. Bateman, A.J. Collier, Mitchell Crawford, Fontaine L. Kemper, James A. Maupin, James T. Miller, Jacob J. Nicolas, Reuben A. Scott, Noah Raines, and Zachariah Raines. John H. Trobaugh, George Scott, and Thomas Weaver were members of Capt. George Chrisman's Boy Company, which was mustered into service April 3, 1864.[5]

Necessarily from the date at hand the above lists are not complete. Doubtless other names should be included but the writer has no knowledge of them.[6]

Chapter Fourteen Endnotes

[1]J.N. Andrews, *History of the Sabbath and First Day of the Week*, vol. 3, (Battle Creek, Mich.: Seventh Day Adventist Publishing Association,1873), 290.
[2]Woodrow Wilson, *A History of the American People,* vol. 4, (New York: Harper & Brothers, Publishers, 1906), 190, 192.
[3]Greeley, Horace, *The American Conflict*, vol. 1, (Hartford: O.D. Case & Company. 1864, 1865), 82.
[4]Edward A. Pollard, *Lee and his Lieutenants*, (New York: E.B. Treat & Co., 1867) 39.
[5]Christopher Allen was in the Nottaway Light Artillery.
[6]William Allen Maupin was Captain of Company no. 5 of the 58th Virginia Regiment. See Chapter 37.

The Civil War: The Invasion of the Town

Stonewall Jackson's defeat of Gen. James Shields at Port Republic, June 9, 1862, marked the end of his Shenandoah Valley campaign, and when he left the Valley to join in the Seven Days Battle before Richmond, his fame had soared to the skies.

It is important to have in mind the positions of the three armies before the opening of the famous battle of Port Republic. Stonewall Jackson had fallen back up the Shenandoah Valley, after notable victories in the lower end of it, closely pursued by Generals John C. Fremont and James Shields. Fremont pursued up the west side of the Shenandoah River, and Shields advanced up the east side of that noble stream.

Passing through Harrisonburg on June 5, Jackson wheeled to the left and marched to Port Republic, determined to bring the mastery of the Valley to a decisive issue. He halted Gen. Richard S. Ewell's division at Cross Keys to await the onslaught of Fremont, and his own division he put in camp, strung from the Dunkard Church at Mill Creek to the bluffs across North River from Port Republic. Jackson established his headquarters at Madison Hall, the home of Dr. George W. Kemper, Sr., and his ammunition train and a herd of beeves were concealed in a hollow in the nearby fields.

On the afternoon of June 6, Union cavalry followed General Ashby some three miles from Harrisonburg and came in contact with him on a long low ridge crowned with trees. In the resulting skirmish Ashby was killed. His blood soaked a spot of soil in the farm of Joseph Good. Late in the evening he was brought to Port Republic and laid out in a corner room of the home of Benjamin Franklin Kemper, now owned by Charles F. Saufley.[1]

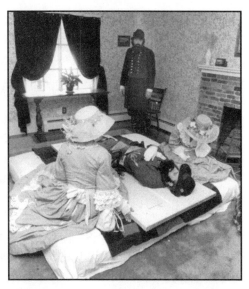

Reenactment: Jackson visiting Ashby's body in the Frank Kemper House

His horse was also killed. John Eston Cooke says that this horse was the same Jackson had ridden at the battle of Manassas, and belonged to Capt. James W. Thompson of the Stuart Horse Artillery. He lent this animal to both Jackson and Ashby. The famous white charger of the latter had been killed at the bridge over the North Fork of the Shenandoah near Mt. Jackson on June 2.

In the skirmish in which Ashby lost his life, Col. Sir Percy Wyndham, an English officer who had taken service in the Union cause, commanded the First New Jersey Cavalry and was captured. He was taken a prisoner, with others, to Port Republic and General Jackson had a conversation with him in the Lee Hotel. Jackson asked him why he, an Englishman, had entered the service of the enemies of the Confederacy when the aristocracy of his country favored the independence of the South. Sir Percy replied that Ashby had become so famous, that he had joined the Union Army with the intention of capturing or killing him. Some of

121

Ashby's troopers were in town and were told of this conversation by Wilson C. Harper, a twelve-year-old lad who had heard it. Deep and dire were their muttered threats. Sir Percy was taken to Jackson's headquarters at Madison Hall for safety.

After Ashby had been laid out and all the last sad rites preparatory for burial performed, Jackson entered the room and remained some time alone with his old cavalry commander. What thoughts this sad communion with the dead brought to his mind does not take a quickened imagination to guess.

The following day, Saturday, the funeral cortege wound its slow way along the Mountain Road up the east side of South River to Waynesboro, where the dead paragon of chivalry was shipped by rail to the University (of Virginia) for temporary interment.

Due to the proximity of Fremont's army, the Confederate signalers placed on top of the Peaked Mountain by Maj. Jed Hotchkiss, were compelled to abandon the station for fear of being captured. This gave Col. Samuel S. Carroll, commanding the advance of Shields's army the advantage of reaching Lewiston early in the morning of Sunday June 8 without being observed. He had overcome almost insurmountable difficulties in his route, due to incessant rains, swollen streams, and muddy roads.

That Sunday morning, June 8, dawned with unequaled splendor over the mountains and valleys, and Jackson was preparing to spend the day in religious exercises; the Beau Brummels among his officers and staff were ingratiating themselves into the favor of the belles of the town, when word was brought to headquarters that a cavalry force of Shields's army was advancing up the Swift Run Gap Road and was hard by. Instantly there was a scurrying to homes and places of safety.

Jackson had taken steps to prevent a surprise from this quarter. Intelligence of the nearness of his leading troops being reported to Jackson, he instructed Capt. E. Sipe to take a small cavalry force during the night of the 7th and go down the river and verify the report, and also to get all other information obtainable. Somewhat later Capt. G.W. Myers was ordered to go with his company of cavalry to the support of Capt. Sipe and to picket the road. Capt. J.J. Chipley and his company of cavalry were retained in the town. The next morning Jackson decided to go himself and look the situation over upon the reception of the following report:

Major - General Jackson:
    The enemy have had a scout of 20 near the bridge this morning at Port Republic. On our approach they fell back. We pursued them, but did not see the scout at all. After passing General Lewis' about 2 miles we found ourselves in front of a regiment of cavalry. They are now just below General Lewis,'
    E. Sipe, Captain commanding scout

    This report contained information of grave importance and led to the following:

Headquarters Valley District,
June 8, 1862
    Major - General Ewell, Commanding, &:
    General: The general commanding directs me to inclose this dispatch, just received. He is going down in person to see into it, but requests that you will not advance your pickets until you hear further from him.
    A.S. Pendleton, Assistant Adjunt General

    But before Jackson had time even to start down the river to investigate, he had to look to his own personal safety by taking refuge on the hills beyond North River.
    Mrs. Sue B. Craig, of Warrenton, relates that she was

taken, on account of the death of her mother, to the home of her maternal grandparents at Madison Hall in her early infancy, and was twelve years old at the time General Jackson was the honored guest of her grandfather, Dr. George W. Kemper, Sr. She was sitting on the front porch that beautiful Sunday morning looking at Capt. James McD. Carrington's Battery, which was placed near a large tree in the meadow in front of the house, when a dispatch was brought to headquarters containing the information that the Union Cavalry was near and rapidly advancing on the town. Jackson, she says, came out of the house, went hurriedly down the steps, and mounting his horse rode at a brisk gait through the town, making his escape across North River Bridge by a narrow margin of time. Major A.S. Pendleton was the only member of his staff who crossed the bridge with him.

John Kenney of Company B, was at breakfast in the hospitable home of Dr. George W. Kemper, Jr., who lived about the middle of town, when told of Jackson's hurried departure. He decided that something unusual was afoot; so he rose from the table, grabbed his haversack, which had been well-filled with food by Miss Fanny Kemper, and following in the footsteps of Jackson; he was saved by fast running. Col. S. Crutchfield and Lieut. Edward Willis, attempting to follow a little later, were captured by the enemy.

By this time Col. Samuel S. Carroll, commanding Sheilds's advanced brigade, was in possession of the town. With about 150 of the First Virginia (W. VA) Cavalry and four pieces of artillery commanded by Capt. Lucius N. Robinson, he had reached Yost's Hill, and had planted two guns on this hill to command the ends of North River Bridge. He then ordered Maj. Benjamin F. Chamberlain, commanding the cavalry, to enter the town and take possession of the bridge. This officer had been injured by a fall from his horse and as his troopers hesitated when they arrived at South River, Capt. Earle S. Goodrich was sent to urge them forward. This he successfully accomplished. They crossed South River at the Middle Ford, which was back of the old Palmer House.

At that time a public road connected Chestnut Street with the river. A mill race runs parallel with South River for about half the length of the town and is midway between the river and Water Street, which it also parallels. A road led from the ford across a bridge over the mill race to Water Street. In a corner formed by the road and the race stood the Palmer barn. Clay Palmer, then about seventeen years old, pulled the family rockaway out of the barn and onto the bridge over the race, and had returned to the barn for the horse to draw it beyond the reach of the enemy when they rode up to the vehicle, which stopped their progress. Several of them dismounted and threw it in the race. Clay climbed into the haymow and looked out of the door to see what was taking place. One of the troopers saw him and fired at him. Fortunately the bullet missed its intended mark and Clay hid in the hay.

Crossing the bridge, Captain Goodrich led the cavalry to Main Street, and drove part of the Confederate cavalry out of town on to the Staunton Road, and part across North River Bridge. He had the coveted bridge in his possession.

At this juncture Colonel Carroll rode into town bringing with him two more pieces of artillery, one of which he planted at the end of the covered bridge so as to sweep it, and the other at the corner of Main Street along which part of the Confederate cavalry had retreated. Before entering the town he had been informed of the location of Jackson's parked train and a large number of beeves herded nearby, the area scantily guarded. Stationing himself midway between the two cannon, that each might have his attention, he ordered part of the cavalry, which is now under its own officers, to proceed out on the Staunton Road and capture or stampede the supply train and herd of beeves. These were just behind a slight rise of land in the fields and the ammunition train was strung along the pike for several miles.

At this end (the southwestern end) of the town, Main Street is entered at a right angle by the old road to Harrisonburg which crossed North River at Pirkeys Ford near the home of Jacob B. Nicholas. At a distance of 200 yards from Main Street this road is entered by the Staunton Road. It was at this point that the advancing Federal troops were to receive the surprise of their lives.

When the troopers were seen advancing up the street, a small company of wounded Confederate soldiers who had been guarding headquarters, were collected and posted near where the street makes its second turn. They delivered a withering fire upon the head of the column as it came up. The enemy fell back and pressed upon its rear which was turning to the right on Main street. But even the rear was not to escape without punishment. Captain James McD. Carrington placed two pieces of artillery in position to rake the street.

An illuminating article by James Dinwiddie, First Lieutenant Charlottesville Artillery, describes the repelling of the oncoming Union troopers. The following excerpt deletes his references to a map:

On the evening before the battle of Cross Keys our artillery—Carrington's battery, Charlottesville Artillery—was halted on the ground which was the battlefield of Cross Keys. About dark we were ordered to proceed to Port Republic and occupy Kemper's Hill. Knowing Dr. Kemper and the location of his house...we took possession of the knoll just above his house, and sent word to Colonel Crutchfield, our chief of artillery, telling him where we were. He told us we were not at

Kemper's Hill, but ordered us to stay where we were until further orders. This was about midnight Saturday night. (ed. note: Never before was the bluff on North River opposite Port Republic known as "Kemper's Hill." Due to ownership at different time this high ground could with propriety be called Scott's, Lewis's, or Bateman's Hill but never Kemper's Hill. There is a hill so named on the battlefield of Cross Keys and it may have been this hill that Carrington was ordered to occupy.) Early Sunday morning, we arose and cooked and ate breakfast. While I was sitting on a mess-chest reading a Testament immediately after breakfast our Quartermaster-sergeant, Charley Harman, of Charlottesville, came up from town in a gallop, telling us the Yankees were coming into town. We made sport of it at first, and pointed to General Jackson's horse down at Dr. Kemper's. But while we were speaking a shell passed over us with a sharp explosion, another penetrated the ground near us, and we saw General Jackson and his staff gallop away furiously. In a few minutes Dr. Dabney, of the General's staff, came back to us, and some twelve infantrymen, the guard at headquarters, under Captain Campbell, also joined us in the field. Our artillery horses, which were grazing in this field, were hitched up with all the haste possible. Dr. Dabney said he had been cut off where the road comes into the main street of Port Republic and that the fate of our whole train depended on us. This train had passed along the 'pike towards Staunton, was in sight, and covered the double track of the 'pike for ten miles. We pulled down every other corner of the worm fence making little V-shaped barricades, with openings between them. We rolled up two cannon by hand and placed them in the opening so they could sweep the 'pike. Captain Campbell and his men got into the fence barricades.

While the horses of these two guns were being caught and the other guns hitched up, the enemy appeared around the corner. They rode furiously up the street. We put three loads of canister into each gun and poured it into them. Captain Campbell and his men also fired from the fence corners. The enemy melted away and retreated around the corner towards the bridge beyond which Jackson's whole army was lying. As soon as the street was cleared we had hitched up our other

127

four guns and ran them down the little road and around Dr. Kemper's house and placed them in position, sweeping the Main street of the town to the mouth of the bridge. We filled the guns nearly to the muzzle with canister and swept the street like a broom. The enemy left their two Howitzers in the street and passed into the road toward the ford. We soon saw infantry pouring down the road. As soon as the head of this column reached the bridge we ceased firing, and General Taliaferro came across with his brigade...
There is no doubt of the fact that the Charlottesville Artillery saved the bridge and the Confederate train that day. Had we not been where we were no human power could have saved the train or the bridge. . .

There was a plank fence back of Dr. Kemper's house through which we had to fire. The fence was made of about four planks nailed on horizontally to the posts. I was sitting on this fence when Jackson passed the place late in the day after Fremont's retreat. He looked at the riddled fence and said: "That may have been a raw battery, but they knew how to fire at the right height, and they did grand work today." At that time this company had just received their guns and had never been drilled. Lieutenant John Timberlake and my-self were the only two in the company who had ever been on a battle-field before, so far as I can remember. Captain Carrington at that time hardly knew how to load a cannon; but he was brave and thoughtful...I think when we were or-dered to join Jackson's army we had been in possession of our guns one week and had never made a single manoeuvre on the field. At night we taught the men how to load and fire, and that was all the knowledge of artillery which they possessed.[2]

Notwithstanding the repetition, a letter of paramount interest in this connection by Prof. R.L. Dabney, D.D., Jackson's Chief of Staff, to D.H. Pannill, Esq. is descriptive of Dabney's part in driving Colonel Carroll and his men out of Port Republic. It was published in the Richmond Times-Dispatch, Aug. 30, 1903, and later in *The Life and Letters of Robert Lewis Dabney* by Thomas Cary Johnson. It reads in part:

I had lodged in a little tent in an orchard, about two hundred yards from the house (old Dr. Kemper's) where the General lodged, but had seen him about breakfast time and he told me that he did not intend to begin any fighting on the Sabbath day, and I should preach to the Stonewall Brigade. I had accordingly gone back to my tent, and was preparing a sermon, when I saw the servant hastily jerking up the tent pins. I asked him why, when he replied in about these words, "Why, Major, don't you know the Yankees done come, and the General done started across the river, and he ordered me that all these tents and baggage must be packed and be moved to the rear in five minutes.' I sprang up and told him to bridle and saddle my horse, while I belted on my arms. His answer was, 'Bless your heart, I can't stop for that, the General's orders is too strict.' I equipped the horse myself, and started to follow the General. The southern end of the village street turns at right angles between the village and old Dr. Kemper's. When I came near that spot two staff officers—Dr. McGuire and Quartermaster Harman—galloped rapidly to the rear, each of them waving me back, and shouting to me that the Yankees were already in the street, and it was simply impossible for me to join the General. Indeed, two of our staff, trying to get to him a few minutes earlier, were already captured. Colonel Crutchfield, colonel of our artillery, was one and he was in the street with the Yankee Colonel Carroll during the battle that followed; escaping that same day, he returned to us and told us what he saw from the Yankee side, which was very instructive to me. The thought which flashed on my mind when I was stopped was that the bridge and our trains must be in immediate danger from these Yankees and my duty was to rally whatever I could for their protection. So beginning to look around I first saw a captain with about fifteen Confederate riflemen. He said he was Captain Moore, of the Second Virginia, who had been posted as picket at the forks of the river just below, and had been driven away by a greatly superior force. I asked him if his men were stampeded. He replied proudly, 'No;' that he could control his men, and the faces of

129

his men confirmed this. I told him it was a critical time and we must do what we could to check the advance of the Yankees. 'Follow me, and I will show you an advantageous position, and you must stay there at all hazards until I bring you some supports.' This he promised to do.

The Staunton road, issuing from the village, makes a second right angle near the old Kemper house, so that between this angle and the first one mentioned lies a straight line of turnpike of some hundred and seventy or two hundred yards, making a capital range for a close rifle fire. I quickly put Captain Moore and his men over there in the field behind a big board fence, ordering them to lie down on their breasts and fire low through the lowest crack upon whatever enemy turned the other corner. Carrington's Battery had come to us the day before so ill-equipped and trained that Colonel Crutchfield had ordered them to stay for the present with the baggage train; they had columned and were going south at a gallop. I raced after them and ordered word to be passed on to their captain to halt the column and come to me. I then asked him what ammunition he had, and he said he had enough canister cartridges for two guns. 'Have you friction primers, Captain?' 'Yes, but no lanyard strings.' I said the whip lashes will do for them; turn out these two guns and follow me. I started him back at a gallop through an old orchard down into Dr. Kemper's front meadow. Meantime, I heard a sharp volley from Moore's riflemen; he told me afterwards that the head of a Yankee column of Cavalry turned the lower corner of the turnpike, but his first volley sent them back. Knowing that my only chance was audacity, I ran my two guns across the meadow, so as to rake the main street at short range, and ordered the men to load with canister. Just then Captain Myers, of Ashby's cavalry, was passing by with a little company of about twenty-five. I ordered them to halt, form and support the guns. This he did. He was one of the cavalry pickets, but being on the direct road to Lewiston, had not been stampeded by Carroll, like the other cavalry picket. I then said to Carrington, 'I don't want to fire into friends; so as Jackson may have gotten some of his men into the street by this time, wait until I reconnoiter once more.' I rode forward to the head of the street behind an old shed; the road was so dusty that at first I saw nothing, but I watched it until I saw a blue column of Yankee cavalry unmistakably emerging from the dust in good canister range; then galloped back and ordered Carrington to fire. The enemy replied by a shell, which was excellently aimed, I knew by the buzz, and shouted to my men, 'Down, men,' and all squatted like partridges in the grass. Sure enough, the shell burst about four yards ahead of them, apparently the very worst place for them; but strange to say, all the fragments ricocheted over them whereon I ordered them up to reload and fire; so we kept up this fire until we cleared the street and Jackson retook the bridge.

A few well-aimed shots of canister and the enemy retreated in confusion. Part of them crossed over to Water Street in order to get out of the line of the guns and galloping down the street to the road leading to the ford they had crossed earlier in the morning, they wheeled into it and fled beyond the river. The remainder retreated down Main Street to the middle of the town where they huddled together in a very uneasy condition.

New events pressed one upon the heel of another. Dashing up the hill on the north side of the river, Jackson ordered the long roll to be instantly beaten. General William B. Taliaferro, commanding the Third Brigade, was forming his regiments for inspection, and hearing sounds of strife over the hill, he was in the act of moving troops in that direction when Jackson rode up. He directed Taliaferro to take a position on the hill near the river and just above the bridge. General Charles S. Winder, commanding the First Brigade, received like orders.

The batteries of Capt. William T. Poague, Rockbridge Artillery, Capt. Joseph Carpenter, Virginia Artillery, and Capt. George W. Wooding, Danville Artillery, were now coming up. One Parrot gun of Poague's Battery was placed in position for effective firing upon the bridge. Wooding's and Carpenter's Batteries were placed farther down the river to command Yost's Hill.

The story that Jackson was cut off from his troops by Capt. Lucius N. Robinson, Battery L, First Ohio Artillery, when he had planted a gun at the mouth of the bridge, is without a foundation of fact. Captain Poague relates the incident thus:

I recollect well the incident you ask about. General Jackson finding one of my guns ready to move, directed me to hasten with it towards Port Republic, he himself going along and posting it in the field overlooking and commanding the bridge. I was surprised to see a gun posted at the farther end of the bridge. For I had just come from army headquarters, and, although I had met a cavalryman who told me that the enemy were advancing up the river, still I did not think it possible they could have gotten any guns into place in so short a time. It there upon occurred to me that the gun at the bridge might be one of Carrington's, who was on that side and whose men had new uniforms something like those we saw at the bridge. Upon suggesting this to the General, he reflected a moment, and then riding a few paces to the left and in front of the piece, he called, in a tone loud enough to be heard by them, 'Bring that gun up here,' but getting no reply, he raised himself in his stirrups and in a most authoritative and seemingly angry tone he shouted, 'Bring that gun up here, I say!' At this they began to move the trail of the gun so as to bring it to bear on us, which when the General perceived, he quickly turned to the officer in charge of my gun and said, in his sharp quick way, 'Let 'em have it.' The words had scarcely left his lips when Lieutenant Brown, who had his piece charged and aimed, sent a shot right among them so disconcerting them that theirs in reply went far above us.[3]

And to this agree the words of Captain Robinson as recounted by the correspondent of a Northern journal soon after the incident:

Yesterday I met Captain Robinson, of Robinson's Battery, on his way home to Portsmouth, Ohio, to recruit. He was at the battle of Port Republic, where his brother lost three guns, and was wounded and made prisoner. Captain Robinson, who appears to be a very modest and veracious man, relates that while he was working one of his guns, Stonewall Jackson, whose form was familiar to him, came within easy hailing distance, and, standing erect in his stirrups, beckoned with his hand, and actually ordered him to 'bring that gun over here.'

Captain Robinson replied by eagerly firing three shots at the ubiquitous Presbyterian, but without even the effect of scaring him. 'I might have known,' said he, 'that I could not hit him.[4]

Captain J.K. Boswell, Chief Engineer, gives such clear and succinct account of what did happen between Jackson's departure from Madison Hall and the capture of the gun at the end of the bridge, that it is here quoted as a corrective of widely-circulated errors still current:

On the morning of June 8, I heard firing in the direction of Port Republic, and saw you, with several members of your staff, riding rapidly in the direction of the bridge. I mounted my horse and followed, crossing the bridge just as the enemy's cavalry entered the town. Lieutenant Willis, who was a short distance behind me, was captured. I found you on the hill a short distance off, and was directed by you to find whether the enemy was in the town. I soon returned with the information that their cavalry were on the bridge, when you ordered up the Thirty-seventh Virginia and rode down to the bank of the river. The enemy brought up a gun and planted it in the south end of the bridge and fired one shot at the Thirty-seventh Virginia as it advanced, but the gun was soon captured by that regiment.[5]

Colonel Samuel V. Fulkerson, commanding the Thirty-seventh Virginia Regiment, was ordered by Jackson to charge through the bridge and disperse the enemy at its far end. He deflected to the right from the road and approached the bridge on its upstream side. Arrived at its entrance, a terrific volley was fired at the enemy, and with a mighty yell, they charged through and fell upon the gunners. The enemy's gun had been doubled-shotted with canister and had they fired with deliberation, the head of the advancing column would have been destroyed. But the missiles of death went over their heads and in a few minutes the bridge was in the possession of the Confederates for the second time. Colonel E.T.H. Warren, commanding the Tenth Virginia Volunteer Infantry, was hurried into the town to occupy the fords.

When the enemy cavalry, still shaken from its repulse, saw Fulkerson advancing towards the bridge, they broke and ran in every direction by which they could retreat, leaving the artillerymen and their support in the lurch. Seeing that he could not hold the town, Colonel Carroll ordered the two pieces of artillery to be withdrawn. But the Confederate infantry fire was so heavy that the limber-horses of the gun at the bridge ran away with the limber and it was abandoned. Lieutenant Charles H. Robinson, brother of the captain, stayed to the last in his effort to save it, and was wounded and captured. The other piece was left in concealment near South River.

General Taliaferro says in his report of the fight that had he known the topography of the town he could have captured most of the fleeing enemy; for his men hastened to the lower ford, the one at The Point, not knowing there were other fords leading into the town. North River was much swollen from recent rains and the backwater made the ford at The Point impassable. Had it not been so, he could have crossed here and thus placed himself between Colonel Carroll and his main body which was now at Lewiston. Perceiving the enemy crossing at the Middle Ford, Lieut. C. Duncan of the Thirty-seventh, detached a part of the regiment and hurried forward to intercept them. He fired upon them but was not in time to cut them off. They retreated to Yost's Hill where, meeting their infantry support, they attempted to make a stand. But the high places on the opposite side of the Shenandoah River had been crowned with Confederate artillery, the well directed fire of which soon drove them back to Lewiston.

In this attack on Port Republic, Colonel Carroll reported his loss in killed, wounded, and missing as follows: Seventh Regiment volunteers: 8 killed, 2 captains, 1 lieutenant and 27 men wounded. Battery L, First Ohio Artillery: 1 killed, 1 lieutenant missing. Total loss 40. Battery L lost two pieces and limbers and fourteen horses.

Three causalities in Colonel Fulkerson's regiment in their advance on the bridge were reported by the Confederates. Colonel Carroll captured four, possibly five, of Jackson's staff officers when he first came into the town; namely, Col. S. Crutchfield, Lieut. Edward Willis, Lieut. H. Kyd Douglass, Dr. Hunter McGuire, and perhaps another whose name is not given. The enemy left the town so precipitately that Colonel Crutchfield was overlooked and left behind. Lieutenant Willis had been taken across South River and turned over to a soldier. He captured his guard and when the way was clear marched him into town.

An interesting story is told of the capture and escape of Dr. Hunter McGuire. The Old Brick Church, located in the middle of the town, and the old Dundore house just across Main Street from the church, had been converted into temporary hospitals. In these Dr. McGuire had performed the surgical operations necessitated by the various wounds of his patients, and he, too, was hoping for a day of rest and relaxation when word was brought of Colonel Carroll's advance. Bestriding his horse, which was conspicuous because of his blazed face and white legs and feet, he ordered up the ambulances to carry the wounded to a more secure place.

Deeming that the wounded were not being handled with proper care, he was exhausting his vocabulary of profanity when Jackson, who was riding by, overheard him and stopped to inquire if he could not do as well without so much swearing.

Dr. McGuire stood by his patients and was captured. The part of the enemy cavalry that fled down Water Street from Carrington's guns had him in their charge. When they turned right to South River, he continued straight ahead and made his escape.

Colonel Thomas T. Munford reported that he had recaptured one of Jackson's staff officers between Lewiston and Elkton. This officer may have been Lieut. H.H. Lee.

The damage done to property in the town during the fight was inconsiderable. Two boys, William Harper and Charles Lee, were looking out of the attic window of the kitchen of the Lee Hotel when the artillery began firing. William asked Charles what he would do if a shell struck the kitchen. He answered that he would continue to look out of the window. He had scarcely spoken when a shell struck the gable close to the window and went out through the roof. The boys scampered to the stairway and Charles, in his hurry, fell down the steps. Several minor buildings at different places in the town were injured and two or three shells lodged in John Harper's barn.

At the very beginning of the fight, one shell reached the home of Henry Crawford and pierced the kitchen roof. Miss Cassie Crawford was making soap in a large iron kettle placed on the kitchen stove—she seems not to have been an observer of Sunday—when the shell came through the roof and fell into the kettle. It did not explode but ringed the floor and walls with soft soap.

Hardly had the attack on Port Republic been repulsed

before Gen. Richard Ewell was engaged with Gen. John C. Fremont at Cross Keys. General Ewell had been left near Union Church to check the progress of Fremont, the "Pathfinder of the West." This he successfully did for he struck him so stunning a blow that he did not recover from it in time to go to the assistance of his colleague east of the river the next day.

A suitable conclusion of the account of the fight in the streets of Port Republic is a paper on the subject contributed by Lieut. Leroy Wesley Cox, one of Charlottesville's few surviving Confederate veterans, who served on the firing line throughout the four years of the war. Lieutenant Cox was the youngest of four sons of Dr. William Cox. These young men volunteered for service in the Confederate Army at the beginning of the war. One of the brothers, Lucian W. Cox, was assigned to Company B, Nineteenth Virginia Regiment, and was killed in battle Dec. 22, 1862. Lieutenant Cox was gunner No.1 in Capt. J. McDowell Carrington's Battery. Lieutenant Cox prepared this paper in 1895, and is a vivid description by the mature man of the part he and his young comrades had in driving the enemy out of the town. His paper follows:

I entered the Confederate service in my 16th year as a private in Captain R. G. Crank's Company, Border Guard, Wise's Legion... Wise was moved East, and after the fall of Roanoke Island, I came home and joined a battery, which was forming at the University of Virginia...There were few men in this company that had ever seen any field service before. I was then in my 16th year.

On the Sunday morning, June 8th, 1862, one of the drivers, John Risk, allowed me to ride one of his horses to water. I saw our Quartermaster, Sergeant C.H. Harman, riding up the street from the direction of the bridge in Port Republic, in an unusually fast gait for him. I stopped, and he said to me, "Tell the men to come to camp at once. The Yankees will be upon us in about fifteen minutes." I hurried up, not letting my horse drink very much for fear that it might founder him.

I think that I was about the last one to get to camp, for, boy-like, I wanted to see what was going on. When I started to camp, I did not allow the grass to grow under my horse's feet. I was riding a large dapple- gray, bareback. When I got to camp I found everything in confusion, the men hitching up and a general breaking of camp. I understood that an order had been given that we should hitch up and get away from there as quick as possible.

In a very few minutes a few infantrymen, possibly eight or ten, commenced firing from a fence near us. I also saw two or three cavalrymen near this fence firing their pistols at some Federal cavalry that was moving towards us up the road, having just turned out of the street. I saw that one of our cavalrymen that I was standing by was shooting very wildly. I asked him to lend me his pistol and told him that I'd get one every crack. He made no reply, but fired again up in the air, and struck spurs to his horse and rode off. The infantrymen also fell back up the rode. About this time our last piece was hitched up.

Lieut. J.H. Timberlake was sitting on his horse near us as the drivers were preparing to mount. I ran up to him and said, "Lieutenant, for God's sake, don't let us leave without firing a shot; if we do, we will all be captured." At this, he seemed to grow at least six inches, standing in his stirrups, drawing his pistol or sword, I forget which, and said, "I will have my two pieces stay if they are captured." At this, he rode after his other piece which had already moved off at a trot.

The driver of our lead horse, Dr. Gardner, turned his horse toward the advancing column. The driver of the wheel horse, a big Irishman (a substitute in our company by the name of Brown) jumped off his horse at the head of the lane, or turn, in the road, which was behind a high rail and stake fence. We at once dropped the trail of the gun and I hollered for Sam Shreve to bring me a double charge of canister. He said, "There is none." "Then bring me anything," I cried. At that he brought me a bag of powder and a round of uncut shell. Our gun was a 12-pound iron Howitzer--we had six pieces in our battery. Julious Goodwin put the powder and shell in the mouth of the gun and I rammed it home and jumped around and pulled off the shot, without even elevating the breech of the gun, not having time to work the screw, as the charging part was in a half-close pistol range from us. We took them by surprise, and they at once fell back, around the turn in the road, or street, out of our sight before we could reload. I think that we fired another shot in the direction of the bridge, but I am not entirely clear about that.

After the first check of the attacking party, Lieutenant Dinwiddie got two of his pieces in position, followed by Lieutenant Timberlake and his other piece, and fired straight down the street, using canister upon two pieces of the enemy's artillery, which had possession of the southern mouth of the bridge. The idea was to stop them at any cost. The remainder of the battery took somewhat different positions as they came up.

I can not say how many times the Yankees fired, but remember one of their shells cutting the limb from a big hickory tree nearby. In the whole skirmish I do not think that anyone was hurt, the only thing that I saw bloody was a horse that Edmund Drew went down the street and got after the firing ceased. It was wounded in the thigh by a piece of shell apparently. It was a strawberry roan.

I have seen a good deal of hard fighting during the four years' service in different commands, and will here say that I never saw men stand up better and fight harder than this battery when it was given the chance. I have been taxing my memory, and can only remember that there were three men at the gun when the first shot was fired by us. They were Julious Goodwin, Sam Shreve and myself. Dr. Gardner drove the leader and Edmond Drew (a colored barber in our company) drove the wheel horse.

A laughable incident occurred. The driver of the Captain's wagon (which was a two-horse wagon) jumped up on one of his horses and hollered to the company's cook to bring on the other horse and wagon. He was near enough to be stopped before he got very far...From the position that this one piece took, that made the first stand and fired the first shot, the enemy could not make out our strength, else, they would have had a perfect walkover.

(L.W. Cox's account of the battle of Port Republic as he recalls it.)

I have read Mr. L.W. Cox's account which is enclosed to you of this date and join with him in saying that it is a correct account of the affair from our standpoint.

Julious S. Goodwin

Later in the day, the battle of Cross Keys was fought and won by the Confederates and the battle of Port Republic, beginning with a skirmish in the streets of the town was fought at Lewiston the next day.

Chapter Fifteen Endnotes

[1]The house was purchased in 1993 by the Society of Port Republic Preservationists for use as a museum.

[2]*Richmond Times Dispatch*, (12 July 1891).

[3]William Allan, *Stonewall Jackson's Campaign in the Shenandoah Valley of Virginia*. The Pall Mall Military Series, (London: Hugh Rees, Ltd., 1912), 267-268.

[4]John Eston Cooke, *Stonewall Jackson: A Military Biography* (New York: D. Appleton Company, 1876), 179, 180, note.

[5]*Official Records of the Union and Confederate Armies*, series 1, vol. 12, part 1, (Washington, D. C.: Government Printing Office), 719. (hereafter known as *Official Records.*)

Chapter 16

The Civil War: The Battle of Port Republic

After hearing of Ewell's success at Cross Keys, General Jackson perfected his plans for the defeat of General Shields. Determining to take the initiative, Jackson ordered Gen. Richard S. Ewell to move at an early hour on the morning of June 9 to Port Republic, leaving Gen. Isaac R. Trimble, with his brigade, and Col. John M. Patton with the Forty-second Virginia Infantry and the First Battalion of Virginia Regulars, as a support, to hold General Fremont in check. General William B. Taliaferro was ordered to occupy the town during the night of the 8th. The remainder of the army was massed on the bluffs on the far side of North River except General Charles S. Winder, who camped in the fields just south of the town.

At the rising of the moon, which occurred about midnight, Jackson had a temporary bridge put across South River so that his men could cross the stream dryshod. The bridge was constructed by placing the running gear of wagons end to end and laying plank lengthwise on them. It is said in history books that Jackson personally superintended the construction; if he did, then he was responsible for the failure of his first attack on the enemy, for several of his officers reported that they experienced much difficulty in crossing and consequently were delayed in reaching the field of battle.

Worn out from the fatigues of a long day, Jackson entered the doors of Cherry Grove, the ancestral home of John I. Harnsberger for such rest as he could get in the few hours he permitted himself to sleep, and to meet his officers to give them their instructions for the forthcoming encounter. John I. Harnsberger told the writer that his paternal grandfather, Stephen Harnsberger, lived here at that time, and being a widower, had John Tiele and family living with him. Mr. Tiele's eldest daughter was a young lady of eighteen summers. In later years she would point out where Jackson, Ewell, and others sat in the parlor, and the large rocking chair which Jackson occupied.

It was here, too, he was sought by Colonel Patton, anxious as to the part he was to play in the plans for the morrow. "I found him at 2 a.m.," says Patton, "actively making his dispositions for battle." Major John D. Imboden, who was in command of a mule battery, received a note from Jackson directing him to report with his command at Port Republic before daybreak. Of this meeting Imboden wrote:

I went up, softly opened the door and discovered General Jackson lying on his face across the bed fully dressed with sword, sash and boots all on. A low-burnt tallow candle on the table shed a dim light, yet enough by which to recognize him. I endeavored to withdraw without waking him. He turned over, sat up on the bed and called out, 'Who is that?'"[1]

The second day's battle of Port Republic has been so well described by Gen. G.F.R. Henderson of the English Army, and Col. William Allan of the Army of Northern Virginia, in particular, and by other historians that nothing more than an outline of it, partly condensed from the official reports of the battle, will be given here.

At 3:45 in the morning Winder received orders to have his brigade in the town at 4:45. He met General Jackson who told him to cross his brigade over South River and march down the Swift Run Gap Road. He sent Lieut. J.M. Garnett, his aide-de-camp, to recall Col. John T. Neff, commanding the Thirty-third Virginia Infantry from picket duty some three or four miles from Port Republic on the road leading to McGaheysville. Neff found the North River bridge blocked by wagons, ambulances, artillery, and infantry. It was with great difficulty and much loss of time that he got his regiment across this bridge and across South River. Not knowing where his brigade was, he marched to the sound of battle and did not rejoin his brigade until the battle was virtually over.

The plain on which the battle was fought stretches between four and five miles down the right bank of the Shenandoah River from the town. A short distance below the town, the plain is about one-fourth of a mile wide, increasing to near a mile at Lewiston. East of the plain are foothills of the Blue Ridge, covered to their summits with underbrush and timber. Just below the home of Samuel H. Lewis—an ex-brigadier general of the State militia—the road from Mt. Vernon Furnace passes through a ravine, and crossing the main road at a right angle leads to a ford at Lewis's mill. This road was fenced on both sides. Still House Run, a shallow stream, issues from this ravine, and passing the rear of the home of Robert P. Fletcher (present Lynnwood), flows into the Shenandoah. The ground is terraced, and the first level reaches from the Shenandoah to the foothills. The grain in the wheatfields was ripening to a golden yellow, an Arcadia was this spot so soon to be marred by the scars of war, stained with blood, and cumbered with the dead and wounded of the contending hosts of Mars.

General Erastus B. Tyler, commanding the Union Army, had chosen a defensible position. Just below the Lewis house, on rising ground at the road crossing and on the east side of the main road had been a charcoal kiln and on

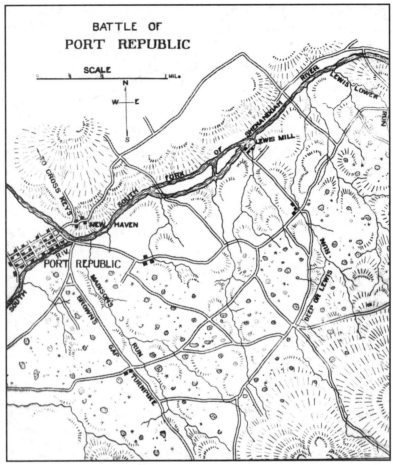

A map of the battle found in May's papers

this coal-hearth Col. P. Daum, Tyler's Chief of Artillery, planted six guns of the batteries of Capt. Joseph C. Clarke, Capt. Lucius N. Robinson, and Capt. James. F. Huntington. From the coal hearth to the river is a little over half a mile and General Tyler formed his infantry in the road between them. Near the river on his right was the Seventh Indiana, Col. James Gavin; in succession to his left were, Twenty-ninth Ohio, Col. Lewis P. Buckley; Seventh Ohio, Col. William R. Creighton; Fifth Ohio, Col. Samuel H. Dunning; and First West Virginia, Col. Joseph Thoburn. Sections of Clark's and Huntington's batteries were placed on the right near the river to prevent a flanking movement by the Confederates. Two pieces, a twelve-pounder howitzer and a six-pounder smooth-bore, were planted in the rear to guard the ford.

The key to the position was on the left and here a company of the Fifth and one of the Sixty-sixth Ohio Infantry were deployed in the woods as skirmishers; the Eighty-fourth and the One hundred and tenth Pennsylvania Regiments were also well up in the woods. Colonel Charles Candy, commanding the Sixty-sixth Ohio, was immediately in the rear of the battery and upon him and his devoted men fell the weight of the blow later delivered by General Richard Taylor. These gallant men fought until they were ordered to retreat. Had they not fought so well, the battle may have resulted more decidedly in favor of the Confederates.

Having crossed South River, General Winder placed himself at the head of his "Stonewall Brigade" and began his march down the river. Jackson rode with him. With the Second Virginia Regiment, Col. James W. Allen, in front with a company as skirmishers, Winder advanced a mile and a half, when the cavalry reported the enemy's pickets near. General Jackson being nearby ordered Winder to drive in the enemy's pickets, occupy the woods in front and attack.

The sun rising above the mountaintops dissipated the heavy mists of the morning and revealed the gallant Union infantry, with flying colors, and whose burnished arms gleamed in the sunlight, stretched from the river to the timberline. Their cannon, advantageously located, scowled menacingly.

Capt. Joseph Carpenter was ordered to advance two guns of his battery, take position on the left of the road and shell the enemy pickets. One or two rounds dispersed them. Captain William T. Poague came up at this time and with his two Parrott guns advanced to within 1,800 yards of the

145

Union battery on the coal-hearth and opened fire. The reply was prompt and effective, the Union battery firing with great accuracy. The Confederates saw that so long as this enemy battery remained active they stood small chance of defeating the infantry it so gallantly supported. So Colonel Allen was instructed to take his regiment, the Second Virginia, with the Fourth Virginia as a support, and Carpenter's battery through the woods to the left and rear of the enemy battery. Unable to get his guns through the thick undergrowth, Carpenter returned and his battery was placed near Poague's guns. The short-range artillery duel was sharp and the Confederates withdrew their guns. During this time, Col. Allen had pushed on to within one hundred yards of the coal-hearth, and engaging the enemy, was driven back.

Meantime, the remainder of Winder's brigade was hotly engaged. The Twenty-seventh Virginia Regiment had been ordered to support Captain Poague's battery in a wheatfield to the left of the road. The Fifth Virginia Regiment was placed to its left and rear to support one of Poague's guns, which had been moved out of reach of the battery on the coal-hearth.

Observing these dispositions, Colonel Carroll sent forward three regiments against the Virginians who suffered terribly from rifle and artillery fire. When the Seventh Louisiana Regiment came up in support, the Confederates advanced with some success, driving back the three regiments, supported by four guns, a short distance. Carroll then threw forward two more regiments and the stubborn conflict became dreadful. The storm of fire was beyond human endurance and the Confederates broke and fell back upon their guns. When the Thirty-first Virginia Regiment arrived on the field Winder tried to rally his men but Carroll sprang forward and drove them back a half mile through the wheatfields. Winder was joined by the Fifty-second Virginia

Regiment but their advance was halted. Two regiments under the command of Colonel Scott were concealed in the woods east of the road. They rushed forward, made a vigorous attack on the enemy, causing him to retire some distance, but were in turn driven back.

The inadequacy of the temporary bridge across South River almost proved fatal to Jackson's plans. It appears that in the middle of the stream, the front end of one wagon was placed next to the rear of another wagon and the discrepancy in height left the ends of the planks without support. When stepped upon, the other end rose in the air and dumped the unfortunate soldier into the river. The men refused to wade the stream, and remodeling the bridge somewhat, crossed in single file. Ewell said the trouble he had in crossing this same bridge not only delayed him but separated his command.

It was now too late in the day for Jackson to hope to return to Cross Keys to deliver the finishing strokes to Fremont after defeating Shields, so he sent orders to General Taliaferro, guarding the north bank of the Shenandoah, and to Trimble and Patton to retire from the front of Fremont, to lose no time in marching to Port Republic, burning the bridge behind them, and join the main body.[2]

So far the Union Army had been successful. They had repulsed Winder's every attack, and themselves taking the offensive, they drove back the Confederates in confusion and pursued them fiercely. But wait! A terrible surprise was in store for them.

By this time Ewell had arrived on the field. He found that his Eighth Louisiana Brigade, commanded by Gen. Richard Taylor, and guided by Major Jed Hotchkiss, Jackson's topographical engineer, had been sent into the woods to attack the enemy battery on the coal-hearth in flank and rear. They followed a road that led them to the

Aerial view of Port Republic battlefield, shows the coaling and Lewis Mill

ravine opposite the battery, and going somewhat higher, crossed the ravine and charged the battery. The charge was so sudden and unexpected that the cannoneers abandoned their guns, but in the following engagement were driven back. Before retiring, a Confederate officer, Lieut. Col. Peck, of the Ninth Louisiana Regiment, cried out, "Shoot the horses," which was done, thereby preventing the artillerists from moving the guns.

"Three times," wrote Taylor, "was the captured battery lost and won, the enemy fighting with great determination." The third time, the fighting was terrific. It was close quarters, hand to hand, and the bayonet was used. Lacking other arms, the artillerymen used their rammers. But at this moment Ewell came crashing through the brush and his presence alone equaled a brigade. The hornets' nest remained in the hands of its captors.

The greater part of Ewell's division had by now arrived on the battlefield. Again the Confederates made a forward movement all along the line before being ordered to retreat

Bogota, home from which the battle was watched by the Strayer family

from the field. And none too soon, for Taylor was turning all the captured guns on those they had served so well. Just at this time, Taliaferro came up with his brigade. The Union Army fled precipitately. Taliaferro was sent in pursuit forcing them to abandon the only gun they were seen to carry from the field. Many of the enemy were soon captured. Sergeant Samuel L. Gray, of the Thirty-seventh, actually captured at one time a Federal captain and all of his men, all armed, and although fired upon by them, seized the captain's sword and made the men throw their arms. This was the greatest individual exploit of the battle. The enemy was pursued five or six miles towards Conrad's store. The pursuit was then handed over to the cavalry under the command of Gen. Thomas T. Munford.

The Confederates began immediately to administer to the needs of the wounded and to bury their dead. They were engaged in the humane service of burying the Union dead when Fremont appeared on the western bank of the Shenandoah River and poured shot and shell upon them. The Confederates withdrew from this vicious attack by taking the Furnace Road to Browns Gap.

Tyler's army consisted of eight regiments, a detachment of the First (West) Virginia cavalry, and three batteries of artillery. He says in his report that his forces "could not have exceeded 3,000 men." Colonel Henderson, in his *Life of Jackson*, says Tyler could not have had "more than 4,000 all told." His casualties were in killed, wounded, and missing, 1018. He also lost seven guns.

The number of Confederate troops actually engaged in the battle was 5,900. Their losses in killed, wounded, and missing were: Taylor's brigade, 290; Winder's, 199; Elzey's, 128; total 816.

The battle of Port Republic was the culmination of Stonewall Jackson's Shenandoah Valley campaign. His fame as a military strategist rocketed to the skies; military students the world over study this campaign. When he fell at Chancellorsville, the star of the Confederacy paled and finally went down in the angry clouds of defeat and despair.

Chapter Sixteen Endnotes

[1]*Battles and Leaders of the Civil War*, vol. 2, (New York: The Century Company, 1887), 293.
[2]See Chapter 24, "Bridges of a River Town," for more on the burning of the bridge during the Civil War.

Chapter 17

The Fourth Horseman: Recent Wars

Spanish-American War (1898-1899)

Cuba had been for centuries a province of a brutal, insolent, and treacherous European power. She had often revolted against intolerable conditions and was as often put down by treachery and force. In 1895 she rebelled for the last time against her foreign masters and was successful.

The United States sent the battleship Maine to Havana to render necessary aid to our nationals. This grand warship was destroyed by an explosion in the harbor of Havana about half past ten o'clock on the night of Feb. 5, 1898. Two hundred and fifty-four men and two officers lost their lives in this appalling act of Spanish treachery. War between the United States and Spain grew out of this fiendish act.

But two men of Port Republic rallied to the colors: William S. May and Harry Leon Bateman. They belonged to Company C, Second Virginia, U.S.V. They were trained in the manual of arms at Camp Cuba Libre, Jacksonville, Fla. Leon returned weakened from fever and William came back hale and hearty, wearing the stripes of a sergeant.

World War (1914-1918)

When the cataclysmic shock of arms began in 1914, America hoped to maintain her neutrality under the leadership of her great president and foremost statesman. But when it was found that there could not be peace with honor, she acted quickly and decisively.

The following list of people in and near Port Republic who were in the service of their country during this time, is due to the kindness of Leon W. Smith.

Volunteers
Leon W. Smith, Field Artillery. He was in the battles of St. Michael and Argonne.
James T. Smith, Signal Corps.
J. Ellis Lee, Signal Corps.
J. Lincoln Spitzer, North Carolina National Guard. Mustered into Federal service. Shell-shocked and gassed.

Drafted
Earle B. Wagner, Engineer Corps.
Ollie Mace, Engineer Corps.
J. Harry Lamb, Engineer Corps.
Russell Armentrout, Medical Corps.
Harry M. Dinsmore, Signal Corps.
John Via, Infantry Corps.
Charles Fisher, Infantry Corps. Died of flu at Camp Lee.
B. Leo Bauserman, Quartermaster's Corps.
W. Russell Downs, Aviation Corps.

The last two did not go to Europe.

Several others who were employed in other parts of the country but claimed Port Republic as their home were: Carl F. Good, Meade O. Good, and W. Gray May.

The writer is indebted to the kindness of Emmet G. Johnson for the names of colored servicemen: John C. Johnson, saw service in France; Emmet G. Johnson, Frank Bell, Alexander Ray, and Albert Richardson were in camps of training.

Chapter 18

Famous Fights,
Fair and Foul

In former times it was thought that the people of Port Republic were too pugnacious, that they were quick to engage in fisticuffs to decide difference of opinion, as well as to prove which was the "best man." No more mistaken opinion was ever held by anyone. A quiet and peace-loving people, they have at all times endeavored to avoid broils and personal combats. True it is that they have always been quick to resent an insult and not slow to engage in personal encounter in self-defense. From its very beginning the town had been the gathering place for the people of a large scope of country. Here were the churches, the schools, the stores, the shops, the hotels--and the fights. These trials in the manly art were usually between two or more outsiders. A resident never became involved in such a contest if he could avoid it with honor; but when he found a fight was inevitable no one fought with more spirit and endurance than he.

Not long before the Civil War, Capt. George W. Eustler and Jack Sigler had an argument which ended in a fight. In the fury of the conflict and while the blood was hot, Captain Eustler drew a knife which pierced Mr. Sigler's side and cut off a small piece of the lower end of his liver. This is the one exception of both combatants being of the town.

On Aug. 4, 1869 John Robinson pitched his tent in the George Nicholas store lot and entertained the public with his usual fine show.[1] The day was warm, the air invigorating; the red blood coursed rapidly in the body, and perhaps the heartbeats of some were quickened by a draft from the bottle. Altogether it was too suitable an occasion to let pass without a fight. The Raines brothers were present in force, three or four of them. And present too was John L. O'Donnell, a blacksmith of Mt. Vernon Furnace. He was a man of powerful build, strong of body and limb. Fearless and honest he stood as a mighty oak. His clear steady eye surveyed the turbulent crowd and he soon saw that he himself was the object of the unfriendly glances of the Raines brothers. Deciding to fight, they were not long in forcing one on O'Donnell. Like Fitz-James he refused to fly and stood as a solid rock to meet the onslaught. But human strength and endurance were unequal to the strain. He was outnumbered. Besides he was foully struck on the head with a rock. He told Zachariah Raines, father of the brothers, that if he would stretch a rope across the street and he and his sons would stay on one side of it, he, O'Donnell, would whip them all, one at a time. The offer was declined. The rope was not stretched across the street. There was no further fighting. A short time later the quarrel was renewed with one of the brothers and resulted in a fatality.

Jake, the crack fighter of the Raines brothers, met more than his match when he was pitted against Albert Harris, a colored man of the town. Raines was not an overly large man but he was strong and athletic. He had trained himself for country fights in which no rules were respected. From start to finish the dominant idea was to win the fight by fair means or foul if necessary; the later, however, not to be so rank as to cause outside interference. Raines' athletic exercises consisted of running, jumping, wrestling, and boxing. He could drop on a knee and evade a smashing blow aimed at the upper part of his body, at the same time delivering a heavy uppercut on his opponent's stomach; or else seize his man near the hips and throw him over his head. If he did the first he would quickly gain his feet and clinch his opponent from the side, often scoring a throw. If he did the second, he would whirl around and spring upon his prostrate enemy. In such a case his manner of fighting showed at its best for no one in the vicinity excelled him in a rough and tumble fight.

Albert Harris was a son of Matthew Harris, "Uncle Mat," a respectable colored man and long a blacksmith in the town. Harris was a little over six feet tall, of well-proportioned physique, and weighed something over two hundred pounds. He could "strike" with his fathers sledge using but one hand, and hold at arm's length the cone-shaped anvil weighing over one hundred pounds.

The memory of childhood days recalls him as a sullen man who seemed to be always displeased at something. However, no rude act or uncivil word of his to any white children who played at his father's shop is remembered.

In 1870, John Robinson once again brought his show to Port Republic and pitched his tent in the Mill Yard. (Per P.C. Kaylor)

Albert J. Sigler ran a barroom at this time in what is now known as the Saufley house (Frank Kemper house). The crowd was jovial and in the mood to enjoy any free entertainment outside of the tent. After much refreshment at the bar it was agreed by several that such a fine crowd should not disperse without seeing a first-class fight. Accordingly, arrangements were soon made for a fight between Raines and Harris. It took place in the down-street lower front room of the Saufley house. The room was cleared of furniture and the combatants were stripped to their waists. Harris discarded his shoes also. He thought he would be less apt to slip on his feet if barefooted. The two men were

Benjamin Franklin Kemper House: a man points to the window where Ashby's body lay

taken to the room and placed facing each other.

What a spectacle: a white man and a black man confronting each other and about to decide by fisticuffs which was the "best man." One need only to look at them. Raines stood in his soft pliable shoes a little less than six feet tall, strong, wiry, with not a pound of surplus flesh; athletic, and confident that the training of almost a lifetime for such encounters would give him the victory.

Two perfect human animals were this white man and this black man. As they glared at each other they were carried by their elemental passions, back to the childhood of the world when the hands were used as weapons of offense and defense ere anyone had seized a stick and brained his enemy.

But what was that? Raines has struck and the fight is on. He aims a heavy punch for below the waistline. Harris wards off the blow with his left hand and strikes at the head with his right. Raines drops on one knee, thus evading the blow, lands lightly with a punch to the body and springs to clinch. Harris seizes him by the arms close up to the shoul-

156

ders, breaks his hold, and throws him across the room. He does not advance upon him. He prefers to strike blows rather than to clinch and scuffle. Raines springs up and advances warily. After some feinting he lands a heavy right-hander on the chest and a lighter blow with the left hand on the face. Harris promptly knocks him down with a terrific drive to the jaw. Raines regains his feet in a bewildered frame of mind. He looks groggy. Water is thrown on the floor in the belief that the shod feet of Raines will stick to it better and the bare feet of Harris will be more apt to slip. But it is of no avail. Raines is not whipped in body but is defeated in mind. His confident air is gone. Both advance. After some feinting and the exchange of a few light punches, Harris delivers another knockout blow. Fearing he will win if the fight continues, outsiders interfere and stop it. It is called a draw but Harris is in the lead.

Another encounter that immediately swept into the channels of notoriety was the one between Major William S. Downs and Bill Jones. The latter was of an unsavory reputation. It was known that in the past he had had connections with an outlaw gang. When this gang was broken up and dispersed, Major Downs and Jack Sigler had gone over the mountain to a hollow in its east side, arrested Jones, whom they found in hiding there, and brought him to Port Republic. He was soon released from custody and fled from the town.

Years later, about 1868, Jones got Henry Raines to help him to "get even" with Downs and Sigler. They came to the town and went to the sawmill where Sigler was at work. Raines at once attacked him but Sigler ran across town and took refuge in John Watson's store. Watson sent word to Downs, who was at work at his tannery, of what was going on. Arming himself with a knife and taking his son Jack in his arms, he walked down Water Street to assist his brother-in-law. Turning into the cross street at the Saufley home, he and Jones came face to face. Putting his son Jack on the ground at one side, he gave his undivided attention to his enemy. The encounter was short and bloody. With knife in hand, a swift movement of his arm laid open the cheek and throat of Jones. The knife was of inferior metal and the point turned up when it struck the jawbone, else the cut would have proved fatal. Jones fell to the ground and bellowed like a bull. Fearing the worst, Downs sent for Dr. Kemper. He declined to give medical attention saying the neighborhood would be better off if Jones died. Major Downs himself then went for the doctor. He explained that he was married and had children and that if Jones died all would suffer. The doctor consented to go see Jones and sewed up his wound. To the end of his life his face was disfigured with an unsightly scar.

It is remembered from childhood when this man was but once seen by the writer, that the scar was long and ugly.

Chapter Eighteen Endnotes

[1]A travelling showman.

Chapter 19

The Post Office

Apost office was established at Port Republic in 1811. The first note in the Post Office Department at Washington of a post office at Port Republic is a record of the appointment of Joseph Graham as postmaster on Jan. 15, 1811.

Immediate cash payment for postage stamps was not required in all cases by our early postmasters, as is now demanded of all buyers of stamps, postal cards, stamped wrappers, etc. Dr. George W. Kemper was debtor to James O'Brian:

To Postage on letters & papers from 1st July 1845 to 30th June 1846,	$6.02
Postage from 1st July to 31st of Dec. 1846	1.94
Do Janry 1st to 30th September	2.58

The account grew to $12.94 before it was settled.

The first through train running on schedule on the Shenandoah Valley Railroad between Hagerstown and Waynesboro made the run April 18, 1881. Newton L. Wagner was mail carrier and received the first sack of mail for Port Republic from the railroad mail clerk on Aug. 22, 1882. Mr. Wagner continued in the service for a few years and resigned. He was succeeded by Elias Grim whose assistant was Abner Brown. Mr. Grim retired about the end of the year 1888 and was followed by James H. Chandler. Mr. Chandler died in the fall of 1893 and his place was taken by his son Harry.

Mail Carrier, Herman Hudlow, with horse and wagon in front of the John Waller Palmer Store and Post Office

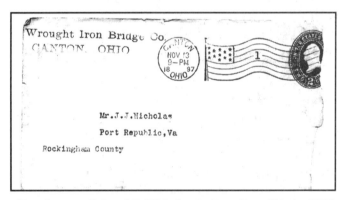

Envelope mailed to J.J. Nicholas in Port Republic in 1897

James Harry Chandler has been in the mail carrier service for forty-three years, assisted in the past by two sisters and at present by his son Burgess. For several years he made two trips a day, then the trips were increased to three daily, and for a number of years there was a Sunday mail to be carried. In all these years in the service, he has traveled approximately fifty thousand miles, something over twice the circumference of the earth.

The names of those who have been postmasters at Port Republic are:

Postmaster	Date Appointed
Joseph Graham	January 15, 1811 (Established)
Fontaine Graham	January 6, 1827
Catherine Graham	March 3, 1829
Benjamin F. Kemper	May 27, 1837
Hugh Bruffy	October 28, 1839
James O'Brian	December 9, 1842
John W. Lee	April 14, 1854
James A. Lewis	August 22, 1865
Charles Lewis	March 2, 1870
George M. Nicholas	March 2, 1875
John W. Palmer	May 10, 1882
John W. Lee	May 22, 1885
John W. Palmer	June 20, 1889
Annie L. Palmer	July 30, 1889
Sarah E. Lee	April 1, 1893
William H. Harnsberger	September 28, 1894
Jennie H. Palmer	December 14, 1897
Virginia H. Hinton	June 29, 1899
Nellie N. Palmer	October 25, 1900
Carroll H. Palmer	October 11, 1909
Mrs. Will M. Dinsmore	March 18, 1914
J. Harry Lamb (Acting)	June 12, 1933
Earl B. Wagner	August 1, 1933
Mrs. Ethel A. Miller (Acting)	May 8, 1939
Mrs. Annie G. Pearl	February 13, 1940

Chapter 20

Going to the Polls

Just when Port Republic was made a polling place may be a moot question. Politics tingled in the blood of the people else it would appear almost incredible that they would go from six to twelve miles to a place to vote. But this they seem to have done.

The earliest date of the establishment of a voting place in the town by an Act of the General Assembly, so far as the writer knows, is in "An Act authorizing a separate election in each of the counties of Loudoun and Rockingham," and passed Jan. 8, 1846, as follows:

Be it enacted by the general assembly, that whenever hereafter an election shall be holden in either of the counties hereinafter mentioned, in which all the lawful voters of the county are required to vote, there shall be at the same time a separate poll opened and held for such election, that is to say: In the county of Loudoun, at the post office at Purcell's store on the Leesburg and Snicker's gap turnpike road. In the county of Rockingham, at the house now used as a schoolhouse in the town of Port Republic. The said separate polls shall be conducted according to the rules and regulations prescribed by the several acts of assembly now in force concerning general elections in the commonwealth.

This act shall be in force from the passing thereof.

For a number of years the people of the precinct did their voting in the old schoolhouse on lot No. 50, the one deeded to George W. Kemper in 1824 by Jacob and Lydia Christ. In Acts of the General Assembly of Virginia Session of 1850-1851, pp. 218-225, there is a table showing the places at which separate polls had been established by law in each county; on page 224, under Rockingham, it is stated, "...at the schoolhouse in Port Republic . . ."

In county government a precinct is a subdivision of the county for election purposes, and there is reason for believing that Port Republic was a polling place even as early as 1843. The larger part of a political handbill issued by the Democratic Central Committee for Rockingham County dated April 10, 1843, is at hand. It is torn from the top left diagonally down to the right-hand side, and many names of persons in and near Harrisonburg are missing.

The first part of the Committee's call to arms against the opposing party is in these words:

Democratic Citizens of Rockingham! It having been ascertained within the day that Mr. A.H.H. Stuart, of Staunton, is in the field, as a Whig candidate for the Congressional District, in opposition to William Taylor the Democratic candidate selected by the later Democratic Convention held in Harrisonburg on the 30th of the last month, the Central Committee of Vigilance for this county, appointed by the Convention held at Richmond on the 2nd of March last, deem it their duty to pursuance of the powers conferred on them by the said Convention, to enlarge their own Committee, and to organize subordinate Committees in the different precincts of the county, with power to increase those said committee.

The committee appointed for Port Republic was composed of Capt. John Dundore, Jas. O'Bryan, John Strayer, Leroy P. Daingerfield, Selah Holbrook, Capt. Robert Hooke, and Jack Kiblinger. All these committeemen lived in Port Republic or in the immediate neighborhood. The above address to the voters of the county leaves the impression that Port Republic was a precinct in 1843.

Chapter 21

School Days

For no lack of effort, very little information has been obtained about the schools in the early history of the town. Here and there in old daybooks and account books mention is made of buying books for pupils and of wood for fuel for the schoolhouse.

It is known that one of the early schoolhouses of the town was close by a spring of excellent water on the east side of South River. This is the schoolhouse mentioned in Joseph Trout's daybook, dated Feb. 19, 1824. His daughter, Sarah Jane, attended the school in this building the site of which is now known to but a few. At that time a lane, or road, between Dundore's tanyard and Galliday's property, led from Water Street to the river, which was spanned by slab benches. The school children crossed the river on this insubstantial bridge.

The following list of early school teachers has been gleaned from musty pages: James H. Triplett, 1837; William A. McKinn, 1851-1852; Richard P. Fletcher, 1845; Maria B. Yost, 1850-1851; Bettie A. Pace, 1851-1852; Martha Rankin, 1853-1854; George A. Wood, 1854-1855; G.F. Mayhew, 1859-1860.

The Old Brick Church was also used as a schoolhouse. The names of some who taught school in this building are: Mrs. Hume, Sewell McCann, a Mr. Weed of Richmond, and Ben Wheeler of East Virginia.

In an account book of Dr. George W. Kemper, Sr., is found a "School Acct" for the years 1848-1861. Port Republic was in School District No. 10 and whatever amount of the school funds was appropriated to the district by the school commissioners was divided by 3½ cents and the quotient called "days." These "days" were apportioned among the teachers of the district according to the number of pupils of indigent parents that each teacher had. This is shown by an entry, "district No. 10 allowed $66.00—at 3 ½ cents—1714 days." Each teacher had a certain number of days "subscribed" to him and it was "ordered" that he be paid for the number of "days" he taught.

Teachers' names found:

1848	J.T.S. McCann, S. Hudlow, Thos. Ryan, A. Mohler, J. Harshberger, and C. Lewis
1849	Three new names appear: J. White, H. Hudlow and D.J. Pirkey (conditionally)
1851	J.G. Raynes, F. Jones, Miss Pace and McKim
1852	Jos. L. Pollard and Fauntleroy, Jr.
1853	Miss Moore, S. Filler and John Miller
1854	Fannie Burton
1857	New names are H. Beahm, Mellie Miller, D.T. Wheeler, and Black
1858	Dan'l Randall, D.M. Layton and Fulton
1859	Maynew, Mellie Ann Bunch, and Angeline Eutsler
1860	Daniel Randol, G.F. Mayhew, H. Beahm, Mary Miller, S. Filler, Miss McCulloch, Mr. Weed, Lou Palmer, Henrietta Miller, J.N. Hume, G.W. Tillotson, Anna Scott, and H.C. Lewis Rev. Quincy A. Wheat taught private or public school in the town 1869-1870.

After the Civil War, school was held in an old log house in the southeastern corner of lot No. 12 for a number of years. The teachers so far as is now known in succession were: Tip Hume, William J. Harper, Erasmus B. Clarke, Bernard B. White, and Josephine Maupin. Miss Maupin was last to teach in this old house. The chinking had fallen from between the logs at many places, and on account of the severity of the weather, the school was moved to another old log structure on lot No. 14, facing on Main Street, before the winter was past.

The first I.O.O.F. Hall in the town was fitted for a schoolroom and at different times the teachers were: Maggie Palmer, Clay Lewis, Jasper Hodge and others. Miss Palmer was a sister of John W. Palmer.

Robert W. Palmer's abandoned store building housed teachers and pupils for a few years. Mary C. Palmer was one of the teachers who molded plastic minds in this house. She was a daughter of John W. Palmer.

What was called the New Schoolhouse, a two-story four-room structure, was built during 1879-1883. (This schoolhouse is usually referred to as MontView Academy.) The principals of this school were in succession: B.B. White, J.R. Keeler, Frank H. Bowman, Kate Yost, S.W. Houck, J.J. Lincoln, B.B. Mitchell, J.Pence, W.H.G. Bowers, _____ Cawthorne, J.E. Keckley, and P.B.F. Good.

Port Republic High School is a modern twelve-room building and was built in 1922 with four more rooms added in 1934. R.L.Layman was principal for two years. Succeeding him, H.M. Earman, the present efficient principal, has built up the school to such proportions that the present building is not large enough for the number of pupils.[1]

MontView Academy class of 1902-1903

166

Sixth-grade class at MontView Academy, 1916-1917. Front left to right: Harbid Rogers, Herman Huffman, Johnnie Wagner, Jefferson Nicholas, Harry Scott, Arthur Scott, Lester Bauserman Back left to right: Susan Lowance, Virginia May, Lucille Scott, Martha Riddle, Frances Miller, Inez Good, Margaret Dinsmore, and Pauline Riddle

MontView Academy in 1916-1917

Port Republic Graded and High School

The following essay by an eleven-year-old Port Republic school girl is copied from the *Progressive School News*, Harrisonburg, Va., December 18, 1916:

Autobiography of a Grain of Wheat

I was a little grain of wheat way back in the barn. In the fall, the farmer prepared the ground to receive me. Then he came into the barn and mixed me with some fertilizer and I was sown into the ground. Before the snow fell, I began to sprout. It was in October when the little green leaves began to peep out of the ground. About two weeks later, the first snow fell to keep me warm through the long hard winter.

In the spring, all the snow melted away. Then the warm rains fell upon me and the sun shone. Then I began to put forth my leaves. I kept on growing and growing until I grew very tall. I turned to a beautiful golden brown. One day some men came into the field where I was. One of them said, 'This looks like it is ready to cut.' I did not know what he meant, as I asked the other wheat that was growing about me; but they did not seem to know either.

We were all somewhat frightened. The next day the men came back into the field. I was cut, then threshed. The men put me into a sack and put me on a wagon. They took me to the mill. The men at the mill put me into the machinery and crushed me. Then I came out I was no longer a grain of wheat, but beautiful white flour.

Now I thought I had gone through all my troubles but I had not. I was put into a barrel, loaded on a wagon, and hauled to a steamboat. When the steamer started off, I was somewhat scared. The boat went faster and faster. Finally two men came up to where I was. One of them said, 'This barrel goes to Europe, does it not?' The other one replied, 'Yes, it goes to Belgium.' Then I was glad, for I knew I was to help the starving people and thus put to some good at last."

(Written by Virginia May, VI grade, Port Republic, Va.)

Chapter Twenty-One Endnotes

[1]This building was later used as Port Republic Elementary School until its permanent closing near the end of the twentieth century.

Chapter 22

I.O.O.F., the Sons of Temperance, and the Cold Water Army

On July 19, 1849, John Kennedy, by Nicholas K. Trout, deeded a house and lot No. 23 to George W. Kemper, Jr., Robert W. Palmer, Joseph Harnsberger, John Harper, Peachy W. Wheeler, and John Huff, Trustees for the Port Republic Lodge, No. 67, I.O.O.F. and Worth Division No. 44 of the Sons of Temperance. The property had been appraised by George W. Kemper, Sr. and Stephen Harnsberger, and its value set at $100.00, however, $111.00 was paid for it.

How long the I.O.O.F. functioned, the writer does not know, but it was going strong in 1855 as an order on it for money by John Huff indicates. It may have lapsed about the time of the Civil War and was not again instituted util July 4, 1890.

Worth Division No. 44, Sons of Temperance, was organized at Port Republic in 1846. It had a large membership. Like other such organizations, it became disorganized when its members were taken in the military service of the Confederacy. It was revived in 1873.

The moral influence of the Sons of Temperance in the town and neighborhood was wide and lasting. They taught temperance and acted the part. The writer does not recall that they taught prohibition. They relied on precept and example. They did not believe that people can be made good by law. They seem to have been aware of the limitations of the accomplishments of legislation. At a later time prohibition engulfed the prudence and wisdom of the county, and the corrupt prosecutor wounded the

The Town Hall, built jointly by I.O.O.F. and the Sons of Temperance

heart of the unfortunate person whose head had already been cracked by the club of a brutal policeman. "Salvation by force" fittingly describes the times happily past:

> Our books are so full of a number of laws,
> That I'm sure that our lives must be without flaws.

The members of the Port Republic Lodge of Sons of Temperance from 1853-1856 were:

Burton, Robert	Harper, John	McClain, Henry
Burton, George W.	Harnsberger, Stephen	McCann, J. T.S.
Brown, Thomas E.	Harnsberger, Stephen M.	May, Ahaz
Bateman, William L.	Holbrook, John	May, G.W.
Breeden, Hugh	Hupp, B.F.	Madison, Thomas
Burton, Crawford	Huffman, Elija	McCauley, Henry
Brown, John H.	Hess, William C.	O'Brian, James
Britt, George	Jones, William	O'Brian, Hugh B.
Burton, William	Johnson, John	O'Brian, Alexander L.
Crawford, Henry M.	Jackson, Willis	Palmer, William E.
Crawford, Lawrence	Kemper, B.F.	Palmer, Charles T.
Crawford, Benjamin F.	Kemper, George, Jr.	Ryan, Thomas W.
Crawford, Zachariah	Kemper, George, Sr.	Roberts, W. T.

Collins, George	Kemper, William	Raynes, Jacob
Clifton, Henry	Kemper, Marcellus	Randol, Elija
Eddins, John M.	Layton, Fountain M.	Scott, William M.
Eakins, Jas. N.	Lee, John W.	Scott, Amos
Eddins, William	Lewis, Waller W.	Sipe, Peter
Funkhouser, Milton	Lewis, Charles	Smith, Frederick
Gettle, Henry H.	Lewis, John F.	Smith, Bluford
Grove, J. I.	Lewis, H.C.	Sipe, Levi
Grove, William	Lewis, William	Scott, Reuben
Grove, Tobias N.	Lewis, James	Spitzer, Samuel
Huff, John T.	Larkins, Samuel	Trout, James K.
Huff, John	Maupin, William A.	Talley, George W.
Hess, Joseph	May, Daniel E.	Traister, John
Weaver, William I.	Moore, William B.	Wheeler, Peachy H.
	Yost, Jacob H.	Young, George K.

Among the papers of Dr. George W. Kemper, Sr., is an undated one containing a partial list of the young ladies and gentlemen who belonged to the Cold Water Army of the Port Republic Total Abstinence Society. The paper is torn through the middle and the bottom half, with about half of the names, is missing. The names of those despisers of Bacchus on the upper half are:

Charles L. Bankhead	Christian Harnsberger
Robert Fletcher	Juliet O. Daingerfield
Abner K. Fletcher	Virginia Huff
Albert Strayer	Amanda Lackey
Isaac G. Coffman	Susan E. Fletcher
Washington Ham	Elvira G. Fletcher
Joseph H. Fry	Frances Eutzser
William Bateman	Margaret Strayer
James O'Brien, Jr.	Barbara Davis
Chas. I. Kemper	Mary Ann Murray
Lewellyn I. Kemper	Lucy Roberts
William Trout Frances	Jane Mohler
John I. Harnsberger	Sarah Jay Daingerfield
William M. Harnsberger	Isabella H. Daingerfield
William Burton	Margaret F. Daingerfield
Fontaine Talliaferro	

Chapter 23

Port Republic's Own: Storekeepers, Writers, and Professionals

Storekeepers

There is little doubt but what Joseph Graham was one of the earliest merchants of the town, setting up in the mercantile business after the town was laid out. Having a large territory to serve, he did a large business. When he died in 1826, his widow carried on the business. William Alexander is charged on Nov. 7, 1832, "to 6 1/8 yds jeans got at Graham's $4.60 ½." Mrs. Graham was in the mercantile business at this time.

Charles Davis was given an order on Geo. W. Kemper & Co. for $6.00, Aug. 3, 1833. Benjamin F. Kemper and George W. Kemper, brothers, were in the mercantile business for several years. The name of the company was variously written.

Other storekeepers in the town or neighborhood were James M. Stout, who later moved to New Hope, and a Mr. Martin.

Charles Davis is charged "To 6/9 paid to Mich Snider for hat $1.12 ½" on Jan. 22, 1835 and Wm. L. Smith is charged "to $2.00 Mr. Watkin's for hat" Nov. 6, 1841.

The names of storekeepers in the list below were gathered from the account books of Stephen Harnsberger. The year following each name is the date when it is first found in these books.

172

Jas. W. Eskridge	1831
Geo. W. Kemper & Co.	1831
Stout & Stiegle	1832
(Thomas) Holt	1832
D.M. Martin	1832
Quinn	1833
James M. Stout	1834
Michael Snyder	1834
Martin & Kemper	1836
Stout & Martin	1837
B. F. Kemper	1837
(Daniel) Whitmore	1838
(David) Watkins	1841
D. & W. Whitmore	1841
Robt. W. Palmer	1844
Palmer & Lewis	1845
Holt & Kemper	1845
J. W. Palmer	1845

Since the close of the Civil War, there have been as many as three stores in the town at the same time:

John Watson
Albert J. Sigler
George M. Nicholas
Dr. George W. Kemper, Jr.
John King
Samuel N. Harper
John W. Palmer, Sr.
Suddith E. Hershberger
Thomas S. Davis
Edward R. Armentrout
James T. Miller
James A. Maupin
John F. Miller

Robert E. Lee
Olin A. Palmer
Ellis J. Lee
Lee and Downs
Downs Brothers
Charles F. Saufley
Lyle L. Wagner
Leon W. Smith
Ophrey A. Wagner
Earle B. Wagner
Joseph W. Miller
Elias Grim
Mundy, Smith, & Mundy

Neighborhood writers

Port Republic has not been prolific of writers. There have been those and are now a few persons who, had they written while in a reminiscent mood, could have disclosed many important facts and interesting incidents; these would now be in print and not engulfed in oblivion's reticent demesne.

Dr. George W. Kemper contributed articles of merit to medical journals.

Joseph S. Strayer, under the pseudonym of "Wyndham", contributed many interesting articles to the *Rockingham Register*.

John C. Wheat was reporter for the *Spirit of the Valley*.

William L. Dinsmore reported for the *Spirit of the Valley*.

James H. Walker was correspondent of the *Daily News-Record*.

Elizabeth Gibbons reported for the newspaper published in Waynesboro, Virginia.

Mrs. Minor Wagner reports for the *Daily News-Record*.

Olin A. Palmer was a local novelist; the book, *At the Mercy of Fate* is his chief production, printed by himself at Port Republic on his own printing press.

Rev. Quincy A. Wheat wrote on astronomical and chronological subjects. His principal work is *Travel On An Old Road Out of Old Ruts*.

Mundy, Smith & Mundy Hardware Store, featuring Weber wagons, J.I. Case plow works, Studebaker buggies, lead, zinc & asbestos paint

Professionals

This section has produced a fair share of able mechanics and good businessmen. It is doubtful if any section of East Rockingham of equal area can match it in the number of residents who have entered the learned professions. The names of those whom memory recalls for the last thirty years are:

Lawyers
Albert W. Palmer
Morgan B. Stickley
Albert S. Kemper, Jr.
J. Harrison May

Preachers
Isaac S. Long
S. Azo E. Wagner
Arthur W. Miller
Carroll W. Palmer
Samuel J. Stickley
John W. Bowman
Isaac D. Bowman
W. Jennings Groah
Charles E. Long

School Teachers
Lucy V. Lamb
S. Elizabeth Harper
Maggie Rogers
Clara V. Rogers
Eva Patterson
H. Burgess Chandler
Edith R. Shifflette
Annie Groah
Janet J. Miller
Annie Z. Wagner
Valley Miller
Elbert H. Miller

Lena R. Mace
Nellie H. Lamb
Grace Harper
Lettie E. Rogers
Nellie Pearl
Ruth Wagner
Jennie Nicholas
Inez Good
Mattie J. Meyerhoeffer
Frances M. Miller
Eulalia Miller
Veda E. Miller
Selda A. Wagner
O.E. Long
Josephine L. Miller
Mrs. Will M. Dinsmore
Lottie V. Harper
McKinley Rodgers
Elsie Bateman
John L. Wagner
Bessie Nicholas
Frances Good
Kathleen Groah
Frances Wagner
Mareta Miller
Victor Miller
Verta C. Wagner
Virginia Nicholas
Joseph Scott

Doctors of Medicine
George W. Kemper, Sr.
George W. Kemper, Jr.
Albert S. Kemper,
Frank J. Miller,
William J. Wissler
Charles W. Scott
Frank Kyger
William J. Kyger
Thomas L. Lamb

Russell Armentrout is the one pharmacist the town has so far produced

In the writer's investigations, he has found the names of others who practiced medicine in the town: Dr. Michael Archdeacon, about 1770; 1807; Dr. William Douglass (he may have been a doctor of divinity) 1809; Dr. Franklin Walker, 1863; Dr. James A. Hardin, 1863; Dr. George Young, 1864; and Dr. William W. Cropt, 1864.

Those disciples of Hippocrates who have mitigated the suffering and prolonged the lives of the citizens of the town in more recent times include: Dr. Stuart M. Yancey, Dr. Charles P. Harshbarger, and Dr. George G. Tanner.

Chapter 24

Bridges of a River Town

The bridges that have spanned North River at Port Republic have an interesting history. To separate the facts from the fictions added by some careless writers in notices of some of those bridges is trying; but nothing in what follows is set down without a basis of facts.

The first bridge, so the writer has been informed, was built in 1854 by John Beckone. However, in John Dundore's daybook, under the date of June 19, 1852, the "Bridge" is charged, "To 20 Trees 50 feet Long; Ditto 13 Twenty six ft Long; Ditto 7 Twenty ft Long; Ditto 11 fifteen ft Long; Ditto 3 Trees 29 ft Long."

This indicates that work had begun on the bridge in the early summer of 1852, unless the timber was for another bridge. Stephen Harnsberger, Sr., received subscriptions to the bridge fund. What follows is self-explanatory. "Mr. Harnsberger will let Mr. Lee have 200 lbs Bacon and I will credit his Bridge Subscription or settle it otherwise as he may choose. Send a bill. July 6, '52—G.W. Kemper, Jr"

In one of Mr. Harnsberger's account books under date, July 6, 1852, is this entry: "To 204 lbs bacon at 12 ½ per John Lee to bridge, $25.50."

On the same page George W. Kemper, Jr., is given credit October 1854: "By subscription to bridge, $25.00."

A lottery was held in Rockingham County in 1831-1832 to raise funds for the building of a bridge between Port Republic and New Haven; but nothing came of it, for no bridge seems to have been built.

177

The bridge built by Beckone was burned by Stonewall Jackson's orders June 9, 1862. It was destroyed to prevent General Fremont from crossing to the east side of the Shenandoah River to the assistance of General Shields.

George W. Hulvey, of Rockingham County, said at different times, that he had charge of the squad that applied the torch to the bridge. Two wagons were loaded with dry hay taken from the nearby barn of Harrison Bateman and were drawn into the north end of the bridge. The hay was intended to give the fire a quick start. The wagons were not unloaded for time pressed, so they were burned with the bridge. The bridge was a wooden structure with sides supporting the roof. The inside boards had been split and splintered the day before to aid the spreading of the flames should any military plans in which the bridge figured fail. And this really happened. Early in the morning of the 9th, Jackson ordered Colonel Patton to hold Fremont in check until he had defeated Shields, when he would recross to the north side of the river and with the army reunited would overwhelm Fremont. Patton was not confident of being able to keep Fremont from advancing any length of time, so he asked Jackson when he should expect him to return. He replied, "By the blessing of Providence, I hope to be back by ten o'clock." But the Yankees fought well and Jackson was compelled to give up all thought of recrossing the river. He decided to concentrate his whole force and therefore, sent orders to Trimble and Taliaferro to leave Fremont's front and hasten to rejoin the main army, and to burn the bridge after they had crossed into Port Republic.

Captain B.W. Leigh, commanding the First Virginia Battalion, says in his report of the 15th: "At ten o'clock we crossed the bridge at Port Republic. At 10:15 the bridge was burned."

Much ado was made of the failure of Colonel Carroll to burn the bridge when he had the opportunity. General

Shields at Columbia Bridge reporting to Colonel Schriver June 12, 1862, says: "The officer (Colonel Carroll) neglected to burn the bridge at Port Republic. This report that the bridge was burned five days ago deceived me. He held it three-quarters of an hour and wanted the good sense to burn it."[1]

In a letter to General Fremont written on the 8th at the same place he says, "I pushed forward Colonel Carroll with our brigade and four pieces of artillery to move on Port Republic to burn the bridge and check the advance of the enemy."[2] Unfortunately for him, he wrote too many letters concerning the bridge incident and made too many reports of it to harmonize. He had written at Columbia Bridge on the 4th to Carroll and among other things ordered him, "You must go forward at once with cavalry and guns to save the bridge at Port Republic."[3] This was sensible, for whether Shields wished to go to the assistance of Fremont or desired him to come to his aid, owing to the swollen condition of the river, a bridge was necessary to cross it. In fact, Shields wrote Carroll on the 5th at Alma that he was trying to rebuild the Columbia Bridge. Had Carroll burned the bridge at Port Republic, Shields says Jackson's destruction would have been insured from the fact that he would have been placed between Fremont and himself with an impassable river in his front.

As it turned out Jackson burned the bridge and Fremont could not cross the river to help Shields; had Carroll burned it, Jackson would have turned on Fremont and completed what he had so well begun and Shields could not have gone to his aid.

The following report may throw some additional light on the subject:

Luray, Va., June 11, 1862
Captain Olmstead:
According to your orders I prepared to burn the bridge at Port Republic and stationed the pioneers awaiting orders. Colonel Carroll went across the bridge. On his return he gave no orders. Soon the rebel cavalry dashed upon the bridge, and I ordered the men to fire it. The rebels put out the fire. The pioneers guarded the rear by chopping down trees to obstruct the road.
Yours, truly,
D.R. Timmons, Lieutenant[4]

The second bridge was built by Captain John Harris. Captain Harris married Anne Palmer, daughter of Robert W. Palmer, and lived in the house on the east end on lot No. 20. This bridge was carried away by the flood of Sept. 28, 1870. Captain Harris was at Harpers Ferry at the time and recognized a span of the bridge going by.

John W. Woods, of Shenandoah County, built the third bridge in 1874. A Mr. Davis, father of Randolph Davis, a merchant in Port Republic at the time, had the contract for, or the superintendence of, the building of the stone piers. Mr. Davis employed John Morrison, a first class stone mason, to work on the piers. He boarded and lodged at Randolph Davis's, who occupied the old log house on the west end of lot No. 23. Erasmus D. Clarke, the tinner, lived diagonally across the street. One night Mr. Morrison sat too

North River Bridge

Flood, March 18, 1936, South River Bridge and Mill

long at the board of good cheer with congenial friends, and was unable to locate his lodgings. Finding himself in front of Mr. Clarke's house, he called for him. "I am bewildered in the dark," he explained. Mr. Clarke went across the street with him.

These piers could not withstand the flood of 1877 and, failing, precipitated the bridge into the river. The writer, a mere lad at the time, was present at the happening, and saw the several spans of the bridge go lengthwise down the river.

Several years later when the roadbed of the Shenandoah Valley Railroad Company was being built, the best of these stones were boated to the eastern shore of the river and hauled from there to Madison's run and used in the abutments of the railroad bridge spanning that run.

The father of the writer had charge of the colored men who boated the stones to the bank of the river. The writer distinctly remembers when one large stone was turned up on its edge, a large water moccasin snake, with eight or ten little ones four or five inches long, was uncovered. The snake immediately opened wide her mouth, the little ones ran in, and she then began to hiss venomously and strike with fury at anyone who came near. A large stone thrown by one of the colored men struck her in the middle and mashed her. Several of the little snakes crawled out of her at the wound.

A Canton, Ohio, company built the fourth bridge in 1885. It was a combination of wood and iron. A Mr. Borger was the superintendent. It was taken down in 1898 and one span put across Cub Run near where it flows into the Shenandoah River, and another over Mill Creek between Port Republic and the Dunkard Church. (Mill Creek Church of the Brethren) The other sections were dismantled.

The fifth and present bridge was built in 1898 by the Salem Bridge Co., Roanoke, and is an all iron structure. Unfortunately, it is a single-track bridge and will have to be replaced with a double-track one in the near future.

There has been but one wagon bridge across South River. It is the present one built of iron by the Pittsburgh Bridge Co. in 1889. R.A. Scott, H.B. Harnsberger, E.A. Herring, Commissioners represented the people and the county. This is located at the old mill ford. Up to the time of the building of this bridge, there had been a number of foot-bridges constructed at different times across this river. These ranged from a slab with a pair of spreading legs at each end and the benches thus made were placed end to end, to a wire cable suspension bridge.

Chapter Twenty-four Endnotes
[1]*Official Records*, series 1, vol. 12, part 1, 684.
[2]Ibid., 23.
[3]*Official Records*, series 3, 335.
[4]*Official Records*, series 1, vol. 51, part 1, 95.

Chapter 25

Tragedy at the Point

At the confluence of North and South Rivers, there is a ledge composed of stones, gravel, and sand running diagonally downstream across South River. The upstream is shallow but below the ledge, which has a sheer drop of ten or twelve feet, the water is deep and treacherous. It is here that fishermen and others unacquainted with the contour of the bottom of the river have met with fatal accidents.

One known to have drowned at The Point was Charles A. Kemper, son of Dr. George W. Kemper, Jr., who drowned June 29, 1853.

When the rear of Jackson's army was crossing the North River bridge on the morning of June 9, 1862, Lieut. Thomas Waller of the cavalry was left on the far side of the river to watch the enemy. Unfortunately the bridge was burned before he could cross and in attempting to swim the river, it being much swollen from recent rains, he was drowned.

A Federal soldier, a bugler, drowned on June 4, 1864, when Gen. David Hunter crossed his army on a pontoon bridge at The Point. Several of his comrades dived to the bottom of the river in an effort to find him but were not successful. Later when the body came to the surface, Alfred Phillips and St. Clair Poindexter, a colored man, buried it. One took the bugle and the other the pistol that were still on the body of the dead man.

A man named Slater, who lived on the mountain, was crossing South River with his daughter on an old white horse at the ford near the flour mill when misfortune overtook them. The water was swift and the horse weak. It stumbled and fell, throwing the man and woman into the river. The man was old and practically helpless. The daughter made a heroic effort to save him. Both were washed downstream to The Point and drowned.

William Eddins, a colored man about forty years ago, was seining near this dangerous ledge with some of the boys of the town. He got too close and accidentally stepped off of it. As he could not swim, he drowned before help could reach him.

James W. Rumple, Salisbury, N.C., was fishing at The Point on a bright afternoon in July 1893. In the later afternoon there was thunderstorm and when it passed he had disappeared. Careful inquiry failed to locate him. The following day the river was dragged and his body recovered. From the stooped position he was in, it was thought that he was struck by lightning.

Two colored men were drowned not long before the Civil War at the Mill Dam upstream a short distance from The Point; and two colored women met the same watery death about the same distance below it some years earlier.

Thomas Via was also to lose his life in the deceptive gurgling waters at the union of the two rivers. He went bathing in South River with several friends July 14, 1931, and it was noticed that he was in fine spirits and enjoying himself very much. Perhaps it was at the urging of the current that he unconsciously went downstream. His friends vociferously warned him of his danger. With a laugh and a reassuring wave of his hand, he went beyond the limit of safety and down to his death.

The Harper Family

William Harper came to America from Londonderry, North Ireland, about the time of the Whiskey Insurrection in Pennsylvania and settled in Lancaster County in that state. This disturbance occurred in 1794. He was arrested on suspicion of being a participant in the rebellion and taken before President Washington, who after hearing his explanation, ordered his release. This incident so disgusted him that he left Pennsylvania and came to the Shenandoah Valley.

He settled on South River just above the present town of Grottoes, and built a flour mill. While living here there was an unprecedented cloud-burst which washed away his mill. A number of persons were attending services at the Methodist Church at Port Republic at the time. The building stood on the bank of the South River. As sometimes happened when two or more of this sect met together, their emotions were aroused and the sudden rising of the river went unnoticed until it was too late to get to dry land except in a boat and on horseback.

John F. Wagner, a citizen of the town, says the above mentioned cloudburst occurred in 1796. He says he got this information from Mrs. John W. Lee who was a sister of the wife of one William Harper's sons.

Mr. Harper married a Miss Ralston. When they landed in this country she saw a Negro and watermelon for the first time. A man at the landing said he intended to give a watermelon to the prettiest woman on the boat. He gave it to her.

Order for flour from William Harper by John Rush, 1847

On Sept. 17, 1805, John Carthrea, Jr., and Sophia his wife, deeded to William Harper, in consideration of $150, a half acre lot in Carthrea's addition. The lot is not numbered in the deed but it was No. 47. On this lot Mr. Harper built a large log house facing on Water Street which is still the home of two of his grandchildren.

The first-born child of Mr. Harper, a daughter named Jane, died in early womanhood. He had five sons whose names, perhaps not in the order of their births, were William, Jr., Joseph, Addison, Samuel, Wilson and John.

Samuel was a farmer who moved to Lost River in Hardy County.

Addison, when a young man went to live with an uncle in Philadelphia. Becoming involved in a quarrel with his uncle, and fearing he had killed him, he fled. He joined the navy and served under Farragut. (It is said that Addison once whipped Zachariah Raines in a fist-fight, which would be a rencounter of the first order, but the writer has none of its details.)

Addison lived at Brock's Gap, was a captain in the Confederate army, and served several terms in the State legislature. In later years he became a Dunkard preacher.[1]

William Harper, Jr., became a man of considerable wealth. He acquired a large tract of land on the west side of the Shenandoah River, about a mile below the town. There he built a flour mill and a saw mill. An old ledger shows that Mr. Harper had a store account with Robert W. Palmer in 1845. The account is under the heading of "Harper's Mill." Earlier in life, William, Jr., had been a carpenter and while at work on the Yellow Tavern at the southwestern end of Main Street, he fell from a scaffold severely injuring his heel. The injury turned into white swelling and it was necessary to amputate his foot. Harper was repairing his dam on one occasion and using a flatboat to convey sand and gravel when, due to an overload it sank in deep water. As he had but one leg he could not help his men to safety, consequently two slaves drowned.

Joseph was a carpenter and farmer who lived near Tinkling Springs. He and his brother William, Jr. built the Yellow Tavern at the southwestern end of Main Street and built, or did the woodwork on, the John Dundore residence on lot No. 13.

John was born April 1, 1806. He belonged to the State Militia and was promoted to a captaincy. The General Assembly passed an Act, Jan. 26, 1866, incorporating Port Republic. At the first election held under this charter on the following March 31, he was elected Mayor.

He married Sarah Jane Trout Oct. 11, 1846. She was born April 30, 1826. There were eleven children born of this marriage:

William Joseph, born June 24, 1848, died in 1929. He was a school teacher and farmer.

Wilson Chesley, born March 24, 1850. While yet a young man he went to Kentucky, attended a business college in Covington and after graduating, engaged in the mercantile business for several years. Returning to his native town, he took charge of the home farm. He has always been much interested in politics and still remains one of his party's leaders in East Rockingham.

Samuel Nicholas, born Feb. 15, 1852. He married Hannah

Elizabeth Snapp, Oct. 12, 1882. She was born in Hampshire County, W.Va., April 1, 1863. Mr. Harper engaged in the store business for a number of years and later became a carpenter. He was the father of Lottie Virginia, born Aug. 22, 1883; John Robert, born June 1, 1885, died Dec. 29, 1920; Helen Victoria, born Oct. 25, 1889; Irma Grace, born Aug. 27, 1890; and Sarah Elizabeth, born Nov. 27, 1901. Mr. Harper died April 5, 1928.

Jennie Belle, born Nov. 27, 1853. She has always been in the forefront of every good and worthwhile movement of the neighborhood.

Mary, born July 16, 1856; died Dec 3. 1856.

Martha, born July 16, 1856; died July 19, 1858.

Charles Addison, born Oct. 20, 1858; died June 15, 1896. Never strong physically, he devoted most of his time to study. He was by odds the best informed man in general history in the vicinity. When the Shenandoah Valley Railroad began business, he learned telegraphy and became an operator in the employment of the railroad.

Annie Archia, born Feb. 22, 1861, married Charles Edward Snapp, Aug. 27, 1881. Mr. Snapp was an able architect. He removed with his family to Portsmouth, Va.

Elizabeth Rebecca, born April 5, 1864, and on Nov. 24, 1887, married William Stuart Nicholas, who was born Dec. 16, 1861. She died March 14, 1934 and Mr. Nicholas died Sept. 26, 1932.

Annie Olivia, born July 16, 1867, died Dec. 29, 1867.

John Harry, born April 5, 1870. While yet a boy, he entered the employment of C.B. Rouse of New York City, in the clothing department. Due to close attention to business and a good understanding of the needs of the department, he was promoted to the position of buyer. Becoming thoroughly proficient in the clothing business he entered it himself. John died Aug. 25, 1889 and his wife, July 5, 1905.

Wilson C. Harper, now in his eighty-sixth year, tells many interesting stories of local happenings in his childhood days. He says in the early part of the Civil War, a man by the name of Keyton lived in what is now known as the

Downs House. Derrick Bird, a valiant member of Chew's Battery, while he lived in this house married a daughter of Mr. Keyton. It was quite a social event and hither came the invited guests and some who were not invited. Of these latter a number had prepared themselves to shivery the couple. They thought it best to begin their noise making at the beginning of the marriage ceremony. In order to learn when this would begin they held up Mr. Harper, who was a youngster of the town at the time, to the transom over the hall door opening into the guest room, so he could see the couple when they came into the room to be married. "Here they come" cried the little rascal and immediately there was a burst of noise from blows on tin pans, the ringing of cowbells, and other noise making instruments that, combined, equaled the roar of a small size cannon. Miss Tillie Green, a beautiful young lady and an employee of the Port Republic Woolen Mills, was bridesmaid. She fainted when the ceremony and noise began simultaneously. The Rev. Mr. Hyde was the officiating minister. And thereby hangs a story.

There were two ministers on this circuit at that time, Mr. Hyde and Mr. Dammeron. As there was but one parsonage, the rule was that the married minister should have it, or in case both were married, the one first to arrive lived in it. It so happened that these two were unmarried. Mr. Hyde was paying his attention to Miss Tanquary whose brother was the superintendent of the woolen mills and living in what is now the Saufley House. Mr. Dammeron devoted his spare time to Kittie Allen. The one who married first was entitled to live in the parsonage. Perhaps Mr. Hyde poured a libation to the son of Venus. Anyhow, he won the race.

Chapter Twenty-six Endnotes

[1]Benjamin Funk, *The Life and Labors of Elder John Kline,* (Elgin, Ill.: Brethren Publishing House, 1900), 419-420.

Chapter 27

The Kemper Family

Too few of the prominent families of the country have published adequate genealogies. This is unfortunate, for whether evolution is true or not, the curious public want to know something of the pedigrees of eminent persons.

The ancestor of the Kemper family in Virginia was John Kemper who was born at Musen, Germany, July 8, 1692. Twelve families, members of the German Reformed Church, in the mining district about the city of Siegen, decided to accept the suggestion of Baron Christopher de Graffenried, that they go to America to mine iron ore and build and operate a furnace for Alexander Spotswood, Governor of Virginia.

De Graffenried had purchased a large tract of land from the Lords Proprietors of North Carolina and sent over a number of Swiss to take possession of it. They arrived in 1710 and built a town, naming it Newberne. The following year, de Graffenried himself being present, the town was attacked by Tuscarora Indians and those of the colonists who were not massacred were dispersed. Going to Virginia after escaping from the Indians, de Graffenried was requested by Governor Spotswood to examine the soil of certain parts of Virginia, having in view the locating of mines and the building of furnaces should iron ore be found in sufficient quantities. The results of the investigation proving favorable, Spotswood indicated that de Graffenried had relatives in Switzerland who were interested in mines "and by their interest he can procure skillful workmen out of Germany for carrying on the work." The twelve families, whose heads were first-class workmen and mechanics, arrived in Virginia in 1714, and were taken to Horseshoe Bend in what is now the Rapidan River in present Orange County, and there they built a palisade town and fort. The fort was furnished with two cannon and some ammunition. The town was named Germanna after the homeland. The colonists did not proceed immediately to mine and smelt, for the Governor was trying to drive a hard bargain with the authorities in England in order to make more profits out of the enterprise for himself and associates. In 1717 and 1719 more colonists came and were added to the community, and possibly some of the survivors of the unfortunate Newberne settlement came also.

The first iron furnace was built at Germanna, which produced the first pig iron made in America. It was from here that the famous expedition of the "Knights of the Golden Horseshoe" started for the top of the Blue Ridge Mountain in 1716.

For some reason not expressly given in the history of the settlement, the colonists became dissatisfied and decided to abandon Germanna. The original families went north about twenty miles in 1720 and settled on Licking Run on land purchased from the Fairfax estate in what was then Stafford County. With them went Rev. Henry Hager, the first German Reformed pastor in America. He had faithfully served the two sects, Lutheran and German Reformed, at Germanna. The Lutherans, who were the larger body, went west and settled on Robinson's River in what is now Madison County. They built a church that is now standing. The organ, communion service and Bible, given to them by European friends, are still in existence.

The settlement of the original colonists was on a large tract of land known as "Germantown," and lay eight miles south of Warrenton in what is now Fauquier County. Here

Part of a page from Dr. George W. Kemper's Daybook, 1835, shows the account of Stephen Harnsberger. Note that a tooth extraction is $1.50.

at Germantown was built the first German Reformed Church in America.

John Kemper, the first of the name in Virginia, married Ailsey Utterbach at Germanna about 1716. He owned at least eighty acres of the Germantown patent. He was a man of intelligence and good education. He invented the shovel plow and it is no wonder that his farm and the farms of his neighbors were very productive. Some of his descendants have climbed high peaks in the civil and military service of their country and have been rewarded with enduring fame. Those who have remained in the most retired walks of life have been respected and honored in their several communities.

Charles Kemper, whose home was named Cedar Grove, was born June 27, 1756 and died Dec. 1, 1841. He married Susannah Mauzy Nov. 30, 1786. Their eldest child, George Whitfield, was born in Fauquier County Sept. 29, 1787, and died at Port Republic Sept. 16, 1872. He studied medicine and devoted the remainder of his life to its practice, as did a son and grandson in years to come. He came to Port Republic 1807-1808 and, in 1837, bought the Madison Hall property, the old home of Bishop James Madison, and of Charles Carthrea. However, he did not move to this property until some years later. He married Mathilda Graham, daughter of Joseph Graham, April 13, 1812 and became the father of four sons and three daughters. After the lapse of over a half-century, one can still hear mention made of his humanity and the good care he took of his poor patients. He was a power for good in the neighborhood. He was a Justice of the Peace for a number of years and Sheriff of the county from 1851-1852.

George Whitfield, Jr., was born Dec. 16, 1814 and died Aug. 19, 1902. He was the second son and child. He graduated in medicine from Jefferson College, Philadelphia, Pa., and spent his life in the practice of his profession in Port

Republic and vicinity. With all his arduous labors he found time to contribute articles to medical journals. He was a good scholar and deep thinker. Of a magnetic personality, his very presence at the bedside was a help to his patients.

He married (1) Angelina Brown and had seven children, five sons and two daughters. The oldest child, William Meade, was born May 30, 1839 and gave his life to the "Lost Cause" at Chancellorsville May 3, 1863. George Bezaleel was born March 7, 1843 and poured out his life's blood in defense of his native State May 6, 1864, at the Battle of the Wilderness. The elder daughter, Mary Frances, married Gen. William H. Young and resided in San Antonio, Texas. Dr. Hugh Hampton Young, the famous surgeon of Baltimore, is their only child.

He married (2) Margaret Strayer. There were five children of this union of whom Albert Strayer was the fourth. He was born Jan. 29, 1866. Later, he studied medicine at the Medical College of Virginia and graduated from the University College of Medicine, Richmond. He studied under the noted Dr. Hunter McGuire and after graduating, returned home and took over his father's practice. True to the precedents of his forebears, he has always made the alleviation of pain and the curing of disease his main object, and not the amassing of a fortune out of the proceeds of his practice. He married Elizabeth Blackburn Dec. 16, 1897 and has seven children. Albert Strayer, Jr., was born March 20, 1901. He studied law at the University of Virginia. He married Elizabeth Haas, daughter of Judge T.N. Haas of Harrisonburg, and located at Bluefield, West Va., where he has a large and profitable clientele.

The Harnsberger Family

John Harnsberger, the ancestor of the Harnsberger family in Virginia, was one of Governor Spotswood's colonists at Germanna who followed the original colony of 1714 either in 1717 or 1719. These Germans were divided into two religious sects, the German Reformed and the Lutheran. Mr. Harnsberger was identified with the latter and when all the colonists abandoned Germanna in 1725, he went to the present county of Madison with the Lutherans where they established a flourishing settlement.

According to tradition, a certain Stephen Harnsberger crossed the mountains into the Valley and settled in the present Elkton neighborhood not long after the middle of the century. He was the first of the name to come to the Valley.

Of the Port Republic branch of the family, a Harnsberger descendant also named Stephen, bought a fine farm just across South River from the town Feb. 22, 1814. He married Elizabeth Baker, daughter of Michael Baker, of the Brocks Gap neighborhood May 13, 1812.

Stephen was the father of six sons and four daughters. He was a Justice of the Peace for a number of years and also a surveyor. He was what was then called High Sheriff from 1845-1846. In those days the senior magistrate of the county was appointed to the office of Sheriff.[1]

He was an ardent Methodist and one of the main pillars of that church at Port Republic during his lifetime. He was clerk of the Board of Stewards and some of the books containing their proceedings have survived a hundred or more years and were given to the Methodist Church of the town in 1928 by his grandson, John I. Harnsberger.

Stephen Harnsberger was born Jan. 3, 1787 and died May 26, 1870. His wife died Sept. 28, 1849, in the 62nd year of her age.

Joseph Mustoe Chambers Harnsberger, son of the above, was a member of Co. I, 33rd Va. Volunteer Infantry of the Stonewall Brigade, and was in the battle of Kernstown March 23, 1862, in which battle he was severely wounded in the face and neck. He was a gallant soldier and carried honorable scars from the wounds received in this battle to the end of his life. He was born Dec. 30, 1818 and died April 10, 1901.

Another son, William Michael Harnsberger, born May 23, 1835, belonged to a troop of cavalry from East Rockingham with the distinctive name of "The River Rangers." Many of our bravest and most patriotic citizens were members of this troop. William was a first-class swordsman and had often declared that under no circumstances would he surrender. He was put to the test Sept. 23, 1862, when, near Paris in his native State, his troop was retiring rapidly before a superior force of the enemy, he rode too close to a pond and his horse mired. In a moment the enemy was upon him. Armed with his favorite weapon, he was a formidable foe and six Yankees did he kill before they drew off and shot him. He was born May 23, 1835.

Henry Baker Harnsberger, another of Stephen's sons, was born Nov. 26, 1816. He was educated at Dickinson College, Carlisle, Pa. He married Elizabeth Hopkins and acquiring his father's estate, he made it his permanent home.

Henry was county surveyor in 1849 and from 1853-1863. He liked the work and was proud of his office and took all honorable means of succeeding himself as the following, taken from the *Rockingham Register*, May 14, 1858, will show: "We are authorized to announce Henry B. Harnsberger as a candidate for re-election as Surveyor of Rockingham County."

He was a Deputy Sheriff under his father 1845-1846 and

ROCKINGHAM COUNTY, TO WIT:

To   Constable of Rockingham County:—
You are hereby commanded to summon *Henry Hudlow*

to appear before me or some other **Justice of the Peace** for the County aforesaid, on the third Saturday of this Month, at Port-Republic, to answer the complaint of *John W. Palmer*

in a plea of debt not exceeding **$30** due by *Note* And then and there make return how you have executed this Warrant. Given under my hand this *15* day of *September* 185*1*

Summons witness for either
party if required. }   *Stephen Harnsberger*

Judgment for *$11* - Dollars and *62.* Cents, with interest from the *28th* day of *May* 185*1* till paid, and *30* cents cost. Given under my hand this *20th* day of *September* 185*1*.

                                          Stephen Harnsberger

Stephen Harnsberger, Justice of the Peace, summoned Henry Hudlow to answer a complaint by John W. Palmer, 1851

a member of the House of Delegates 1866-1872 and again from 1880-1883. For a while he was the Captain of a company in the Civil War. During the last year of the war he was assessor of foodstuffs for the Confederate Government. As it is not well known that the Confederacy had a tax-in-kind and fought the last year of the war on an almost empty stomach, the principal part of one of these assessments sheets, already filled out by the assessor, is here given:

Tax-in-Kind.
Estimate And Assessment Of Bacon, agreed upon by the Assessor and Tax Payer, and the value of the portion thereof to which the Government is entitled, in accordance with the provisions of an Act of Congress, "to lay taxes for the common defense, and carry on the Government of the Confederate States," and of the Act to amend the same, approved 17th Feb-

ruary 1864. This estimate to be made after, and as of March 1st of each year.

Name of Producer	Quantity of Pork	One Tenth	Quantity of Bacon due 60 lbs for each 100lbs of Pork	Value
Geo. Armentrout	885	88 ½	53 ½	371

I, Geo. Armentrout, of the County of Rockingham and State of Va. do swear that the above is a true statement and estimate of all the pork produced by hogs slaughtered by me, within the year ending the 1st March 1865 to the best of my knowledge and belief.

George Armentrout, Tax Payer.

Sworn to and subscribed before me, on the 23d day of March, 1865, and I further certify that the above estimate and assessment has been agreed upon by said Geo. Armentrout and myself, as a correct and true statement of the amount of Pork produced by him, and of the amount and value of the Bacon to which the Government is entitled.

H.B. Harnsberger, Assessor.

On the back of this interesting paper is printed,

Special Exemption.
No farmer, planter, or grazier, or other person, who shall not slaughter more than two hundred and fifty pounds of Net Pork during any year, shall be subject to the Bacon Tithe.

Henry Baker Harnsberger died Sept. 4, 1904. His wife was born in 1821 and died Jan. 22, 1899. Capt. Henry B. Harnsberger had one son and five daughters. John I. Harnsberger, the son, came in possession of the paternal estate and made it his home. He was born June 3, 1859, educated at Bridgewater College, and made Civil Engineering his profession. He was actively engaged in laying out the town of Shendun, now Grottoes, and later entered the employ of the Gauley Coal & Land Association. He married (1) Adelaide Kemper Dec. 5, 1895. She was born March 3, 1862 and died June 11, 1902. There were two children, a son and daughter. George Kemper Harnsberger, the son, attended the Virginia Polytechnic Institute. Later he became a surveyor. For four generations there have been surveyors in the family. Mr. Harnsberger married (2) Matilda Graham Kemper.

There is a tradition that the elder Stephen Harnsberger was a member of the Spotswood expedition of 1716 and gave his golden horseshoe to a younger Stephen Harnsberger who went to Georgia many years later. It is also said that when Joseph M.C. Harnsberger visited this kinsman in Georgia, he saw this horseshoe. But according to John I. Harnsberger, there was none of the name in the colony of Virginia in 1716, and Joseph M.C. Harnsberger was never in Georgia. (Per John I. Harnsberger)

Chapter Twenty-eight Endnotes

[1]To learn of Stephen Harnsberger's work as president of the new Shenandoah Company, see Chapter 7, Boating.

Chapter 29

John Dundore, a Picturesque Man

John Dundore was the most picturesque man that ever lived in Port Republic. According to the only source of information available to the writer, he came here as a young man from East Virginia. There were Dundores in the county in the last half of the eighteenth century.

Mr. Dundore bought of John Carthrea, Jr., a small tract of land "by estimation" thought to contain two and one half acres, April 2, 1816. This piece of land lies between Water Street and South River, beginning at the lower end of the milldam, which runs diagonally across the river, where the water enters the millrace, and extends downstream to, and probably included, the lot he later sold to Frederick and Samuel Golliday. This millrace is about a quarter of a mile in length and at that time furnished the motive power for several plants.

The deed for this piece of land granted Mr. Dundore the right "to take a sufficiency of water by pump and other fix to get by the force of water out of the dam to grind his Tan Bark that he may require for his yard erected or to be erected on this Ground." As the race runs through the middle of this piece of land and the plants at the lower end of the race might at any time need more water for their successful operation, a reservation is made that "John Carthrea, Jr., his heirs or assigns has the right whenever they or either of them may think it proper to widen the race as wide as twenty feet at the bottom and twenty-five feet at the top.

The increase of the width to be on the northwest side."

It appears from the deed that all buildings, sheds, vats, etc., were in the process of building or yet to be constructed. Just when hides were first taken in to be tanned there is nothing at hand to show, but his tannery became one of the leading enterprises of East Rockingham. He had an addition built to his fine old house just across Water Street from his tannery, which he used as an office.

Mr. Dundore acquired a considerable amount of real estate. In an "Table of Tracts of Land for the year 1863," by the commissioner of the revenue, the Dundore estate is credited with having 206 acres of land on the Shenandoah River, and two tracts of land in the Blue Ridge, one containing 90 acres and the other 70 acres. Also he had four lots in Port Republic. Before the above date, he had sold his tannery and many acres of land.

At different times, Mr. Dundore had associated with him in business Alexander R. Givens, Maj. James Eddins, who had married his daughter Mornen Delinger, and Jacob S. Piper, whose widowed sister, Mrs. Funkhouser, became Dundore's third and last wife.

On Aug. 16, 185-, Mr. Dundore deeded the tannery to Jacob S. Piper of Shenandoah County, on the payment of the cash purchase price of $3000. It was not long after this that financial troubles began to lower upon his house and to fret and worry him to the bitter end of his life.

A man who paid overmuch attention to the rich, Mr. Dundore had not even a kind word for the poor. Purse-proud, haughty, and arrogant, John Dundore strutted the streets of Port Republic and expected servile attention and respect from those he considered his inferiors. It is said that he aped the manners of the English aristocracy. But not so. He may have patterned after them in the style of his clothes—he wore a fine frock coat, expensive waistcoat, knee breeches with appropriate buckles, silk hose, and anything else that would add to his spectacular appearance—but he was infinitely below them in polite accomplishments. There is no doubt that there have been and are snobs among the English aristocracy, but the English speaking people cannot afford to forget the great men this class has produced.

Mr. Dundore bought a handsome coach, the first owned by a resident of the town, which he used when visiting "birds of his feather" and on other important occasions. About this time, Capt. John Harper returned from one of his periodic trips to Kentucky, with a pair of fine matched black horses. An admirer and a good judge of horses, Mr. Dundore bought them for his carriage. He trained one of his slaves as a coachman and dressed him in a showy uniform and high hat. Handsomely dressed, powdered, and with a queue hanging down his back, Mr. Dundore was a striking figure sitting grandly in his fine carriage as it rattled showily through the town.

Mr. Dundore married three times. From the best information at hand he married (1) Jane Martin May 6, 1806, (2) Mrs. Catherine Graham Sept. 26 1838, and (3) Mrs. Eliza Funkhouser. It is known that he had two children, both daughters. Harriet married John Matthews, and Mornen

Dundore/Downs house; shows footbridge across the mill race

Delinger, as mentioned before, married Maj. James Eddins. One daughter of this union married Jacob S. Piper, and another married John W. Palmer.

Mr. Dundore's second wife was the widow of Joseph Graham. She was the mother of Matilda Graham, wife of Dr. George W. Kemper, Sr. Becoming sick and realizing that she was nearing dissolution, Mrs. Dundore called her husband and Dr. George W. Kemper, her son-in-law if senior, or grandson if junior, to her bedside on March 16, 1850, and told them her will. She died the next day.

Mr. Dundore had a suitable gravestone made to mark her last resting place, but his stepdaughter, Mrs. Kemper, would not allow him to have it placed at her mother's grave, so bitterly did she despise and hate him. Fourscore and six years this gravestone remained unused at Madison Hall. The following is an exact copy of the inscription on it:

In memory of Catharine
Wife of John Dundore,
Born in 1778
Died March 17, 1850
In the silent tomb she rests,
Death in Jesus which is Blessed.

Mr. Dundore had a fine brick residence built on one of his lots, No. 13, with a double front porch, the roof of the building extending out to cover the upper porch. The builders were two brothers, William and Joseph Harper. Cabins were built in the backyard for his colored people and a large log house on an adjoining lot for his overseer.

Mr. Dundore owned a number of slaves. On Nov. 10, 1856, he bought a woman named Mary and two boys of John Miller, with the understanding that if they did not suit his wife they could be returned; but if they did prove satisfactory he would pay the price agreed on which was $1,100.

In an account book of the tannery under date of Aug. 28, 1854, he is charged $4.00 for digging four graves. Wilson C. Harper says the fever raged in the town that year and these graves were for his colored folks who died of the fever, most likely.

The following account of the return to his former home of a colored man whom he had sold is found under date Oct. 2, 1855:

St. Cinclare came home here on Tuesday the 15th of September sick & I told him to gone back to Harrisonburg to his Master to be nursed as we had sick Negroes of our own to Nurse but he remained here ever since until the 16th of October at which Time John took him to Harrisonburg.

The "John" mentioned as taking the poor homesick fellow back to Harrisonburg was, probably, John M. Eddins, grandson of Dundore.

These items are of human interest of times now happily past.

Mr. Dundore was alive to the beauties and sounds of his animate surroundings. In the middle of a page in his daybook he wrote, "I heard a dove sing on the 1st of March (1855). Spring comes." The following year he wrote, "I heard the Crooksee Hollow on Sunday evening the 20th of July & from which time we will have frost in 9 weeks so says John Fisher." Whether the "crooksee" was a katydid or not is left to the reader to determine.

At that time children, especially boys, were not dressed so nicely as they are now. Amos Scott was charged Sept. 11, 1851, to three sheepskins for aprons for his boys.

Mr. Dundore had a threshing machine in 1850. It was driven by horsepower. Whether he threshed the wheat of nearby farmers does not appear from his daybook.

But the days of his prosperity passed. A supposedly rich man who was in the iron business in the neighborhood borrowed much money of Dundore which, in the end, was the cause of his breaking up. After all the facts were put before him showing that there was no chance of him ever recovering his money he still could scarcely believe that his friend would fail him in a matter so vital. He made dire threats against his own life, but finally found comfort in the cup.

It was thought by some that Mr. Dundore kept large amounts of money in his office. William J. Downs now owns the property and his family have converted the office into a dining room. They say that an attempt was made to rob the office but the stout oak door resisted all efforts to smash it in. When Dundore learned who was engaged in this nefarious plot, he became so despondent that taking up his pistol he fired at his own head. Fortunately the bullet missed the intended mark and penetrated the wainscoting instead. The hole it made may yet be seen

Ever deeper and wider became the financial difficulties that had engulfed Mr. Dundore. He was old and tottering to his grave. Neglected and in sorrow, he lay down, closed his eyes and passed away. Major William S. Downs provided the clothes in which he was buried.

Fate dealt hardly with this man before and after death. He was buried in Riverside Graveyard and a suitable stone with an appropriate inscription on it was placed at his grave. Just below the graveyard is the milldam that backs the water upstream for quite a distance. The mill pond and the grassy bank between it and the graveyard make an ideal bathing place. Here the youth of the neighborhood gather to disport themselves in the crystal blue water. Someone, forgetful of the respect due to the dead, tore the stone from its setting and carried it to the water's edge to stand on. It was soon broken and the pieces became scattered along the shore. Even the pieces are now lost in the mud and water. Without some restoration, the location of the grave itself will soon be forgotten and the last resting place of this proud and vain-glorious man will have disappeared.

Chapter 30

The May Family

At what time Adam May came from Pennsylvania
to East Rockingham, the remains of the mutilated
and dispersed records of the family do not disclose.
Adam May was a farmer. Among other tracts of land
owned by him was one of eighty acres lying "on the South
side of Mattison's Gap." He bought this parcel of land from
Jacob Lemmons and Elizabeth, his wife, Sept. 16, 1797. This
piece of land adjoined the lands of Sarah Lewis, Henry Mace
and Mathias Almond. On Jan. 20, 1801, he and his wife,
Elizabeth, deeded this property to George Compton.[1]

Formerly the county was divided into military districts
and Adam May, in 1792, belonged to Company No. 4, commanded by Capt. George Huston. Ralph Lofftus, Commissioner, took the tithables of this company in 1792 and Mr.
May had five horses, but no sons sixteen years old nor any
slaves twelve years old, (sons and slaves who had reached
these ages respectively were tithables) for neither sons nor
slaves were listed. As John Carthrea had nine horses and
890 acres of land, Abraham Fisher three horses and 514 acres
of land and George Huston four horses and 703 acres of
land, if the same proportion held with Mr. May he must
have possessed a goodly number of acres of land.

Adam May was the father of fourteen children. The
sons, whose names are at hand, were Daniel, Samuel J.,
Jacob, Adam, Jr., Albert F. and John. The names of but three
daughters are remembered: Gertrude, Sally, and Christina.
Little is known about most of these children.

Adam's son Daniel May was a boat builder and a farmer. He became fairly wealthy. Samuel J. May was a boatman at times. He moved to the Winchester area.

A highly creditable story is told of Jacob May's humanity and patriotism. When the Confederate States arose on the ruins of the National Government in the South, his son joined the Confederate Army. After the battle of Port Republic, Jacob met him on the lower end of the battlefield, and noticing that his son was shoeless, took off his own shoes and gave them to his son with his blessing.

In Joseph Trout's daybook is found this entry on July 24, 1819, "Mr. May, to balance on saddle, $7.00," and this one April 29, 1820, "Adam May, to halter, $1.75." An undated charge of $6.60 for beef is made to Adam May, Jr. in one of Stephen Harnsberger's account books. Probably the Adam May whose name is found in Joseph Trout's daybook was the father of Adam May, Jr., whose name appears in Stephen Harnsberger's account book.

There are reasons for believing that Adam May, Jr., in his early manhood, owned a team of horses and hauled produce of the farms, and the manufactured products of the shops and factories of the town to the markets. But the business with which his name is inseparably connected is boat-building. He seems to have been the outstanding boat-builder of the neighborhood. His charges varied with the times and conditions of the boating business, usually from $6.00 to $8.00 a boat. Stephen Harnsberger paid Jefferson Randall $14.00 for building two boats in 1839. William S. Downs paid Mr. May $6.00 for building one boat in 1859. In his old age, he was toll collector at the North River Bridge. He also made wagons and other useful articles for children as well as household furniture.

Adam May, Jr., and Nancy Raines were married June 28, 1821. Her father Lawrence Raines was one of the first settlers in East Rockingham. She had large intellectual powers, was the happy possessor of a spotless character, and was a good wife and kind mother. She was famed for her womanly virtues; she endured with patience and fortitude the troubles and worries incident to life and with an all too short a life with sweet resignation sat smiling at the approach of death.

Adam May was born May 1, 1798 and died June 14, 1874. Nancy May was born Nov. 25, 1800 and died Apr. 29, 1845. Their children were:

	born	died
Martha Ann	April 2, 1822	May 4, 1863
George Wesley	Aug. 8, 1824	June 6, 1881
Mary Elizabeth	Dec. 14, 1826	July 29, 1830
Daniel Eskridge	Feb. 24, 1829	
Benjamin Ahaz	Sept. 2, 1831	
Isabella Frances	Mar. 29, 1834	
Eliza Jane	Jan. 22, 1837	May 9, 1895
Adeline Cathrine	June 30, 1839	Aug. 25, 1917
James Henry	Mar. 16, 1843	Feb. 16, 1918

Their daughter, Martha Ann May married Harrison Bateman, a farmer and boatman, Jan. 5, 1845. She was the mother of five children.

Adam May Jr.'s son, George Wesley, did some boating on the river in his young days, and later spent several years in hauling goods to market. He had a fine four-horse team, a good wagon, and his preferred market was Winchester. Still later, he engaged in the sawmill and flour mill businesses and used his team to haul his own products to market. He owned forty acres of land across the Brown's Gap Pike in front of the home of Michael A. Scott, Jr., and built thereon a dwelling house and necessary outbuildings. He also owned lots No. 15 and 16 in Port Republic with a dwelling house on lot No. 16.

George Wesley was a man of wide vision and noble character. Honest, industrious, tolerant, and wise, he viewed the future with serenity. Of an amiable disposition, he was very companionable. Many of his quaint sayings are remembered to this day. "Noblest Roman of them all," he died honored and respected by the neighborhood.

Stories are yet told of his quaint humor and goodness of heart. In a ledger of the Dundore tannery, then under the control of Wm. S. Downs, Mr. May is charged Oct. 21, 1856, "To hauling tombstone from Harrisonburg, $1.00." So prosaic is the business side of our most tender acts! The stone, still in a fine state of preservation, marks the last resting place of his first wife in Central Graveyard.

George Wesley May married (1) Sarah Buster, daughter of David and Nancy Buster, July 13, 1848. She was born Oct. 20, 1827 and died March 27, 1856.

Their children were:

James Edward Fisher, born July 13, 1849 died Dec. 1, 1876
Nancy Ellen Shelton, born March 6, 1851

George Wesley next married Eliza Ann Teter May 8, 1857. She was born Feb. 12, 1841 and died Jan 16, 1923.

Among the worthy early settlers in the southeastern corner of Rockingham County, none were more prominent than the Teters, Lutzes and Hoffners. John B. Lutz, with his wife, Elizabeth, and daughter, Susanna, moved from Cumberland County, Pennsylvania to Virginia in 1812. Susanna was born May 5, 1801. In 1818 she was united in marriage to Jacob Haffner. Their eldest daughter, Elizabeth E. Haffner, born Jan. 28, 1822, and John Teter were married Feb. 6, 1840. Eliza Ann Teter was their first child.

George Wesley and Eliza Ann May had seven children:

	born	died
Mary Elizabeth	Sept. 4, 1860 J	Jan. 3, 1918
Alice Gertrude	Jan. 26, 1864	
Martha Ann	Sept. 12, 1864	
Rosa Lee	Aug. 17, 1866	May 20, 1920
John Wesley	Jan. 5, 1868	Jan. 21, 1923
William Scott	Nov. 3, 1870	July 16, 1933
Maud Beatrice	July 19, 1873	

Their son, John Wesley May was a farmer. He married Virginia Hayes Kyger. Of fine business capacity, he was uniformly successful in his business undertakings. He studied vocal music, had a fine tenor voice, and was much in demand where good singing was desired. He was a Justice of the Peace in Stonewall District in 1912.

Another son of George Wesley and Eliza, William Scott May, was an architect of ability. He was often employed to oversee the construction of fine buildings. The one monument to his ability in this neighborhood is the Dunkard Church at Mill Creek which was built in 1920. He kept abreast of current events and was a close student of secular and church history. His mind was well stored with knowledge and he was an entertaining talker. With an attractive personality and good manner, he was welcome at social affairs and other gatherings. He married Beatrice Hyde. There was one child, a daughter, Frances. For a number of years he lived at Coots Store, in the neighborhood. It was there that he died. He was buried in the Mill Creek Cemetery.

Daniel Eskridge, son of Adam, Jr. and Nancy Raines May married Sarah Ann Marica Aug. 10, 1852. At the time of his birth, there was a merchant in the town by the name of James W. Eskridge. Perhaps his middle name was taken from the merchant's surname. While yet a young man, he moved to the State of Illinois and became a Methodist preacher. Two of his sons studied medicine and devoted themselves to its practice.

Another of their sons, Benjamin Ahaz May, enlisted in the Confederate Army, was engaged in the first battle of Manassas and never after heard from by his father's family.

Their daughter, Isabella Frances May, was married to LaFayette Lee. He lived on his farm on the Keezletown Road near Peale's Cross Roads and owned and operated a sawmill. Adaline Catharine May never married. She made her native town her lifelong home.

Eliza Jane May, another of their daughters, married Dr. C.B.F. Jankans; they made their home at Fincastle in Botetourt County. Their children were:

	born	died
Martha A.C.	Oct. 10, 1857	Jan. 10, 1861
Lillian Gertrude	Mar. 30, 1859	Jan. 2, 1861
Charles Burhman	Dec. 19, 1860	
Rosa May	Dec. 15, 1863	
Edith Patton	Mar. 4, 1866	July 30, 1885
Wilbur Gray	Dec. 5, 1867	
Bessie Gaunt	May 6, 1870	

The Jankans's sons studied dentistry and Dr. Wilbur Gray Jankans moved to Fort Dodge, Iowa, where he built up a wide practice.

James Henry May, like his father, Adam, Jr. and brother, George Wesley, also engaged in boat-building and continued at it intermittently until the final breakdown of the boating business not long after the Civil War. He built the last boat that went down the river from Port Republic. In 1878, Major Hutton and an assistant, two engineers in the Service of the United States Government, made a trip of observation down the river in this same boat in order to decide on the feasibility of building locks and dams in the river to make it fit for navigation by small steamboats. The boat had a comfortable cabin in its middle with a passageway on each side. A skiff for going ashore and other purposes attended the boat. John W. Lee, hotel-keeper and post-master in the town, hired the crew for Major Hutton. The crew were, Newton L. Wagner, William H. Harnsberger, Albert Shifflette, Abner Brown, and Clarence L. May. Brown was the cook and Clarence, a mere lad, had charge of the skiff. The first stop was at Milnes where one of the Aleshire brothers was employed as pilot. The stops in succession were Newport, Honey Run, Shannondale Springs, and Charlestown. The boat was abandoned at the last stop and the remainder of the trip was made on foot. The crew were each paid $1.00 a day and expenses for the round trip. There were no results from this investigation except to hasten the completion of the Shenandoah Valley Railroad from Roanoke to Hagerstown.

Before the collapse of boating on the Shenandoah River, James Henry had interested himself in carpentry and later he became a contractor and builder on a large scale. He was a furniture and coffin maker also. Many of the latter, made of hardwood, were very fine. In this connection, the following charge to the account of Mr. May is found in one of William S. Downs' ledgers under date of June 16, 1869. "To 20 ft. Walnut Plank for Daddy Lees coffin, 60 cts." "Daddy Lee" was the father of John W. Lee.

James Henry May married Regina Pforr (see Chapter 31) of Staunton. She was born in Baltimore Jan. 29, 1846, and died in Staunton July 18, 1911. There were ten children:

	born	died
Clarence Lee	Aug. 25, 1865	Dec. 23, 1897
Irene Elizabeth	Oct. 28, 1867	
George Elliott	Dec. 26, 1869	
Mattie Wilsonia	Apr. 16, 1872	
Oswald Herman	Sept. 25, 1874	
Ernest Lynwood	Jan. 17, 1877	
Pauline Regina	June 18, 1879	July 18, 1935
French Augustus	Mary 11, 1882	Sept. 12, 1931

Wilbur Gray   June 6, 1884
James Harrison   Aug. 22, 1889

Of these, Clarence Lee May married Alma Cox of Hanover County, May 12, 1891. Irene Elizabeth May and James Robert Gregory of Staunton, were married April 30, 1890. George Elliott May married Beatrice Glenna Worley of Lynchburg, Sept. 27, 1900. Mattie Wilsonia May and Ryland Jeter Hall, of Westmoreland County, were married April 11, 1903. Oswald Herman May married Willie Reed in 1895. Pauline Regina May and Thomas Claybrook Elder of Staunton, were married June 1, 1901. French Augustus May married (1) Mrs. Kate Flemming of Washington. D.C. in 1912; (2) Mary Bell Hyde of Augusta County, Sept. 13, 1927. James Harrison May married Mattie Belle Jones of Louisville, Ky., June 1911.

Gray May in his shiny roadster

Chapter Thirty Endnotes
[1]Deed Book 00:442.

Chapter 31

The Pforr Family

R egina Pforr, who wed John Henry May, was the oldest daughter of George Pforr and his wife Ann Eliza
(Coleman) Pforr. George Pforr was a native of
Hesse-Cassel, a former landgraviate and electorate of Germany, but now mostly in Hesse-Nassan. His father Henry
Pforr, was a lawyer and mayor of the town, Sundra. He was
born Oct. 24, 1780 and died Jan. 7, 1821.

Henry Pforr had two brothers who also were lawyers.
They were appointed judges of what in a State in the Union
is called the Supreme Court.

In 1841, George Pforr and his sisters, Elizabeth and
Gertrude, with Elizabeth's husband, Andrew Wenck, and
their only child, a boy, and Ann Eliza Coleman, took passage on a sailboat at Bremen, Germany and after eight weeks
on the heaving bosom of the Atlantic Ocean, landed at Baltimore April the 7th.

George Pforr and Ann Eliza Coleman were married in
Baltimore. Making application for naturalization, he was
given full citizenship in this country Oct. 1, 1850. Some years
later he moved to Staunton.

Bernard Pforr, eldest child of the above couple, joined
the Staunton Artillery when the storm of secession swept
Virginia from her moorings and landed her in the Southern
Confederacy. He was brave and soldierly and was promoted
to the rank of corporal. In the battle of Spotsylvania one
discharge of his gun was so destructive that he sprang upon
it and gave three rousing cheers for Jefferson Davis and the

214

Southern Confederacy, and fell to the ground dead, shot down by the enemy.

George Pforr, a younger brother of Bernard's, thought the South was unprogressive and reactionary and decided he would not fight to help establish her independence. So he went North and joined the Union Army under the alias of Charles W. Anderson. He served in Custer's command in the Shenandoah Valley and was one of seventeen who captured Confederate Flags in the Battle of Waynesboro. The one he captured was described by Sheridan as an "unknown Rebel Flag." Sheridan gave them a furlough, sent them to Washington and each was decorated with a medal.

Joseph Trout, Saddler

A tradition preserved in the Trout family that three brothers of the Lutheran connection were compelled to flee from their home in the neighborhood of Frankfort-on-the-Main, and came to America a number of years before the Revolutionary War, is in all probability true. They settled at Germantown, Pa., where many emigrants from their fatherland had preceded them. One, whose name, probably, was Jeremiah, was a Lutheran minister. He became a chaplain in the Continental Army and served during the War of the Revolution. He preached a sermon to the army in the presence of Washington on the evening before the battle of Brandywine.

Joseph Trout was born at Newtown, now Stephens City, Oct. 16, 1787. He married Sarah Whitesides in Augusta County, Dec. 24, 1812, making his home at Greenville. Sarah Whitesides was born in Amherst County, April 18, 1793, and died at Port Republic, Aug. 15, 1873. She was the daughter of James Whitesides and his wife, Ann (Kinney) Whitesides. Mrs. Whitesides died at Port Republic, June 28, 1845. Her husband had lost his life many years before while on a business trip to Tennessee, having drowned in crossing the Tennessee River.

Joseph Trout served for a short time in the War of 1812 as a private in Capt. John C. Sower's Company of Virginia Artillery of Augusta County. He moved from Greenville to Port Republic in 1818. He was a saddler by trade and did a large business. The first entry in his daybook, under the heading, "Port Republic December 24th, 1818," is: "Joseph Grayham Dr To 1 Cirb briddle $1.25"

Andrew McCaslin commenced to work for Mr. Trout Aug. 2, 1820, and Stephen Smith began working for him Aug 14, 1828.

Three medical doctors are named in Mr. Trout's book: Dr. Kemper, Dec. 24, 1818; Dr. Chambers, Aug. 6, 1819; and Dr. Foude, March 1, 1828.

The prices of farm products, either bought or sold by Mr. Trout, over a century ago are of more than passing interest. The various articles were either credited or charged to the accounts of his patrons and are a fair index to the prevailing prices of the various articles in the years mentioned.

Wheat	May 1820	$ .75 per bushel
Corn	October 1820	.50 per bushel
Rye	May 1829	.50 per bushel
Oats	June 1825	.25 per bushel
Potatoes	February 1824	.37 ½ per bushel
Sweet Potatoes	October 1827	.68 per bushel
Turnips	October 1822	.25 per bushel
Apples	October 1828	.16 2/3 per bushel
Bacon	October 1821	.10 per pound
Pork	April 1828	.04 per pound
Lard	1822	.10 per pound
Beef	1821	.03 per pound
Flour	February 1820	3.50 per barrel
Cabbage	September 1822	.02 ½ per head

When Mr. Trout moved to Port Republic there were no free public schools in the county. With those who were interested in the education of their children, the custom was to employ a competent teacher, rent a suitable house, supply wood for fuel, and agree to pay their proportional part of the expense. In 1824 Mr. Trout notes that W. Graham, Peter Miller, Murray, and Austin each delivered a load of wood at the schoolhouse.

It is pleasant to know that Mr. Trout had some books. On Jan. 24, 1825, he made a note that William Harper had borrowed two books: *Indian Wars* and *Endfield's Speaker*.

Some antiquated notions respecting the art of healing were in vogue here in the first half of the past century. The following is found on page 347 of this interesting daybook:

To cure a swelled neck, three nights in succession before the full of the moon, you must look at it when it is rising and say what I see is a rising and at the same time rub your hand over the swelling and say what I see is a falling continue it for three moons.

Doubtless this treatment for a "swelled neck" was as efficacious as were the rites and sacrifices prescribed in the cleansing of the leper as practiced by the ancient Hebrews.

Mr. Trout united with the Methodist Episcopal Church. On page 339 of his daybook is: "On the 24th day of October 1824 I joined the Methodist Church in Port Republic, Rockingham County, Va.—Joseph Trout"

Mr. Trout was not a prohibitionist but an advocate of temperance. May 16, 1831, he gave Charles Lewis credit for a gallon of whiskey, price fifty cents. On page 344 is a recipe for the making of what might be called an old time Methodist drink:

Barrell of 32 Galls 8 Galls Brandy 1 Bushell Grapes put the Brandy & Grapes in the Barrell and let them stand tenn or twelve Days then fill the Barrell up with sider from the press & in three weeks it will be fit for use & a very pleasant Drink.

Mr. Trout had eleven children. Eight were born at Port Republic, the first three were born at Greenville. He died March 26, 1850, and was buried in Riverside Graveyard.

Mary Ann Trout married Thomas W. Ryan on Aug. 14,

1839. Ryan was born in Baltimore, Md., March 29, 1813. He was a shoemaker and saddler, and while he lived in the town did a thriving business. His home was on lot No. 31. He was the father of eight children, all of whom were born at Port Republic. He died at Mt. Jackson, Aug. 12, 1883. Their children were:

Joseph Nicholas, born June 27, 1840; died at Staunton, Nov. 30, 1892. Was Clerk of the Circuit Court of Augusta County from 1864 until his death.
Jefferson Kinney, born Sept. 20, 1841; was killed at the battle of Cedar Mountain, Aug. 9, 1862.
Richard Daingerfield, born Oct. 2, 1845; died at Staunton, Nov. 28, 1876.
John Chesley, born Oct. 26, 1847; died at Staunton, July 21, 1891.
Sarah Matilda, born Aug. 12, 1849; died at Grottoes, Sept. 8, 1898.
James William, born Oct. 17, 1851; died at Grottoes
Llewellyn Kemper, born Oct. 31, 1854.
Mary Archer, born Oct. 30, 1857.

Mary Selina Trout, daughter of Joseph, was born Jan. 12, 1824 and died July 9, 1892. She married John W. Lee on May 18, 1842. He was born near Front Royal, March 18, 1820. He made his home at Port Republic and for a number of years he was proprietor of the Lee Hotel, which was located on lot No. 6. He had a tailor shop in the hotel and for many years the post office also. He died at the home of his daughter, Mrs. John C. Scott at New Hope. They had twelve children, all born in Port Republic:

Sarah Elizabeth, July 17, 1844-Sept. 16, 1894
Joseph William, March 3, 1846-Jan. 15, 1901
Araminta Martha, May 25, 1849-died at New Hope
Julia Thornton, March 1, 1850-Feb. 11, 1882
John Nicholas, Jan. 9, 1851-Feb. 20, 1851
Charles Kelley, Jan. 1, 1852-

Mary Craig, April 1, 1855-
Angeline Kemper, July 9, 1857- June, 1858
Stephen Archer, April, 1859-living
Dora Virginia, Jan. 4, 1861-
Harriette Selina, March 24, June 9, 1869
Lucy Flynn, Mary 2, 1868- [1]

Sarah Jane Trout, another of Joseph's daughters, married John Harper. A sketch of each is found in the chapter on the Harper family.

By early removal to other parts, those children of Joseph Trout not above named, lost connection with the town.

Chapter Thirty-two Endnotes

[1]H.M. McIlhany, Jr., *Some Virginia Families*, (Staunton, Va.: Stoneburner & Prufer, 1903.)

Chapter 33

Zachariah Raines, the Commodore of the Shenandoah

Born in a glamorous locality near Browns Gap, this neighborhood never had a more colorful character than Zachariah Raines. The first object to meet his inquisitive eyes when taken outdoors was the smiling Blue Ridge Mountain. Like it, he grew up strong and rugged. The very air of the mountain gave him courage and inspiration as he explored its deep hollows and climbed its high peaks. He was strong of body and mind and overflowing with energy, which caused him to undertake tasks hard and venturesome. Untutored but possessing strong mental faculties, he soon became the leader in the sports and labors in which he engaged; and so in his mature manhood the habit of command sat lightly upon him. He became a river boatman and his home port was Port Republic. Here he had at his command a well-organized body of assistants, men fitted to do their difficult tasks requiring great agility and physical strength.[1]

The boats, called gundalows, were usually nine or nine-and-a-half feet wide and from 76 to 90 feet long. The side planks were two inches thick and fourteen or more inches wide. To keep out splash-water the width of the sides was increased by placing one-inch thick splash-boards on top of the gunwales.

Many of these boats were built at The Point by Adam May, Jr. He was a famous boat builder and his youngest son, James Henry, was his expert assistant.

Mitchell Crawford was another well-known boat builder. He lived at New Haven, which town was not far beyond North River from Port Republic. An abandoned house and a deep well of fine water are all that remain to mark the site of this ghost town.

Chutes were built in the dams for the passage of these boats. The top ends of the chutes were placed as far below the level of the water going over the dams as the bottom of the boats were submerged in the water, and were closed with a well fitting plank. The chutes fell gradually to the level of the water below the dams. These chutes were excellent passageways for fish in their annual migration up the river. At a certain height in the rise of the river, both boats and fish could pass over the dams.

A storehouse and shed were built on The Point to shelter flour and other freight liable to damage from inclement weather.

South River was cleared of obstructions to Mount Vernon Forge. The product of this forge, a high-class iron beaten into blooms, was loaded onto the boat, which then dropped down the river to Port Republic to await the departure of the flotilla, of which it was a part. Sometimes there were as many as twenty boats in one fleet. When the time of the departure of the fleet arrived, Commodore Raines and his men were in their glory. With earsplitting blasts from long tin horns, much shouting and loud singing, the boats, singly or lashed two together, drew away from The Point and headed down the river. Each boat was usually manned by four polemen and a man each to the front and rear rudders. There were many stations along the river where the oncoming fleet, or certain boats designated by the commodore, would go ashore to discharge or take

ROCKINGHAM COUNTY TO WIT:

I do hereby certify that a Plough and *11* Horses belonging to *Zachariah Rains* worked *2* day *5* on that part of the public road of which I am Surveyor, and that the same was employed by me, as Surveyor aforesaid, which work was done since the first day of June last. Given under my hand this *13ᵗʰ* day of June, 185 *2*

Sworn to before me
Abr Smith J P. *Zachariah Rains*
Waggon

WE, the subscribers, being first sworn, have valued the work of a Plough and *4* Horses (by the day) belonging to *Zachariah Rains* and which were employed by *him* to work on that part of the public road of which he is Surveyor, and do value the same to be worth the sum of *2ow*. Dolls. and *fifty* Cents per day. Given under our hands this *13ᵗʰ* day of June, 185 *2*

Sworn to before me, a Justice of the Peace for }
Rockingham, the day and year aforesaid. }

Abr Smith
H M Harris
Jacob Sipe

Voucher for work done on a public road by Zachariah Raines, 1852

on freight. Occasionally a fleet would not stop at Harpers Ferry but continue by way of the Baltimore and Ohio Canal to Georgetown.

Arrived at their destination and unloaded, the boats were sold, in favorable circumstances, for as much as $25 a boat for the large size and less for the smaller ones. They were not bought for future use as boats but for the lumber that could be got from them suitable for building purposes.

Going no further than Harpers Ferry, the round trip was made in about a week. Eighteen dollars were paid to each man for the trip when conditions were good.

Commodore Raines had an able competitor in Capt. Jacob Sipe, whose name frequently occurs in all the daybooks, etc., of the business concerns of the town at the time, that are now in the possession of the writer. To give some idea of the amount of business done by these knights of the Shenan-

223

doah the following is taken from an insurance advertisement in the Harrisonburg Daily Record, March 24, 1934:

The Shenandoah River at one time was one of the great avenues of commerce of this section of the State. It may not be generally known but hundreds of tons of flour, lumber, iron and other articles of trade were shipped down the river from Port Republic to Georgetown each year.

In the Rockingham Register of Jan. 16, 1841, Jacob Sipe, of near Port Republic, was advertising his shipping business. The advertiser declared that he had taken 5,623 barrels of flour through the "Shenandoah Locks during the past season."

For those engaged in the shipping business on the river during that period it was absolutely necessary that they have large holdings in real estate and other property. This property was put up by them as security for returns from the cargo entrusted.

Zachariah Raines owned considerable land lying east of the head of the Shenandoah River. There were numerous iron ore deposits on it and one in particular was so rich that Mr. Haynes, superintendent of the Abbott Iron Co., put men to work in this mine without the formality of securing a right to do so. Mr. Raines took his case into a magisterial court and employed George F. Compton to handle it for him. Mr. Compton drove a horse and buggy and attempting to cross Mill Creek near the home of Isaac Long, the creek being high, washed horse and buggy downstream against a floodgate and drowned the horse. Mr. Compton was in no good humor when he reached Port Republic and entered the court. Mr. Haynes became unduly facetious which angered Mr. Compton. Turning to his client he advised him to shoot the defendant should he again find him in his mine. There was no more trespassing.

Henry, Reuben, and Zachariah "the Commodore" Raines were brothers. Their father, James Raines and their mother, whose maiden name was Zuriah Davis, were married Sept.

30, 1802. Reuben Raines went to California about 1855 and became wealthy. A few years later he sent his mother a check for $1,000. She took it to Gen. Samuel H. Lewis at Lewiston and requested him to get it cashed for her the next time he went to Harrisonburg. When she left home, some days later, to go to General Lewis for her money, she did not go direct but went down to the home of her son Zachariah Raines, who lived near the south end of Weaver's Bluff, for a short visit and to get a setting of duck eggs, which indicates that it was springtime. Leaving the home of her son to go to Lewiston, instead of going the usual way she took a by-path to the Port Republic Road and was murdered in the woods just before reaching the road. The murderer thought she had the money on her person. The eggs were broken and scattered around. When search was made for her body, bits of her dress were found on bushes here and there, but as the body seemed to have been moved from place to place, it was never found. Years after, the skull of a woman was found on a high mountain peak back of Lewiston.

Commodore Raines was affiliated with the Methodist Church. Of a deeply emotional nature, he was easily aroused by the fluent preachers of his denomination. Once, when meetings were held at the Port Republic Church in behalf of missionary objects and the Commodore being present, he was called on to lead in prayer. He at once embraced the opportunity of publicly informing the Lord that the greater part of the world was groping in deep darkness and that the enlightening sun of Methodism shone upon but a small part of the earth's surface and would he not in His loving kindness be pleased "to send missionaries to convert the heathen in the land where the foot of man never trod and the eye of God has never seen."

A somewhat extended investigation to ascertain the dates of the birth and death of Zachariah Raines has been successful. The record of his father's family is lost or destroyed, and the records of the families of his sons and daughters are misplaced or do not contain it. The husband of one of his granddaughters says that he was born July 15, 1810 and died Feb. 18, 1870; the granddaughter assures that he died Feb. 2, 1870, which she supports by an association of dates.

Zachariah Raines is no ordinary name in the annals of East Rockingham. No history of the county is complete without a liberal sketch of him. No man of the neighborhood has left behind him a memory so pleasing to the imagination. Strong, bold, honest, he was fearless to do right as he understood it. When death faced him, he was not afraid. He died, held in high respect by all who knew him.

In a beautifully located graveyard near the foot of the mountains that always drew forth his admiration, he lies peacefully and at rest.

Chapter Thirty-three Endnotes
[1]See Chapter 7, "Boating: A Commercial Enterprise."

Chapter 34

Michael Amos Scott, a Self-made Man

Born Sept. 21, 1806, Michael Amos Scott was inured from early childhood to hard work. His father lost his life in the War of 1812, leaving a wife and ten children: five boys and five girls. The boys were bound out to lighten the mother's burden.[1]

In early manhood, Michael Amos left his home, which was in the neighborhood of what is now the city of Roanoke, and came to Port Republic. He was industrious and saving, and it was not long before he had enough money to buy the water power at Scotts Ford on North River and to build a mill. The ford was named for him. He was interested in boating to the extent of going, at times, with the products of his labor, usually flour and lumber, to the Georgetown market.

On March 1, 1836, he bought a large tract of land of Thomas M. Mansfield and his wife Cassandra, paying therefore $1,000. This tract of land lies on the east side of the Shenandoah River and extended about a mile eastward towards the mountains. The large part of his land lay on the north side of the Brown's Gap Pike. That part lying on the south side did not reach the river by a quarter of a mile. The entire tract was heavily covered with timber. On an elevated spot, he built a commodious house, commanding the beautiful scenery of the countryside and giving a glorious view of the river.

Mr. Scott married first a Miss Hanna. Issue: William

227

H. Scott, born Jan. 29, 1834 died Feb. 25, 1898; Reuben A. Scott, born July 28, 1838 died Jan. 12, 1912; Michael A. Scott, born March 15, 1841, died Nov. 10, 1915; George and Annie. (The dates of their births and deaths are unknown to the writer.) He married second, Agnes A. Palmer, daughter of Robert W. Palmer; and married third, the widow Catharine Bowers, nee Hatfield of Bridgewater.

If there is a future life in which rewards are given to the industrious in this world, Mr. Scott is deserving of the best gifts within the means of the giver for the hard work he did on his stony farm. He built a stone fence with a five-foot base, four feet high with sides inclining to a two-foot top. On the top was built a bar fence several rails high. The fence was built on the north side of the pike and was at least three-quarters of a mile long. The fence contained over fifty-five thousand cubic feet of stones. Those stones were laboriously picked off the ground, thrown onto a wagon with a body of loose-lying planks for the bottom and a plank on edge on each side so the unloading could be done quickly, and hauled to where the fence was being built. It is but a few years ago that this fence was torn down and used in the construction of public roads.

Several children of William H. Scott live in the neighborhood. Michael A. Scott, III lives on part of the original farm.

Mr. Scott died at the advanced age of eighty-two years, seven months, and twenty-one days, May 12, 1899, and was buried in Riverside Graveyard. His second wife, Agnes A. Scott, died May 29, 1862, "aged about 50 years." Side-by-side they are resting in unbroken sleep.[2]

Chapter Thirty-four Endnotes

[1]Children from poor or indigent families were often "bound out" or indentured to people who would provide shelter and sustenance in exchange for labor. Contracts detailing the terms of the indenture—the length of time, type of labor expected of the individual, and material goods provided—were recorded and filed in the county courthouse.
[2]May included the following corrections and comments on this chapter provided by Amos Scott's great-great granddaughter, Eva Patterson Baker:

1. Only Amos Scott. He had a brother Michael. See Franklin County, Va. records also check deed and tombstone.

2. See Census of 1810 for Franklin Co, Va. William Scott father of Amos had 4 males 1-10 years old; 2 males 10-16; 1 male 26-45; 2 females 1-10; 3 females 10-16 and 1 female 16-45 years.

3. Bought the mill at Scott's Ford 1856. See Deedbook 29, page 544, Rockingham County records. Mathias Diehl was in partnership. Scott's Ford was named for Jacob Scott son of Robert Scott who patented land on North River 1747. First called Coal's Ford see Chalkley's Vol. II, page 30.

4. Agnes Palmer's father was James. See marriage bond and *Palmer History* by Stickley.

5. Could have been Michael A. Scott the II but not the III. Uncle Michael A. Scott raised him, as he was born to Jane Smith while she was keeping house for Uncle Mike. No proof. See Uncle _____ estate settlement 1919-1920.

Amos paid $1,080 for 102 acres 1836 and bought the rest at later dates.

Chapter 35

The Hooke Family

A mong the old families of the Port Republic neighborhood none are more highly respectable and respected than the Hooke Family. The ancestor of the
Port Republic branch of this family was Robert Hooke,
"Captain Robin," as he was usually spoken to and of. He
was born Sept. 5, 1780 and died Jan. 25, 1858. He was a
Lieutenant in a company of Virginia Militia in the War of
1812. He married (1) Sarah Beard, Aug 16, 1815. She did not
live long. He married (2) Elizabeth Fisher, Dec. 14, 1821.
She was daughter of Abraham and Elizabeth Fisher, was
born Aug. 21, 1801, and died Dec. 13, 1882.

Abraham Fisher was a man of affairs in the neighborhood. He owned a large farm and his name frequently occurs in the daybooks and ledgers of the businessmen of the
town in his time.

Robert Hooke bought of Samuel Fisher and his wife,
Lydia, Aug. 1, 1837, a large farm bordering on North River,
for which he paid $3,500, "lawful money of Virginia." In
the several previous conveyances of this tract of land, it is
described as adjoining the lands of John Pirkey, a Mr. Yount,
William Lewis, George W. Burton, and a Mr. Kemper. The
tracts of the two latter are described as "lots." This tract of
land was conveyed by John Weaver to Richard Austin; by
him to John Miltenbarger; by him to Abraham Fisher; his
heirs to Samuel Fisher; and by him to Robert Hooke.

Joseph Mauzy surveyed this land May 14, 1834. William Lewis's land adjoined it on the east side. Mr. Mauzy, in

Riverside, the home of Robert ("Captain Robin") Hooke

a note on the diagram, says, "The Patent for Mrs. Lewisses Land was granted to Robt. Scott the 16th of August 1756."

Captain Hooke built a large fine brick dwelling house on the left bank of North River about half a mile above Port Republic. His large farm reached from Mill Creek downstream along the bank of the river for about three-quarters of a mile, and extended back from the river to beyond the Port Republic-Harrisonburg road. It was a valuable estate. The unmarried members of the family lived and

Capt. "Robin" Robert Hooke's son, Robert J. Hooke with his bride, Calpurnia Firestone

died here. A grandson, Grover S. Hooke, lived here in recent times. About 1924 the State School Board bought the house and thirty acres immediately around it and converted the place into recreation grounds for the teachers and students of the State Teachers College (now James Madison University) at Harrisonburg.

Robert Hooke's children were:

	born	died
Sarah Beard	Oct. 12, 1822	Dec. 14, 1892
Archibald H.	Apr. 20, 1824	Mar. 22, 1877
Elizabeth Louisa	Oct. 19, 1825	July 22, 1910
James Lewis	May 25, 1827	Nov. 26, 1918
Mary Margaret	June 11, 1829	Apr. 2, 1890
Abraham Scott	Dec. 14, 1830	Apr. 20, 1912
George W. Kemper	Feb. 21, 1832	Oct. 15, 1863
Rebecca Jane	Oct. 1, 1832	Dec. 4, 1913
Robert J.	Apr. 1, 1835	Nov. 22, 1861
Cynthia Maria	Mar. 25, 1837	Sept. 12, 1923
Amanda A.	Nov. 29, 1839	Oct. 18, 1910

Cloverdale: Home of Harrison Bateman; his widow, Rebecca Hooke on steps

Of Robert's children, Sarah Beard Hooke married David Trissel, of Dark County, Ohio. Rebecca Hooke married Harrison Bateman. Robert J. Hooke was a member of the River Rangers and was promoted to a sergeancy. He died in a hospital at Charlottesville of typhoid fever. George W. Kemper Hooke, died two years later in the same room and hospital at Charlottesville and of the same disease.

Another son, Sergeant Abraham Scott Hooke was an ultra Confederate sympathizer and served through the Civil War with honor. He was a Member of the River Rangers, a cavalry troop recruited in East Rockingham and was in many hard-fought battles. He was in the Gettysburg campaign and saw the ebb of the mighty Confederate wave whose flow carried the Southern cause within a stone's throw of success. After this he fought with firmness but with little hope of success. When the bitter end came he returned home and gave his time to repairing the damage done to the paternal estate.

He married Sophia Frances Null, daughter of George Null. She was born June 28, 1848 and died Jan. 18, 1926. There were ten children born of this marriage:

	born	died
Laura Virginia	Jan. 27, 1867	Sept. 10, 1925
George Robert	Dec. 19, 1868	Aug. 16, 1923
James Archibald	Oct. 11, 1870	Apr. 30, 1932
Elizabeth Olive	Sept. 26, 1872	
Josie Margaret	Feb. 2, 1874	
John W.	Oct. 12, 1875	May 5, 1905
Mary Rosella	Oct. 23, 1877	May 25, 1921
Charles Cleveland	Nov. 2, 1880	
Sophia Katharine	Aug. 4, 1882	
Grover Scott	Oct. 23, 1884	

In 1905 Abraham Scott Hooke retired from active farming. He bought Lot No. 9 in Port Republic in 1911, built a commodious modern house and made it his home to his death. He was a reader of worthwhile books and had a store of useful information. He was a member of the Port Republic Methodist Church.

Of another of Robert's daughters, Cynthia Marie Hooke, there is an interesting story of the nerve displayed in defeating the efforts of a squad of Federal soldiers to invade her home. One of her brothers was at home from the army for a short stay when a small party of Yankees was seen unexpectedly coming towards the house. The brother did not have time to get his horse before fleeing to cover. His sister Cynthia was determined that the horse should not be taken, so she led it upstream and hid it in some high bushes on the riverbank. Returning to the house, she picked up an empty pistol and walked around to the front of the house. She met the Yankees coming through the front yard gate. A flourish of the pistol and the men in blue decided that they were very unwelcome guests and departed, leaving the premises in the possession of the young heroine.

Chapter 36

The Palmer Family

etween 1810 and 1820, James Palmer, a soldier in the
Revolutionary War, moved from King William
County to Rockingham County. His son, Robert
Waller Palmer, was born in the former county, Sept. 30, 1803
and died at Port Republic, Sept. 2, 1861. He had married
Sarah Harrison Austin, who was born April 15, 1815, and
died March 3, 1884. Their children were named John Waller,
Agnes, William and Clay.

Robert Waller Palmer was a successful shopkeeper. His
ledger carries the names of all the prominent people of the
town and neighborhood at that time. Perhaps the last in-
voice Mr. Palmer made of his merchandise was Sept. 20,
1860. As owner of a small town store and with a large family to support, he had done well.

John Waller Palmer, his son, was born at Port Republic,
Oct. 6, 1827. His first marriage was solemnized April 13,
1848 when Annie Maria Eddins, daughter of Maj. James
Eddins, became his wife. Her mother was Mornen Delinger
Dundore, daughter of Capt. John Dundore.

In 1851, John W. moved to Augusta County and engaged in the mercantile business; and in 1856 he returned
to Port Republic, and was engaged in the same business at
different times to within a few years of his death. He was
postmaster at Hermitage while living in Augusta County,
and held the following offices of trust after his return to his
native town: postmaster, three years; school trustee, seven
years; notary public, five years; and served several terms
each as county supervisor and magistrate.

Water Street in the snow: John Waller Palmer Store, Frank Kemper House

Mr. Palmer's store house on Water Street was the largest and finest in East Rockingham. None but the best material was used in its construction and first-class workmen only were employed. The shelving and counters were objects of beauty. This fine building was destroyed by fire, Sept. 27, 1928; many persons thought the fire was of incendiary origin.

John W. Palmer had five children by his first marriage who were born, Mary Catharine, Sept. 1, 1850; Charles Minor, Sept. 19, 1853; Annie Laura, Sept. 22, 1861; Robert Vernon, May 21, 1864; and Viola Maria, Oct. 30, 1866.

Charles Minor Palmer married a Miss Bear of Elkton, and entered a partnership in the store business at that town; Annie Laura Palmer married Morgan J. Stickley, a lawyer, and moved to Concord, N.C.; Robert Vernon Palmer studied medicine and was a successful practitioner near Alexandria. Viola Maria Palmer married Charles Lambert of Waynesboro, a carpenter.

Their mother, Annie M. (Eddins) Palmer died at Port Republic, May 24, 1867, and was buried in Riverside Graveyard.

John Waller's second matrimonial alliance was with

Mary Catharine Funkhouser, daughter of Rev. Joseph Funkhouser of near Keezletown. She was born in Shenandoah County, April 9, 1840. The children of this union were born: John Waller, Jr., Aug. 6, 1870; Olin Austin, July 3, 1872; Virginia Harrison, Feb. 13, 1877; Nellie Neff, March 24, 1879; and twins, Caroll and Albert.

John, Jr. had the makings of a good merchant in him but died in early manhood. Olin was a printer and writer. In his boyhood he published a small paper for several months, named if memory does not fail, *The Advance*. In 1912 he published *At the Mercy of Fate*, a tale of the Shenandoah Valley. Virginia married a John Hinton and lives in West Virginia. Nellie married Rev. George Mays. Caroll entered the Methodist ministry, and Albert is practicing law in North Carolina.

John Waller Palmer owned several properties in the town and a nearby farm which his first wife inherited from the Dundore estate. He was quick to participate in controversies and not slow to engage in lawsuits. He took legal action to have William S. Downs ejected from several properties the latter claimed and of which he was in possession. The litigation extended over a period of years and permanently estranged the two. During all this litigation a certain rock mentioned in the boundaries of these disputed properties was much discussed. It is described in an old deed as "a rock in the Shape of a Half Moon the circular part thereof being towards the South in the river." The part of the rock marking the corner is named in the above deed as its "North east corner." With this established corner, a little "sweet reasonableness" on both sides would have prevented a lawsuit.

These men were both Methodist and belonged to the church. Happening to meet one day, Mr. Downs inquired of Mr. Palmer why he no longer attended church meetings.

This was an acceptable opportunity for a blow at his enemy so Palmer replied that he did not care to be so closely associated with hypocrites. Knowing that this thrust was intended for him alone, Mr. Downs replied, "That's all right, brother Palmer; come to church next Sunday and sit by me."

When the fateful decision had to be made whether Virginia remain in or withdraw from the Union, Mr. Palmer was a secessionist. It is reported that he openly declared that if Virginia did not go out of the Union, he would go to South Carolina and "wade in blood up to his knees" He did not engage in active military service the first year of the war. However, when the bridge at Port Republic over the North River was burned, he built a flat boat and ferried persons and such freight as was suitable to be carried by the boat over the river. The boat was propelled by a pole, and both of his shoulders became callused by pressing them against the pole. Though no military honors were placed upon his brow, this service was of inestimable benefit in those troublesome war times.

Two of John Waller's brothers were Confederate States' soldiers: William L., a member of Company B, Tenth Virginia Infantry, who was wounded in the battle of Cedar Mountain and returned home to die at his mother's house in Port Republic, Sept. 11, 1862, and Henry Clay who was a member of the same company.

An old resident of the town was Jonathan Bateman. There is a tradition that he and Mr. Palmer were partners in the manufacture of beehives. The venture was not of long duration and the partners separated with mutual aversion. In process of time, Mr. Bateman became very ill and it was thought that his end was near. Desiring a reconciliation, Mr. Palmer called on him with that object in view. Explanations and regrets were made by both and Mr. Palmer rose to take his leave. "Jonathan," he said, "I am happy at this understanding. All now is forgiven and forgotten." To which Mr. Bateman replied, "Well, Waller, if I die I forgive you; if I get well I don't."

After the war, John Waller changed his political creed and became an ardent Republican. He was a politician of no mean ability. On account of his superior intellectual faculties and influence with the rank and file of the Republican Party in East Rockingham, he was heartily disliked by the Lewis family. An authentic story of an amusing argument between Mr. Palmer and John F. Lewis as to whether General Lee was a greater general than General Grant is still told. Leaning far back on his horse and in his pompous manner, Mr. Lewis exclaimed, "Ho! Ho! Ho! General Winfield Scott says General Grant is the greatest general the Civil War produced; but John Waller Palmer says General Lee is." Mr. Palmer quickly responded, "Oh! No! John F. Lewis and General Winfield Scott say that General Grant is the greatest general the Civil War produced; but John Waller Palmer and the world say that General Lee is."

Mr. Palmer lived to the ripe age of ninety-two years. He returned to mother earth and slept with his fathers June 26, 1919.

William Allen Maupin, Blacksmith and Soldier

The subject of this sketch was born in Albemarle County, May 31, 1815. His father, William J. Maupin, ran a distillery at White Hall. William A. grew to manhood in the home of an aunt who lived at Charlottesville. He learned the blacksmith trade and became an expert workman. When he removed to East Rockingham about 1838, his father, who was born March 10, 1770, came with him and died at Port Republic, Aug. 17, 1853 and was buried in Riverside Graveyard. Mr. Maupin located in the community of Screwsburg, now LeRoy. He bought property adjoining the Hanna estate and built a large up-to-date blacksmith shop at the crossing of the two public roads at LeRoy. A few years later, 1850, he removed to Port Republic and established his shop at the southwestern end of Water Street. He did a large business. The trade became almost hereditary in his family, for two sons, a son-in-law, and one grandson followed in his footsteps.

Mr. Maupin announced his candidacy for the office of Commissioner of the Revenue for District No. 1, in the *Rockingham Register*, May 14, 1858. In this announcement he says, "I conceive it due not only to them, (the voters) but also to myself, to say, that I have been a resident of the county for upwards of twenty years, taking a lively interest and an honest pride in the prosperity in my adopted home." Later, he withdrew from the race.

Shortly before the parting of the way between the North and the South, Mr. Maupin was appointed Colonel of the Fifty-eighth Regiment of Virginia Militia. When the clouds of blood and fire lowered upon the land, Colonel Maupin notified William S. Downs that he had been appointed Captain of Company No. 5, of the Fifty-eighth Virginia Regiment and sent him the roster of the company. This notification was not dated. However, Captain Downs, who succeeded Capt. J.E.A. Harris, was ordered to notify his men to assemble in Harrisonburg, July 25, 1861. This roster is of peculiar interest to the people of East Rockingham. It follows:

W.S. Baugher
Hawkins Austin
J.S. Keller
M.A. Scott
John S. Kiger
Elijah Randol
W.K. Hughes
Joshua Harlow
Jas. Reese
G. Phillips (for W.S. Baugher)
Jackson Frazier
J.L. Mohr
McCahay Shiflett
John D. Matheny
Jas. W. Murray
Newton Wagner
Fielding Matheny
Isaac Liskey
J.H. Licklighter
Wash Grim

Elias Grim
Benj. Haney
A.J. Collier
James Bateman
Jas. H. Eddins
W.L. Morris
Henry McCauly
B—Cave
Calvin Keezle
J.H. Brown
J.H. Holbrook
W.F. Hammer
Wm. Morris
Wm. Burkett
Jas. Cross
(for Showalter, Peter, son)
W.E. Palmer
Thos. Shiflett
Frank Ellett

Some of the above militiamen lived in Port Republic, others lived in the immediate neighborhood.

The State Militia was not equal to the storm and stress of Civil War, so when Virginia entered the Southern Confederacy, her militia was taken over, reorganized, and re-officered by the Confederate Government. An authority on the subject says:

The officers of the State militia had hitherto exercised the functions of command over the ill-knit concourse of enthusiastic patriots. The militia, however, was hardly more than a force on paper, and the camps swarmed with generals and field officers who were merely civilians in gaudy uniform. By order of the State Legislature these gentlemen were now deprived of their fine feathers. Every militia officer above the rank of Captain was deposed; and the Governor of Virginia was authorized to fill the vacancies.[1]

When John F. Lewis became United States Marshal for the Western District of Virginia, he had Colonel Maupin appointed as one of his deputies which position he held until his death, Feb. 18, 1882.

Colonel Maupin married Mary A. Price, May 10, 1836. She died Sept. 3, 1889, and sleeps beside her husband in Riverside Graveyard.

Laura V. Maupin married a young man, Joseph H. Lamb who had come from the Elkton neighborhood and worked at blacksmithing for Colonel Maupin. Later he set up in business for himself. Due

William Henry Harrison Maupin, Lieutenant CSA, son of Col. William A. Maupin

Maupin/Lamb House on Water Street

to his superior workmanship, he did an extensive business which continued up to within a few years of his death. He died Dec. 5, 1921. His widow, Laura Maupin Lamb, remained a "presence" in this community for many years.

Chapter Thirty-seven Endnotes

[1]G.F.R. Henderson, *Stonewall Jackson and the American Civil War*, vol. 1, (London: Longmans, Green, & Co., 1906), 115.

Chapter 38

George W. Eustler, Slave-trader

T here were several men of the name of Eustler in the town and neighborhood during the decade of 1840. There was George Eustler, Sr., William Eustler, Washington Eustler, and perhaps others.

The subject of this notice was a farmer, storekeeper, cabinetmaker, and slave trader. A few pieces of furniture he made are still in existence. In a bill he made out against George Morris July 1, 1851, he charges him with one bureau $15.00 and one set of Windsor chairs $9.00. As a storekeeper he was not a success and the farm passed out of his hands. It is as a slave trader that he is generally remembered.

Chattel slavery, now held in abhorrence by every civilized man, had its place in the Constitution of the United States; was imbedded in the Constitutions and laws of the slave-holding states, was defended as a divine institution by the churches; and was upheld by the aristocratic elements of the country. When we think of the burdens laid upon these human slaves, of the agony of the indignities to which they were subjected, and of the blows given in payment for labor performed, we can sympathize with those brave and progressive men who denounced the Constitution that permitted such horrors as a "covenant with death and an agreement with hell."

"Man's inhumanity to man" in the desire of the few to live upon the requited labor of the many, is as brutal and strong now as it was in the time of chattel slavery. As a general thing, the chattel slave was fed, clothed, and housed in his old age. Not so with the wage slave who has been forced into the position formerly held by his deceased brother, the chattel slave. The minute an employer at the present time thinks one of his wage slaves is too old to be profitable, the unfortunate man is thrown upon the scrap-heap of unemployment. Henry Ford and a few others are noble exceptions to the above rule. The one thought that makes the present economic system tolerable is that all-inclusive Evolution is working for an amelioration of conditions in all the departments of human activities. But Evolution is so slow!

Mr. Eustler was a dealer in human chattels. In the winter of 1857-1858, he was in East Virginia dealing in slaves. At Charlottesville, Dec. 19, 1857, he wrote to William S. Downs of Port Republic, instructing him to send Ben and Jessey across the mountain to a certain Mr. Brown who "can sell them or not." He also wrote that some Negroes he had bought had not been delivered to him. In another letter to Mr. Downs he writes that he had sold his "family of Negroes for $3,250." He writes as if he were elated at his success and says "all is right now, sir."

In still another letter written at Charlottesville, Jan. 1, 1858, he writes Mr. Downs that he has bought, since he left home, "5 likely Negroes and one scrub." It was about this time, as the story is told, that he brought a number of Negroes home and housed them in his cabinet-making shop. The Negro children had whooping cough which soon spread to the white children of the town. These mistakenly thought the disease more virulent because it began among the slave population.

While on this trip, Mr. Eustler went to the slave marts of Richmond. In them, slaves were bought and sold in as unabashed manner as if they were tobacco or cotton. Red flags were projected from the doors of the auction offices when slaves were to be sold with a piece of paper tied to each flag advertising the human merchandise for sale. A good account of these auction sales is given in a long extract taken from Chamber's Journal for 1850 and reproduced in Frederick Law Olmstead's *A Journey in the Seaboard Slave States in 1853-1854*. One sale, which illustrates other innumerable will be quoted. The white salesman had a mulatto assistant. Among the lots for sale was a colored woman with three children, all girls, one a baby three months old and the others two and three years of age respectively. The salesman signifying to his assistant that he was ready to begin the sale, that worthy led the woman and her children to the block, and after assisting her and the children to mount, he stood by to do any further bidding of the salesman. The heartless proceeding was as follows:

"Well, gentlemen," began the salesman, "here is a capital woman and her three children, all in good health - what do you say for them? Give me an offer." (Nobody speaks.) "I put up the whole lot at 850 dollars - 850 dollars - 850 dollars" (speaking very fast) "850 dollars. Will no one advance upon that? A very extraordinary bargain, gentlemen. A fine, healthy baby. Hold it up." (Mulatto goes up the first step of the block, takes the baby from the woman's breast and holds it aloft with one hand, so as to show that it was a verible sucking baby.) 'That will do. A woman, still young, and three children, all for 850 dollars. An advance, if you please, gentleman." (A voice bids 860.) Thank you, sir, 860; anyone bids more?" (A second voice says, 870, and so on the bidding goes as far as 890 dollars, when it stops.) "That won't do, gentlemen. I cannot take such a low price" (After a pause, addressing the Mulatto), She may go down". Down from the block the woman and her children were therefore conducted by the assistant, and as if nothing had occurred, they calmly resumed their seats by the stove."

The saddest result of such a happening was that it was more degrading to the whites than to the blacks.

In the slave-holding states, chattel slavery was a cancer on the body politic, and a running sore in their social life. It tended to make the whites willful and cruel, and the blacks servile and fawning. Politicians in the South imagined themselves as defending the Constitution when they were only defending human slavery. Were the Constitution, as some seemed to think, a document containing the political faith once delivered by the fathers to the country and for all succeeding time, then it was worth saving. Political institutions that permit human slavery, or the sinking of wage earners to a level almost as low, are beyond defense.

Mr. Eustler had the following advertisement in the *Rockingham Register* and *Virginia Advertiser*, Friday, June 26, 1857:

500 Negroes Wanted.

I will purchase at fair prices, any class of Negroes. I have on hand three families which I will sell at fair prices. They were raised in the Valley and positively did not come from Richmond as they are sound and of good character. Beware of Negroes from the Richmond market as everyone knows the traders in that market are good judges and will buy none but those that are sound and healthy, and the refuse stock is paddled through the country; or if any of my acquaintances wishes to buy a scrub or a defective Negro, give me a call and you will not go away without one. I also will swop by getting the advantage a little, say $25 or $50 in a Negro, if you have one that don't suit you, come and see me, my friends, if there is such a thing.

Geo. W. Eustler

Address Port Republic, Rockingham Co., Va.

In 1853 there was a state tax on "Slaves over 12 years old, 60 Cents." John H. Austin, a constable then living in the neighborhood, emancipated Aaron, a slave, and paid $1.25

to have the deed recorded. Downs and Piper, tanners at Port Republic, gave Mr. Eustler credit, on March 10, 1857, "By 1 girl $200."

Mr. Eustler was a militia captain in 1845. In later life, he seems to have been proud of his title. When old age overtook him, Captain Eustler made his home with his widowed daughter, Mrs. Evaline Baugher, who owned "Westwood," the former home of Leroy P. Daingerfield. Sickness came and abode with him; death stood by his bedside; and a visit by the Rev. G. Moseley Murray, Rector of Grace Memorial Church at Lynnwood, was welcomed. The Captain made a profession of religion, was baptized, and received into the Episcopal Church. Shortly after this he died and ascended to heaven. He, his wife, one son, and one daughter are buried in Central Graveyard. The inscription on his gravestone is unusual in that it had no dates. It is:

Capt. Geo. W. Eustler
Age 75 Yrs.
Asleep in Jesus.

No effort has been spared to learn the dates of the birth and death of Captain Eustler. The following, under date of July 27, 1934, is from Rev. Charles G. Leavell of St. Stephen's Mission, Yancey, and has come to hand:

I have just looked up the information you desire. It is somewhat unsatisfactory, as the date of birth is not recorded by the rector at that time, a Rev. G. Moseley Murray. A number of others baptized by him do not have their date of birth recorded either, so this does not seem to be unnatural.

George W. Eustler was baptized at 'Westwood' November 1, 1886 by Rev. G. Moseley Murray. The name of his parents is not recorded in the usual manner, perhaps because it seems to have been an adult baptism.

'George Washington Eustler' was buried at Port Republic in November, 1886, the Rev. G. Moseley Murray having charge of the service. The exact date of burial is not recorded for some reason. The Rev. Mr. Murray must have been a bit careless, although the month and year are recorded, November, 1886. There is no record of his being confirmed.

From the above information we may assume that Capt. Eustler (the title would not naturally be given in an ecclesiastical recording) was ill at 'Westwood', and perhaps felt the end coming. He had possibly been attending services at Lynwood, or at least knew the rector there, The Rev. G. M. Murray. Calling for him, he was baptized as he no doubt wished to be, but had not made up his mind fully until this time. He could not be confirmed, as the Bishop did not come for confirmation until 1887 (a number were confirmed then), and by that time his soul had departed this life and he was buried at Port Republic the same month (at least) of his baptism.[1]

Chapter Thirty-eight Endnotes
[1]Rockingham County, Virginia, Register of Deaths. The date of his death is recorded as 12 November 1886.

Chapter 39

William S. Downs, Spared From the Gallows

William S. Downs was one of the most noted persons among all those who have at any time made Port Republic their home. He came to the town an ex-horse racer and with a comprehensive knowledge of the tanning business. Many anecdotes of him still linger in the minds of those who knew him personally. His son, William Stonewall Jackson Downs has related a number of these to the writer.

One, illustrating the barbarity and inhumanity, a consequence, of the South's "peculiar domestic institution," is here given. Mr. Downs had accepted the position of superintendent of John Dundore's tannery. He worked several Negro slaves, belonging to Dundore, in the tanyard. Downs and one of these unfortunate colored men were at work on hides in a vat on the side of the tanyard lying next to the tailrace, which was six or eight feet below the surface of the ground. Thinking that the colored man had answered him impudently, Downs made a dash at him and the poor fellow sprang across the vat and fell into the tailrace. Seizing him and dragging him into the tan house, Downs tied a rope around the upper part of the victim's body, and passing the other end of the rope over a joist in the ceiling, drew him up until his toes just touched the floor. He then applied the blacksnake whip to the bare back and the "correction" was so severe that the poor slave was unable to return to work for several weeks.

Tamed bears were kept at the tannery at this time. Men doing business with the concern brought their children with them to see the bears. One of the slaves would wrestle with a particular bear to the great delight of his rustic audience.

On April 10, 1851, Mr. Downs and John S. Owens rented a tanyard at Wardensville, now in West Virginia, of Henry W. Frye. Mr. Downs was engaged in the tanning business at Wardensville for five years and came from that town to Port Republic.

In an "Article of agreement made and entered in to this 31st day of March 1855, by and between Jacob S. Piper of the County of Shenandoah and State of Virginia, of the one part, and William Downs of the County of Hardy and State aforesaid, of the other part," shows that Mr. Downs was considered to be "of the County Hardy" as late as the spring of 1855.

In this article of agreement it is agreed "that the said Jacob S. Piper rent and to use let, for a term of five years, to commence on the first day of May next, a Certain Tanyard property, lying and being in the County of Rockingham at Port Republic." It was agreed that they "are to go equal partners" subject to certain conditions, one of which was that the "said Downs is to do and have purformed all the Labor that may be necessary to carry on the said Tanyard profitably, to manage the yard in every respect such as buying & selling at the North also to peel and to put up the bark in the mountain, all of which the said Downs is to do and have purformed at his individual expense." The contract concludes: "It is further agreed that either of the parties have the right to rescind this contract at the end of either year after the third year by the party wishing to withdraw, giving the other party three months previous notice in writing of his intention to do so."

As a matter-of-fact the company of Piper and Downs did not survive the shocks and strains of the first year as will appear later. A bond for $500.00 dated Sept. 24, 1855 in which Mr. Downs and another person promise "to pay J. S. Piper the sum of Five hundred dollars, it being for the first year's rent of the tanyard property in Port Republic," is at hand. It is attested by Margaret C. Miller. It was the custom at this time that when a bond was paid to tear the signature or signatures partly or altogether off. It was so in this case and consequently it is not known who signed with Mr. Downs.

It appears from a letter written at Strasburg, Sept. 11, 1857, by Mr. Piper to Mr. Downs that the latter had very recently bought the tanyard property. Mr. Piper writes, "I now give my opinion that you have bought a very great bargain and I hope you may have good luck and do a fine business." He wrote further, that he had transferred part of the bonds to his grandfather but he holds "the five hundred dollars Bonds falling due from 1st May 58 to 1st May 62, the Bonds I hold are the 5 bonds executed for the stock." After suggesting that Mr. Downs "select a companion so you may be permanently situated and keep the property through life," he paused, "until money due is badly needed which was not in the distant future."

A few items taken at random from Mr. Downs' book may be of interest:

Joseph Randol
1855 Dr.
Aug. 1 To 6lbs Sole Leather @ 30ct $ 1.80
Sept. 29 To 1 Side Upper   2.25
1856
Jan. 30 To 1 Sheepskin   .63
1856 Cr.
July 11 By 1 Nite Lodging   1.00
July 23 By 1 Quart whiskey   .25

Zachariah Raines was charged $2.55 for 8 ½ lbs of sale leather, July 23, 1860

Robin Hooke, $1.00 for 2 ½ lbs., July 23, 1861.

A.J. Sigler, $4.55 for 6 ½ lbs., July 11, 1862.

Charles McClung, $36.00 for 9 lbs., Sept. 17, 1863.

Robert Showalter, $9.10 for 26 lbs., Sept. 17, 1864

Evan Watson, $.25 for 1 lb., June 1, 1865.

James A. Maupin was charged $2.00 for half pound plug tobacco, Aug. 9, 1864.

John Ketton, $4.00 for a watermelon, Aug. 15, 1864

Confederate States were given credit for three beef hides valued at $57.80, Feb. 6, 1863; for 160 lbs. per Peyton, at 40 cts. per pound, March 11, 1863; for five hides, per Capt. McKune, at $103.60, March 19, 1863 and one sheepskin $20.00, Sept. 20, 1864.

Daniel Boone was given credit, Feb. 4, 1865, for 12 ½ cts. for one pint of brandy. Farm hands were paid $1.50 to $2.00 per day. Brandy and labor, at least, were cheap.

Mr. Downs mentions six medical doctors by name, George W. Kemper, Senior and Junior, 1855; James A. Hardin, 1863; Franklin Walker, 1863; George Young, 1864; and Wm. W. Cropt, 1864.

An intriguing, undated note, not in the handwriting of Mr. Downs, is found in one of his daybooks: "John C. Clarke came to Texas in 1821 or 22, died in 1862. Enquire if John C. Clarke had a sister that married Doct. Lee of South Carolina."

On April 17, 1858 William Downs bought of George W. Eustler and Minerva, his wife, two lots, Nos. 39 and 40, lying just beyond Upper Alley and being in the Carthrea Addition. There was a dwelling house on each of these lots with necessary out-buildings. The one on lot No. 39 which Mr. Eustler used as a cabinet shop, has been moved back from the street to an alley, and is now used as a horse and cow stable. Facing Main Street on lot No. 40, was a long low dwelling house. This house is still standing and is called the "Longhouse" on account of its shape. It was in this house that he first lived after his marriage.

Dundore/Downs house, c. 1903. Pictured are: Back row: "Madge," DeWitt Downs, Cassie Crawford, Mrs. Long (wife of the mail carrier) and her child, Old Charley (horse) and Charles Kyger, son of a tannery worker. Front row: William Stonewall Jackson Downs, William S. Downs, Annie Downs, and her baby Russell.

On the same date as the purchase of the above lots, he bought lots Nos. 41, 42, and 43 of Alexander R. Givens of Augusta County. These also are in the Carthrea Addition.

In 1868 he acquired the fine old colonial mansion now occupied by his son William S. J. Downs. It stands on a half-acre lot formed by dividing lots Nos. 27 and 28 and faces Water Street.

In that mighty tragedy, the American Civil War, acted on half a continent, William S. Downs did not play a conspicuous part. Those were the times that tried men's souls and all Virginia should have been for or against the Confederate States of America. They should have displayed their colors, and have not tried to play the role of neutral. John F. Lewis manufactured iron for the Southern Confederacy, who in turn converted it into cannons and shells to kill and cripple Yankee soldiers, and when occasion demanded he would declare himself a loyal citizen of the United States. Such "loyalty" smacks of opportunism.

It seems when the North and South appealed to the arbitrament of arms to decide which interpretation of the Constitution of the fathers was right, that Mr. Downs belonged to the State's Militia. On old muster roll of the time has the following notification and order below it:

Wm. S. Downs is hereby appointed Capt. of company No. 5 lately commanded by J.E.A. Harris: Wm. A. Maupin, Col, 58th Regt.
Capt. W.S. Downs will notify his men to be in Harrisonburg on Thursday, July 25th, 1861, supplied with such arms as can be found and 10 days provisions.
W.A. Maupin, Col.

The names of the members of the company are given in the chapter on Colonel Maupin.

How long it was before Mr. Downs was detailed to what was to him the more congenial, and to the Confederacy profitable business of tanning hides, there is little data at hand to show. But an unsigned order indicates that it was not for long. It follows.

Manassas Sept. 13th, 1861
Mr. Wm. S. Downs, comes to Manassas, and the camp generally of the S.C. Army, for the purpose of procuring hides for his Tannery in Rockingham Cty, any facility extended to Mr. Downs, in his important purpose will, oblige.
Most Respectfully yours obt

This order, of course, emanated from Gen. Joseph E. Johnston's quartermaster's department. Considering the large number of horses in the cavalry at that time in and near Manassas, there is no doubt but that Mr. Downs secured a large number of hides.

The next paper found in connection with this business is as follows:

Manufacturing Department
Quartermaster's Office
Staunton, Va., March 21, 1863.
Wm. S. Downs, Esq.,

Sir, My agent Mr. James Ijains reported to this office that he purchased about One Hundred sides Leather of you for the Confederate Government to be finished about the last of Feb'y. As the weather has been bad for your business, I have supposed you may have been disappointed in the drying process. Let me know, if you please, by return mail, when it may be sent for & I will send a wagon for it with the money.
Very truly Yr. obt, st., R.H. Phillips, Capt. & A.Q.M.

The above shows that Mr. Downs was doing all he could in the line of his business in "aiding and abetting the rebellion." He manufactured a particularly high grade of harness leather. From first to last, the Confederacy did not have sufficient leather to equip her cavalry. Many of her cavalrymen not only furnished their own bridles and saddles, but horses also. The following order is of interest in this connection:

Headquarters Camp of Instruction,
Richmond, Va., June 27th, 1864
(Extract) Special Orders, No. 149

XIX The following conscript from Rockingham Co Va is hereby detailed until 1st January 1865 as a Tanner at the expiration of which time, unless this detail shall be renewed, he will report at this camp, or be considered a deserter:

Wm. S. Downs, By order Maj. T.G. Peyton,
L.O. Peters Lieut. and Adj't.

In the latter part of 1864 the tanyard property was burned by the Yankees. This put Downs out of the business temporarily.

There is a tradition, as told by Mrs. Laura V. Lamb, that on Saturday, June 7, 1862, an advance cavalryman of Shield's army came into Port Republic and stopped at the "Longhouse" where Mr. Downs lived. Mr. Downs came out into the street and became engaged in a conversation with the Yankee. There was the space of a few feet between them. Harry Maupin, a Confederate soldier and a brother of Mrs. Lamb, came around the corner at the southwestern end of Main Street and shot at the Yankee. The bullet whistled by in the narrow space between the two.

When Gen. David Hunter made his raid through the Shenandoah Valley, he passed through Port Republic on his way to Lynchburg. As his army neared the town, one of his officers rode up onto the bluff on the north bank of North River to reconnoiter. While thus exposed, someone in the town, a Confederate soldier some assert, fired at him and either killed or wounded him. An investigation was instituted and someone told Hunter that Mr. Downs possessed a long range rifle. The rifle was so well hidden that it was not found but Mr. Downs was arrested and carried off with the enemy army. He was court-martialed and sentenced to hang. A walnut tree on the farm of William Craig Patterson beyond the Pennsylvania Ford was selected to hang him on. When John F. Lewis heard of this untoward occurrence, he put his son Sheffley on a horse with a message to Hunter in which he exculpated Mr. Downs. Instead of releasing him, Hunter sent him to a military prison.

Years later when he was making an effort to have the United States allow him claims for damage done to his property by her armies, Mr. Lewis again came to his rescue as what follows will show:

United States Senate Chamber,
Washington, May 15,th, 1874.
Major Downs
Mr. dear Sir

"I received your letter & called upon the Commissioners of Southern Claims & they say they can not allow your claim because the evidence proves that you were not loyal at the beginning of the war. I told them that you had always told me that you were a Union man. They seem determined not to pay any one that they can get an excuse for refusing.

Yours truly
John F. Lewis

The Civil War over and the sword having decided that the South had no rights the North was bound to respect, Mr. Downs settled down to the serious business of restoring his property and making a living. He became overmuch engaged in litigation as will appear in another place.

An account, sworn to as just and true on Oct. 16, 1869, shows that Mr. Downs was a Justice of the Peace at the time. On May 17, 1870 Mr. Downs issued a handbill announcing himself as an independent candidate for the office of magistrate in Stonewall Township at the election to be held the 26 inst.

A bill from the *Alexandria Gazette* shows that he was a subscriber for that newspaper before the war. He was a subscriber for the *American Union*, of Harrisonburg after the war.

William S. Downs and his twin brother James B. Downs were born Jan. 13, 1822 in Middleburg, Loudon County. Ellen Downs, mother of the above, was born Jan. 21, 1797. The name of the father is forgotten. He was a drinking man, which so angered his family, that his name was not written in the family Bible record.

William S. Downs and Mary Ann Sigler were married by a Rev. Houck, Jan. 9, 1858. Mary Ann Sigler had been born Feb. 9, 1825. The children of this union were:

De Witt Clinton was born Nov. 10, 1858
Henrietta Margaret Feb. 15, 1861
William Stonewall Jackson Dec. 11, 1864
Virginia Elizabeth Oct. 7, 1866
Sagourney Catharine April 17, 1870
William S. J. Downs and Annie Elizabeth Sheets were married
Jan. 17, 1899.
Annie Sheets was born Oct. 1, 1866. Issues:
Isaac William Russell was born May 6, 1900
Robert Clinton July 31, 1903
James Edward Jackson July 6, 1905
I. W. Russell Downs married Margaret Dickerson June 6, 1928.
Issue: Carolyn June, born Feb. 16, 192__.

William S. Downs and his wife were members of the
Methodist Episcopal Church at Port Republic. Mr. Downs
fought invisible powers and after the manner of St. Paul
won the fight. He died Oct. 28, 1902, aged 80 years, 9 months
and 15 days. Mrs. Downs had preceded him by almost a
decade to the last resting place. She died Nov. 9, 1893, aged
65 years and 9 months.

Early in his business career, William S. J. Downs became entangled in the machinery of the tan shop and his
right arm was so mangled that it had to be amputated. In
later years Mr. Downs abandoned the tanyard, but is actively engaged in other business enterprises.

Robert C. Downs is a farmer and a man of affairs.

Chapter 40

Jacob Jefferson Nicholas, a Man of Many Talents

John Jacob Nicholas was the ancestor of the Nicholas family in Rockingham County. He was born in Germany Sept. 8, 1724. While yet a young man he emigrated to Pennsylvania. Like so many others in colonies adjoining the Old Dominion, he moved to Virginia and settled in Rockingham County near Peaked Mountain. He was one of the founders of Peaked Mountain church. He married Barbara Zeller who was born Feb. 27, 1733.

His son, Jacob B. Nicholas, the father of the subject of this sketch, was born Oct. 26, 1814, and died at Port Republic Aug. 10, 1897. While a young man, he was engaged in tanning business. He married Elizabeth Koiner whose father objected to the match. Mr. Koiner became so angry at the couple that family relations were severed. In the course of time he became very sick and his daughter returned home and nursed him back to health. In gratitude for her filial care, he bought the Peter Fitch farm which lies on the right bank of North River about a mile upstream from Port Republic, and made her a present of it.

Their children were:

	born	died
Silas C.K.	Sept. 2, 1841	March 15, 1865
George M.	Mar. 1, 1843	Aug. 15, 1912
Jacob Jefferson	Aug. 13, 1847	Feb. 20, 1927
John A.	Feb. 10, 1850	July 26, 1881

Charles	Oct. 10, 1853	William S.
Dec. 16, 1861	Sept. 26, 1932	
Franklin L.	Oct. 9, 1859	

Jacob Jefferson Nicholas was born on the Shenandoah River near East Point and not far from the old homestead of John J. Nicholas, his grandfather, who may have been a son of the immigrant. When he was seven years old his father moved to the newly acquired Fitch farm.

Of a strong robust nature, farm work seemed to agree with him. At the early age of seventeen, he quit the farm and went to the aid of his country in the last year of the Civil War. After Lee's surrender, he returned home and by industry and economy, helped to repair the damage done by the war and to coax prosperity to return to his war-stricken country.

His two elder brothers, Silas C.K. and George M. were also in the Confederate service. They were in Capt. C.M. Kemper's cavalry company. Captain Kemper was at home for

The house of Jacob Jefferson Nicholas near Scott's Ford

a few days in the latter part of March 1865 and penciled the following note, with its heart-breaking news, to their father:

March 30, 1865
Mr. Nicholas,
    Sir,— I am sorry to inform you of the death of George and Silas. George died at Beverly and Silas was killed on the 15th at Ashland. I will stay at grandpa Kemper's to night. I would come up but I am very much fatigued. I send you a notebook, the only thing that was saved. The Yankees got his watch and portmanteau. Yours, resp., C.M. Kemper

The facts were not as bad as the note indicates. George had been shot in the leg and the blood filling his cavalry boot froze and the leg was amputated. Silas was, indeed, dead and buried. Abraham Scott Hooke, a member of the company, carried a pine box three miles on his horse in which to bury him. Later on he was exhumed and brought home and now sleeps in Port Republic Cemetery.

On May 30, 1872, at Lacey Spring, J. Jefferson Nicholas married Mary Lee Lincoln, daughter of Jacob and Caroline Homan Lincoln. She was a distant relative of the martyred president Abraham Lincoln. The following year, J. Jefferson bought the old Dundore estate at Port Republic of John W. Palmer and built a large dwelling house thereon which, from its situation, was appropriately named "Belle View."

Six children were born of this union:

Bessiel L., who married Dr. Stuart L. Yancey, now living in Gainesville, Fla.
Carrie T., who now owns the homestead
Jacob B., killed in early youth by a stroke of lightning
John H., deceased, was a farmer and flour mill proprietor.
Grover C., farmer and now mechanical engineer and builder in Washington, D.C.
Edna V., deceased

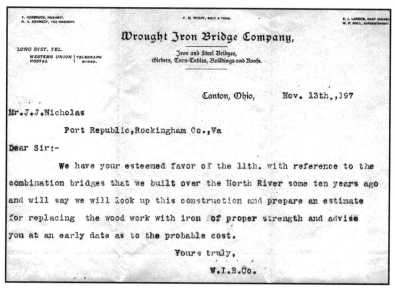

Response of Wrought Iron Bridge Co. to an inquiry from J.J. Nicholas, 1897.

Jacob Jefferson was an industrious man and made a success of farming. Of an enterprising nature, he bought the water power property on South River of J.T.L. Preston in 1889, erected an entirely new mill building and installed a modern flour mill.

This venture proving a success, he built two more flour mills, one at Mossy Creek and the other at Harriston, both in Augusta County. The latter was known as the Nicholas Milling Company, his son, John H. Nicholas, being the junior member.

He was an outstanding man of the neighborhood and took an active interest in all things conducive to the advancement and good of the town. Of excellent judgment and unquestioned integrity, he was invariably consulted about roads, bridges, schoolhouses, and other undertakings of a public nature.

Jacob Jefferson was a member of the Confederate Veterans. Not long before his death he assisted the committee in charge of erecting suitable markers at historic places, to locate one on the battlefield of Port Republic.

He was a good honest man. To those whom he liked, he gave, in a quiet way, sound advice and extended many favors. Being a normal man, he loved his friend and hated his enemies. He was of a charitable nature and was among the first to help the deserving needy.

Mr. Nicholas was a member of the Mt. Horeb Presbyterian Church and sleeps in the beautiful cemetery of the same. His passing was mourned by all who knew him.

Mrs. Nicholas was a woman of fine character, kind and charitable. She lived a cheerful and contented life, visiting the sick and condoling with the sorrowful. She did not withhold a giving hand to the necessitous. She passed beyond our ken Sept. 26, 1934, and was buried by the side of her husband two days later.

Several years ago she told the writer what she thought was the cause of death when she was but a child. The death of not one from old age or disease had come to her notice while the Civil War was going on, and she thought the war only was responsible for the death of the people. Shortly after it was over, a friend stopped in at her home and announced the death of an old gentleman of the neighborhood. Child that she was, she asked, "How could he die? The war is over."

Samuel Godfrey Spitzer, Cabinetmaker

T he father of Samuel Godfrey Spitzer came from Germany and settled in the New Market neighborhood.
It was here that the subject of this notice was born
Sept. 22, 1817. While a young man he came to Port Republic and worked at the cabinetmaker's trade with Isaac J.
Grove. Mrs. Grove's maiden name was Pirkey.[1] When Mrs.
Grove came to die, the weakening of her body did not en-
feeble her mind. She died as she had lived—a good woman
without fear of fire and flame in the future.

Samuel Godfrey Spitzer married first, Martha Fitch.
There were four children of this marriage; Arthur, Elizabeth, Lucretia, and Charles. All these went West and did
well. He married second, Margaret Hulvey, May 9, 1854.
She was a half sister of Prof. George W. Hulvey, Superintendent of Rockingham County Schools. Papers are at hand
that show a constable by the name of George W. Hulvey
performed duties connected with that office in this neighborhood in 1848-1850.

Mr. Spitzer bought house and lot No. 44 of John W.
Palmer in 1858. This was a very desirable property and remained in the possession of the family for near three-quarters of a century. It is now owned by Samuel L. Randall.

Of this second marriage there were six children,
namely: Mary Catherine, Millie Caroline, Annie Belle,
Emma Jane who married Robert Bruffy, Nannie Wheat and
George William.

Mr. Spitzer died March 10, 1879. Mrs. Spitzer, who was born May 4, 1838, died May 26, 1916.

George W. Spitzer was born Jan. 4, 1875. He married Julia Virginia Mace. Their children were: Roy William, born July 2, 1914; Margaret Anna, born July 9, 1916; Harry Mace, born Sept. 2, 1918; Carrie Belle, born April 16, 1920; John Samuel, born Sept. 28, 1922; Charles Arthur, born Sept. 4, 1924, and Phyllis Virginia, born April 7, 1936.

A private by the name of Spitzer was in the Confederate Army at the battle of Port Republic. A Yankee officer was at an upstairs window in the Lewis house directing the artillery fire of the Yankees by signals. The Captain of the company of which Spitzer was a member saw him. The Captain ordered him to shoot the officer. Spitzer fired at him and the officer disappeared from the window and was seen no more.

Chapter Forty-one Endnotes

[1]The following words were crossed out in one of May's manuscripts, yet are included in the other two. The reason why and, indeed, the person who deleted them are unknown. They are included here for the reader's perusal: "She was an Infidel. This opprobrious name coined by the Mohammedans and applied by them to disbelievers in Islamism was early adopted by the Christians and used by them to designate all those of independent minds."

Chapter 42

Harrison Bateman, Fifty Years a Boatman

H arrison Bateman was born near Mt. Sidney, Augusta County, June 30, 1812. In 1814 his parents, William and Elizabeth (Allen) Bateman, made their home in Rockingham County for the remainder of their lives. They were born in this county, the father in 1789, and the mother April 1, 1792. William Bateman died Jan. 22, 1855. He was a soldier of the American Army in the War of 1812.

Elizabeth Bateman was a descendant of an old family of the Shenandoah Valley. In 1734 Benjamin Allen, Riley Moore, and William White moved from Monocacy, Md., and built their cabins on the banks of the North branch of the Shenandoah River, about twelve miles south of the present site of Woodstock. The Allen family became numerous and some of them moved to Rockingham County. Mrs. Bateman died March 5, 1879, surviving her husband by nearly a quarter of a century.

Harrison Bateman was twice married. His first wife was Martha Ann, daughter of Adam, Jr., and Nancy May. She was born April 3, 1822. They were married Jan. 5, 1845. She died May 4, 1863. The children of this marriage were:

	born	died
Nancy E.	June 14, 1847	June 13, 1859
Infant son	April 1, 1849	1850
William H.	Oct. 25, 1845	Nov. 6, 1882
James E.	Sept. 25, 1851	Nov. 6, 1915
Martha A.	June 6, 1855	Feb. 15, 1927

His second wife was Rebecca Jane Hooke whom he married April 21, 1867, Rev. Isaac Long the officiating minister. She was born Oct. 1, 1832, and died Dec. 4, 1913.

William H. Bateman was a farmer and tax collector in Stonewall District. On Oct.29, 1868, he solemnized his marriage with Annie Etta Moore. She was born Jan. 1, 1847 and died Sept. 15, 1895. The children of this union were:

	born	died
Elmo Allen	July 16, 1869	
Nannie M.	Sept. 15, 1871	
Percy H.	Jan. 3, 1874	Nov. 22, 1896
Harry Leon	Aug. 3, 1879	

Harrison's oldest son, James E. Bateman, acquired the old William Harper Mill property and operated a sawmill and corn mill for a number of years. Coming into possession of one of the finest wheat-growing farms in this section, he devoted the remainder of his life to farming. He married Elizabeth Jane Patterson who was born March 10, 1855, and died Dec. 13, 1897. Their children were:

	born	died
Edward Ernest	Aug. 24, 1875	
Elber Lloyd	May 22, 1878	Sept. 12 1899
Mary Elizabeth	Sept. 10, 1880	
Martha Elsie	April 23, 1885	March 11, 1908

Harrison Bateman spent fifty years boating on the Shenandoah River, during which time he saved enough of his hard worked earnings to buy two farms lying at the head of the river whose bosom had witnessed so many of his former activities. He was a farmer and stock-raiser in the latter years of his life.

By an Act of Assembly the town of New Haven was established on the land of William Lewis and Gideon Morgan. The latter became embroiled in a difficulty with a man

Workers in front of H.B. Alexander's Cannery (once the Harrison Bateman barn)

at a large rock opposite Goose Lane where it enters the Port Republic-Harrisonburg Road, and unfortunately, killed him. Mr. Morgan immediately left for the West and was never after heard of. In due time his real estate was advertised for taxes and Mr. Bateman bought it to round out one of his farms.

On Sunday morning, June 9, 1862, two wagons were loaded with very dry hay from Mr. Batemen's barn, drawn onto North River Bridge and set on fire in order to burn the bridge after the last of the Confederates had crossed it into Port Republic.

The day after the Battle of Port Republic, General Fremont and General Milroy rode to Port Republic to decide on the feasibility of building a bridge across the river. Meeting Mr. Bateman in the road, General Fremont asked him where Jackson had gone. Mr. Bateman answered that he did not know. "You're a liar" rejoined General Fremont. Mr. Bateman retorted, "God knows whether I lie or not, sir." General Fremont, leaning towards him, pulled his whiskers and said, "You are an old gray-headed philosopher."

Mr. Bateman died Aug. 23, 1889, respected by all who knew him. He was buried in Riverside Graveyard.

Chapter 43

Thomas Madden, Wheelwright

Thomas Madden was born in Denbigh, Ireland, July 10, 1850. The family came to America in 1854 and settled at Lynchburg. Mr. Madden learned the wagon-making trade and worked at it for several years in that town. He came to Port Republic in 1873 and bought the Sigler property in 1880, building thereon, an up-to-date wagon making shop. His wagons were so satisfactory that the fame of them spread to nearby counties. Men came from considerable distances to place their orders for wagons with him.

He married Jan. 6, 1876, Sarah Frances Lee, daughter of Luncefield Lee. She was born Oct. 15, 1847. They had two children, Edward Kenton, born Sept. 18, 1881, and Virginia who was born June 2, 1885.

Mr. Madden was an honest and good man. He had an inexhaustible fund of good humor and was at all times an agreeable person. He was a great reader and the subjects that interested him, ranged wide. He was an authority on the history of Ireland and many interested in that subject were indebted to him. He died Nov. 12, 1928, lamented by all who knew him. Mrs. Madden's death had preceded his by twenty-six years, June 7, 1902.

Luncefield Lee, father-in-law of the subject of this sketch, was born August 1819. He married Mary Elizabeth Gully. She was born August 1825, and died May 12, 1868.

Mr. Lee had two brothers, LaFayette and Harvey; and

two sisters: Susan who married a Mr. Hawkins, and Jane who married a Mr. Yancey.

One of his sons, Warfield Lee, belonged to the River Rangers, a troop of Cavalry from East Rockingham, captained by Charles Marcellus Kemper, oldest child of Benjamin F. Kemper and his wife, Eliza Holbrook. It was this Warfield Lee who disseminated the myth that Gen. Robert E. Lee was born after the death of his mother.

1810 Census of Port Republic.

	Males Years of age					Females Years of age					Persons not taxed	Slaves
	Under 10	10-16	16-26	26-45	45 and up	Under 10	10-16	16-26	26-45	45 and up		
William Cochran	1	0	0	1	0	1	1	1	0	0	0	5
James Cochran	0	0	0	2	0	0	0	1	1	1	1	0
James Burgess	0	2	2	1	0	2	2	0	0	0	0	0
John Dundore	1	0	0	1	0	2	0	1	0	0	0	0
John Smith	1	0	1	2	0	1	0	1	1	0	0	2
Samuel Harby (Harris)	-	0	0	1	0	2	0	2	0	0	0	0
Reuban Scantling	0	2	1	0	1	0	0	1	1	0	0	0
Holland Ferguson	1	0	0	1	0	2	0	0	2	2	0	3
Alexander Satson	1	0	0	1	1	3	3	2	1	0	0	0
Josiah Emmet	0	1	1	0	1	1	0	1	0	0	0	0
Samuel Tingley	1	0	0	0	1	1	2	1	0	1	0	0
William Douglass	3	0	0	1	0	1	0	0	1	0	1	1
Edward Day	0	0	1	0	0	0	0	1	0	0	0	0
John Clarke	1	2	1	1	0	1	0	0	0	1	0	0
Joseph Graham	1	1	0	1	0	4	2	0	1	0	0	6

	Males Years of age					Females Years of age					Persons not taxed	Slaves
	Under 10	10-16	16-26	26-45	45 and up	Under 10	10-16	16-26	26-45	45 and up		
Margaret Boyer	0	0	0	0	0	0	0	0	0	1	0	2
John Carthrea	1	2	1	1	1	2	1	0	1	0	0	9
George Wolfe	3	0	0	1	0	0	1	0	1	0	0	0

(1810 Census of Rockingham County, Virginia, Geneaology Room, Rockingham County Library.)

1860 Census of Port Republic.

(From the eighth Rockingham County census records, 1860: families known to be involved with Port Republic. It includes heads of households and those others with occupations listed.)

Breeden, Allison	63	Blacksmith		
Powell, Alfred	26	Shoemaker		
Randall, Richard	22	Miller		
Johnson, Martin	40B	Farm laborer (black)		
Mary	35			
Benjamin	16			
Virginia	14			
William	12			
John	10			
Henry	7			
Mary	95			
Bateman, Harrison		Farmer	7,000	
Lee, John	40	Tailor	800	
Rose, Same L.	62	Tailor	1,500	
Jones, W.A.	25	Painter		
McNutt, Catherine	40	Weaving		
Mary	35	Weaving		
Martha Randall	18	Weaving		
Eliza Moore	17	Weaving		
Groves, Isaac	45	Cabinetmaker		
Jackson, Willis	60	Shoemaker		
Palmer, John	32	Farmer	10,300	4,500
Bateman, Jonathan	59	Chairmaker	1,411	100
Dundore, John	77	Farmer	7,700	20,500
Eddings	45M	Farm laborer (black)		
Brown, Thomas	33	Saddler	250	200
Spitzer, Samuel	42	Cabinetmaker	500	100
Crawford, John	65	Farm laborer		75
Crawford, John	26	Farm laborer		75
Huffman, Mary	25			
Maupin, William A.	45	Blacksmith	600	250

Son		Blacksmith		
Son		Blacksmith apprentice		
William Brown		Blacksmith apprentice		
Harris, Briscoe	32	Miller		40
Harper, John	48	Farmer	10,000	4,000
Eddings, Mornen	54F		1,000	1,000
Hiram	25	Tinner		250
Downs, William S.	38	Farmer		
Burkhead, William	45	Farmer		
Lewis, Charles		Constable	650	650
James		Tailor		
Smith, Bluford	35	M.E. Clergyman		400
Palmer, Robert	56	Merchant	4,000	7,000
Henry	16	Merchant clerk		
Smith, Robert	44	M.E. Clergyman		250
Kemper, George W.	45	Physician	5,500	10,800
William		Merchant clerk		
George		U.Va. student		
Eutsler, George	47	Cabinetmaker	4,000	250
Grady, William	38	Shoemaker	300	50
Edwards, Thomas	40	Miller		100
Larkins, James H.	27	Manufacturer of Woolen goods	1,200	
Kemper, Benjamin	48	Farmer	10,000	4,000
Charles	22	Constable		
May, Adam	62	Toll-gate keeper	100	
Benjamin	26	Boatman		
James H.	17	Boatmaker		
Bateman, William	31	Blacksmith	150	100
Madden, William	38	Cooper		100
John Thomas	28	Cooper		
Ryan, Thomas	46	Shoemaker	400	200
Joseph	20	Printer		
Jefferson	17	Merchant clerk		
Good, Annias	52	Farmer	12,000	3,500

Has 3 black women listed: Mary, 21, Susan, 2, Lydia, 2 mos.

Another black family: Johnson, Franklin, with 12 members of his household; listed as a farm laborer, along with two other men, Daniel Williams, age 22, and Mark Alexander, age 26

Old Bibles

A German Bible that belonged to Christopher Mohr was published in Germany in 1717. He married a Miss Wagner in Germany and when they came to this country, they brought it with them. Mrs. Taylor Wagner of this town, is a great granddaughter of Mr. Mohr and now owns the book.

The writer has in his possession several Bibles, the oldest of which are:

A Bible published in 1812 containing the names and births, fourteen in number, of a family by the name of Snow. The dates of the birth of the first two are lacking but the date of the third, Jean Snow, is Dec. 14, 1780, and the last, Ruth Jane Snow, is Aug. 27, 1806. Below these are the names and births of six colored people. A family named Snow lived in the neighborhood of Port Republic in those early days.

On another page in this Bible is found the name of John H. Austin, son of Ely H. and Harriet Austin, who was born March 27, 1843, and died of a wound received in a battle in Albemarle County, Sept. 5, 1862. Following the above is John F. Wood, born March 4, 1842, and fell in battle at Allegheny Mountain Dec. 13, 1861; and James N. Wood, who was born Sept. 30, 1844. Austin and Wood are old family names in our neighborhood.

Reuben May's Bible, published in 1829. "Reuben May, his bible, his hand and pen, January 26, 1832," is written on a flyleaf. There is no family record in this Bible, but there are two other names written in it, Francis May, and Erasmus May, December 2, 1844. Reuben and Francis used black ink,

Erasmus used blue ink. The last gives the date when he wrote his name. All are in different handwriting.

A German Bible published in Germany in 1833 given to the writer by his mother. "Wehn" is written on a flyleaf with a pencil.

A Bible published in 1837 in which are written the names and births of the children of Jefferson Randall.

Bibliography

Abbot, John C. *The History of the Civil War in America: Comprising a Full and Impartial Account of the Origin and Progress of the Rebellion, of the Various Naval and Military Engagements, of the Heroic Deeds Performed by Armies and individuals, and of Touching Scenes in the Field, the Camp, the Hospital and the Cabin.* Vol. 1 and 2. Springfield, Mass.: Gurdon Bill. 1863 and 1866.

Allan, William. *Stonewall Jackson's Campaign in the Shenandoah Valley of Virginia.* The Pall Mall Military Series. London: Hugh Rees, Ltd. 1912.

Andrews, E. Benjamin. *History of the United States.* 6 vols. New York: Charles Scribner's Sons. 1917.

Andrews, J.N. *History of the Sabbath and First Day of the Week.* Battle Creek, Mich.: Seventh Day Adventist Publishing Association. 1873.

Armstrong, James Edward. *History of the Old Baltimore Conference.* Baltimore: King Bros. 1907.

Asbury, Francis. *Journal of Rev. Francis Asbury, Bishop of the Methodist Episcopal Church.* 3 vols. New York: Lane & Scott. 1852.

Bancroft, George. *History of the United States of America.* 6 vols. New York: D. Appleton and Company. 1885.

Bennett, W. W. *Memorials of Methodism in Virginia.* Richmond, Va.: W. W. Bennett. 1871.

Book of Mormon, The. Fifth Independence ed. Independence, Mo.: Press of Zion's Printing and Publishing Co. n.d.

Bruce, Philip Alexander. *History of Virginia.* 6 vols. Chicago and New York: The American Historical Society. 1898.

Buckley, James M. *History of Methodism in the United States.* 2 vols. New York: Harper & Brothers. 1898.

Chalkley, Lyman. *Chronicles of the Scotch-Irish Settlement in Virginia extracted from the original court records of Augusta County, 1745-1800,* 3 vols. Rosslyn, Va.: Commonwealth Printers. 1912. Reprinted Baltimore, Md.: Genealogical Publishing Co., Inc. 1999.

Chandler, J.A C. and T.B. Thames. "Colonial Virginia." *Richmond Times Dispatch*. 1907.

Cooke, John Esten. *Virginia: A History of the People*. American Commonwealths. Boston: Houghton, Mifflin and Company. 1890.

_____. *Stonewall Jackson: a Military Biography*. New York: D. Appleton and Company. 1876.

_____. *Surry of Eagle's Nest or the Memoirs of a Staff-Officer Serving in Virginia*. Chicago: Donahue & Company. n.d.

Crafts, W. A. *The Southern Rebellion: Being a History of the United States from the commencement of President Buchanan's Administration through the War for the Suppression of the Rebellion. Containing a Record of Political Events, Military Movements, Campaigns, Expeditions, Battles, Skirmishes, etc.* 2 vols. Boston: Samuel Walker & Co. 1865. 1867.

Dabney, R. L. *Life and Campaigns of Lieut.-Gen. Thomas J. Jackson*. New York: Blelock & Co. 1866.

Duyckinck, Evert. A. *National History of the Late Civil War, Civil Military and Naval*. 3 vols. New York: Johnson & Miller. n.d.

Ex-Cadet, An. *The Life of Lieut. Gen. T. J. Jackson*. Richmond, Va.: James E. Goode. 1863.

Foote, William Henry, D. D. *Sketches of Virginia, Historical and Biographical*. Philadelphia, Pa.: J. B. Lippencott & Co. 1856.

Ffirth, John. *The Gospels and Labours of the Rev. Benjamin Abbott*. Harrisonburg, Va.: printed by A. Davisson for James Dillworth. 1820.

Funk, Benjamin. *The Life and Labors of Elder John Kline*. Elgin, Ill.: Brethren Publishing House. 1900.

Gordon, John B. *Reminiscences of the Civil War*. New York: Charles Scribner's Sons. 1905.

Grant, U. S. *Personal Memoirs*. 2 vols. New York: Charles Webster & Company. 1886.

Greeley, Horace. *The American Conflict*. 2 vols. Hartford: O. D. Case & Company. 1864. 1865.

Hardesty, H.H. *Historical and Geographical Encyclopedia.* Special Virginia edition, Rockingham County supplement. New York: H.H. Hardesty & Co. Publishers. 1884.

Harper's Encyclopedia of United States History. 10 vols. New York: Harper & Brothers. 1906.

Henderson, G.F.R. *Stonewall Jackson and the American Civil War.* 2 vols. London: Longmans, Green, & Co. 1906.

Howe, Henry. *Historical Collections of Virginia.* Charleston, South Carolina: Babcock and Co. 1845.

Hutchinson, William T. *Cyrus Hall McCormick.* New York: The Century Company. 1930.

Johnson, Robert Underwood and Clarence Clough Buel, editors. *Battles and Leaders of the Civil War.* 14 vols. New York: The Century Company. 1887.

Johnston, Mary. *The Long Roll.* New York: Houghton Mifflin Company. 1911.

Kemper, W.M. and H.L Wright. *Genealogy of the Kemper Family in the United States.* Chicago: G. K. Hazlitt & Co. 1899.

Kercheval, Samuel. *History of the Valley of Virginia.* 3rd edition. Woodstock, Va.: J.H. Graybill. 1902.

Lee, Susan Pendleton. *A Brief History of the United States.* Richmond, Va.: B.F. Johnson Publishing Co. 1896.

Lewis A.H. *Biblical Teaching Concerning the Sabbath and the Sunday.* Alfred Centre, N.Y.: American Sabbath Tract Society. 1888.

Magill, Mary Tucker. *History of Virginia.* New edition. Lynchburg, Va.: J.P. Bell Publishers. 1890.

Martin, Joseph. *Gazetteer and History of Virginia.* Charlottesville, Va.: Mosely & Tompkins. 1835.

Mauzy, Richard. *Mauzy and Kisling Families.* Harrisonburg, Va. 1911.

McDonald, William N. *A History of the Laurel Brigade.* Baltimore: Sun Job Printing Office. 1907.

McIlhany, H.M. Jr. *Some Virginia Families*. Staunton, Va.: Stoneburner & Prufer. 1903.

Morse, Jedidiah. *An Abridgement of the American Universal Geography*. Boston: Thomas & Andrews. 1811.

Official Records of the Union and Confederate Armies. Washington, D.C.: Government Printing Office.

O'Ferrall, Charles T. *Forty Years of Active Service*. New York: The Neale Publishing Company. 1904.

Olmsted, Frederick Law. *A Journey in the Seaboard Slave States*. 2 vols. New York: G.P. Putnam's Sons. 1904.

Parkman, Francis. *The Conspiracy of Pontiac*. 2 vols. Boston: Little, Brown, and Company. 1880.

Peterson, Charles J. *The Military Heroes of the War with Mexico: With a Narrative of the War*. Philadelphia: William A. Deary. 1848.

Peyton, J. Lewis. *History of Augusta County, Virginia*. Staunton, Va.: Samuel M. Yost & Son. 1882.

Pollard, Edward A. *Lee and his Lieutenants*. New York: E.B. Treat & Co. 1867.

_____. *The Lost Cause*. New and enlarged edition. New York: E.B. Treat & Co. 1868.

Pond, George E. *The Shenandoah Valley in 1864: Campaigns of the Civil War*. New York: Charles Scribner's Sons. 1883.

Remsburg, John E. *The Bible*. New York: The Truthseeker Company. n.d.

Ridpath, John Clark. *A Popular History of the United States of America*. New York: Nelson & Phillips, New York. 1887.

Rives, William C. *History of the Life and Times of James Madison*. Boston: Little Brown and Company. 1866.

Rockingham County, Va. Death Register.

Rockingham County, Va. Deed Books.

Rockingham County, Va. Judgments and Orders.

Rockingham County, Va. United States Census. 1810, 1860.

Roosevelt, Theodore. *The Winning of the West*. 4 vols. Presidential Edition. New York: G. P. Putnam's Sons. 1889.

Sams, Conway Whittle. *The Conquest of Virginia*. New York: G. P Putnam's Sons. 1916.

Schools of Rockingham County, Virginia. pamphlet. Circa 1914.

Sheridan, P. H. *Personal Memoirs*. 2 vols. New York: Charles L. Webster & Company. 1888.

Smith, Uriah. *The Biblical Institute*. Oakland, Ca. 1878.

_____. *Synopsis of the Present Truth*. Battle Creek, Mich.: Seventh Day Adventist Publishing Association. 1884.

Smucker, Samuel M. *Among the Mormons*. New York: Hurst & Company, Publishers. n.d.

_____. *The History of the Civil War in the United States. Its Cause, Origin, Progress, and Conclusion. Containing Full, Impartial, and Graphic Descriptions of the Various Military and Naval Engagements, with the Heroic Deeds Achieved by Armies and Individuals, Touching Scenes and Incidents in the Camp, the Cabin, the Field and the Hospital. And Biographical Sketches of its Heroes*. Revised and completed by Dr. L.P. Brocket. Philadelphia: Jones Brothers &. Co.; Chicago: Zeigler, McCurdy & Co. 1865.

Strickler, Harry M. *Massanutten*. Luray, Va. 1924.

_____. *Tenth Legion Tithables*. Luray, Va. 1930.

Taylor, Richard. *Destruction and Reconstruction: Personal Experiences of the Late War*. New York: D. Appleton and company. 1879.

Thatcher, B. B. *Indian Biography*. 2 vols. Chicago: Elliott-Madison Company. 1916.

Thompson, Robert Ellis. *A History of the Presbyterian Churches in the United States*. The American Church History Series. New York: The Christian Literature Company. 1895.

Waddell, Joseph A. *Annals of Augusta County, Virginia.* 2nd edition. Staunton, Va.: C. Russell Caldwell. 1902.

Wayland, John Walter. *The German Element of the Shenandoah Valley of Virginia.* Charlottesville, Va.: The Michie Company, Printers. 1907.

_____. *A History of Rockingham County, Virginia.* Dayton, Va.: Ruebush-Elkins Company. 1912.

_____. *Virginia Valley Records.* Strasburg, Va.: Shenandoah Publishing House, Inc. 1930.

Whitehead, Paul. "A Lucky Mistake and Two Narrow Escapes." *Quarterly Review of the Methodist Episcopal Church, South.* Jan.1892

Wilson, Woodrow. *A History of the American People.* 5 vols. New York: Harper & Brothers, Publishers. 1906.

Withers, Alexander Scott. *Chronicles of Border Warfare or A History of the Settlement of Whites, of Northwestern Virginia, and the Indian Wars and Massacres in that section of the State, with Reflections, Anecdotes.* New edition. Reuben Gold Thwaites, ed. Cincinnati: Steward & Kidd Company. 1920.

Daybooks, Account Books, and Ledgers.
Burgess, James. Account Book, 1802-1814

Downs, William S. Account Book. 1855-1862.

_____. Daybook, 1863-1864.

_____. Daybook, 1864-1865.

_____. Account Book, 1858-1863.

_____. Account Book, 1863-1869.

_____. Ledger, 1869-1894.

Downs, William S. and Jacob S. Piper. Account Book. 1855-1857.

Dundore, John. Daybook, 1849-1857.

Graham, Joseph. Account book, 1821-1826.

Harnsberger, Stephen. Account Book, 1830-1839.

_____. Account Book, 1845-1846.

Kemper, B.F. and G.W. Daybook, 1854.

Kemper, Dr. G.W. Account Book, 1841-1872.

Palmer, Robert W. Ledger, 1845.

Palmer, John W. Ledger, 1861.

Piper, Jacob S. and James H. Eddins. Account Book, 1853-1855.

Trout, Joseph. Daybook, 1818-1833.

Class books. Methodist Episcopal Church, Port Republic. 1812-1813, 1833-1840.

Trustees Minutebook. Methodist Meetinghouse, Port Republic. 1833-1846.

Miscellaneous Account Books with no known owners.

Newspapers
Baltimore Southern Methodist. Baltimore, Md., 11 April 1929. add

Daily News-Record. Harrisonburg, Va. 12 Dec. 1929; 18 Dec. 1929; 2 June 1931; 3 July 1931; 9 July 1931; 17 Dec. 1931; 12 Jan. 1932; 13 Jan. 1932; 21 Jan. 1932; 25 July 1932; 30 Aug. 1932; 24 March 1934.

Richmond Times Dispatch. Richmond, Va., 19 Oct. 1902; 30 Aug. 1903.

Rockingham Register. Harrisonburg, Va., 26 June 1857; 14 May 1858.

The Independent. Port Republic, Va., 17 April 1886.

The Sun. Baltimore, Md., 24 July 1932.

Waynesboro News-Virginian. Waynesboro, Va., 31 Jan. 1930; 2 April 1930; 5 April 1930; 14 April 1930; 12 Feb. 1931; 21 Feb. 1931.

Oral histories and written statements
Eva Patterson Baker; John W. Burford, 25 Apr. 1914; William S. Downs; John I. Harnsberger; M.C. Harnsberger; Wilson C. Harper, Feb. 1932; C.C. Hooke, 28 Dec. 1931; A.C. Kemper; John I. Kemper; Laura V. Lamb, 23 Dec. 1931; John K. Mace, 15 Feb. 1930; James A. Maupin, 20 Dec. 1929; Mary Lee Lincoln Nicholas; John B. Peale; C.F. Saufley, 21 Dec. 1931; John Wagner; N.L. Wagner, 19 Dec. 1931.

Letters
John M. Kemper, Pearsall, Tx. 2 Feb. 1931; Sue B. Craig, Warrenton, Va. 28 Jan. 1932; G. Mauzy. Richmond, Va. 20 May 1863; Richmond, Va. 20 May 1863; To C.H. McCormick from John H. Holbrook, Glenora Va. 10 June 1884; To P.C. Kaylor from Herbert A. Kellar, 9 Oct. 1934; To George May from W.A. Moon, Waynesboro, Va. 25 Oct. 1939; To D.H. Pannill from R.L. Dabney, Austin, Tx. 14 Jan. 1891; to George May from David Funkhouser 4 Apr. 1930.

Miscellaneous papers. Society of Port Republic Preservationists. All letters and written statements, or copies thereof, are now in the possession of the Society of Port Republic Preservationists.

Index

Poague, Capt. William T. 131, 132, 145
Poague's Battery 131
Poindexter, St. Clair 183
Politics 163, 239; appointments 7, 13; elections 187; polling places 162–163; positions 186, 193, 195, 197, 210, 235, 240, 258
Polk, James K. 114
Pollard, Joseph L. 165
Port Republic, Battle of 15, 120, 133, 141-150, 207, 266, 269
Port Republic Cemetery 262
Port Republic Church 225
Port Republic Electric Light Co. 60
Port Republic Elementary School 168
Port Republic Foundry 58
Port Republic Graded and High School 166, 167
Port Republic Methodist Church 234
Port Republic Milling Co. 58, 59
Port Republic Mutual Cemetery Co. 108, 110
Port Republic Total Abstinence Society 171
Post Office 159–161, 235
Powell, Benjamin 119
Preston, J.T.L. 58, 263
Price, Henry 40
Price, Mary A. (Mrs. William A. Maupin) 242
Protzman, Daniel 30, 31, 56, 76
Protzman, Mary (Mrs. Daniel) 56, 76
Public Offices 33, 60, 72
Pullin, C.M. 91
Purce, William 5
Purcell's Store 162
Purdham, Elder Benjamin F. 96

Q

Quinn 173

R

Railroads 188
Raines brothers 154
Raines, Henry 119, 157, 224
Raines, Jacob 119
Raines, Jake 154
Raines, James 14, 224
Raines, Lawrence 207
Raines, Nancy (Mrs. Adam May, Jr.) 109, 207
Raines, Noah 119
Raines, Reuben 119, 224
Raines, Robert 112
Raines, Zachariah 40, 46, 119, 154, 186, 221–226, 252
Raines, Zuriah (Davis) 225
Randall, Jefferson 40, 207, 277
Randall, Joseph 40
Randall, Samuel L. 265
Randol, Daniel 165
Randol, Elija 171, 241
Randol, Joseph 252
Rankin, Bertha 76
Rankin, James 29, 30, 76
Rankin, Martha 164
Rankin, Richard 114
Ray, Alexander 152
Rayn, James William 219
Rayn, Llewellyn Kemper 219
Raynes, George 40
Raynes, J.G. 165
Raynes, J.G.H. 40
Raynes, Jacob 171
Raynes, Laurence 113
Reece, Euen 29, 30
Reece, George 114
Reed, Willie (Mrs. Oswald Herman May) 213
Reese, James 241
Reigns, Bennett 114
Reiley, James 92
Reiley, Tobias 92
Reins, Patrick 114
Religious Organizations 66, 195, 216, 266
Revolutionary War 52, 112, 235

Scott, Lucille 167
Scott, M. Amos 34, 110, 241
Scott, Margaret 77
Scott, Michael A. 110, 119, 227-228, 229
Scott, Michael A. Jr. 208
Scott Mill 57
Scott, Mrs. John C. 219
Scott, Mrs. Robert G. 13
Scott, N.C. 110
Scott, Reuben 171
Scott, Reuben A. 119, 182, 228
Scott, Robert 7, 14, 23, 231
Scott, William 119
Scott, William H. 227
Scott, W.L. 110
Scott, William M. 171
Scott's Ford 58, 227, 261
Seals, William 32
Semple, Mr. 10
Seven Days Battle 120
Seventh Day Adventists 96
Seventh Indiana 144
Seventh Ohio 144
Sewell, Joseph 92
Sheets, Annie Elizabeth (Mrs. William S.J. Downs) 259
Shenandoah River, 212
  beginnings of 1–6; Shenandoah River Company 60; Shenandoah Locks 224; The Point 44, 184
Shenandoah Valley Railroad 64, 212
Shendun 199
Shephard, James 40
Sheridan, Gen. Philip 215
Shields, Gen. James 6, 120, 141, 147, 178
Shields, Preston & Co. 48
Shifflette, Albert 212
Shifflette, Edith R. 175
Shifflette, Robert 118
Shiflett, McCahay 241
Shiflett, Thomas 241
Showalter, Robert 253
Showalter, Peter 241
Shreve, Sam 138

Shuler, Daniel P. 34, 110
Shuler, James E. 34
Shutler, Mary 78
Sibert, John 89
Sigler, Capt. Albert J. 118, 155, 173, 253
Sigler, Jack 153, 157
Sigler, Mary Ann (Mrs. William S. Downs) 258
Sigler property 270
Simmons, John 92
Sipe, Capt. E. 123
Sipe, Capt. Jacob 223
Sipe, Edna 103
Sipe, George 39, 118
Sipe, Henry 114
Sipe, Jacob 40
Sipe, Levi 171
Sipe, Luther 56
Sipe, Maggie 103
Sipe, Peter 40, 171
Sipe, S.H. 110
Sirkle 32
Sixth Virginia Cavalry viii, 118
Slater, Mr. 183
Slavery 117, 187, 203, 206, 244-250
Smith, Amena 75
Smith, Bluford 40, 171
Smith, Frederick 58, 171
Smith, J.H. 91
Smith, Jacob 40
Smith, James T. 152
Smith, Jane 229
Smith, John 29
Smith, Joseph 32
Smith, Leon W. 152, 173
Smith, Prof. Uriah 100
Smith, Randall 92
Smith, Rev. Bennett H. 40, 87, 88
Smith, Stephen 217
Smith, William 27
Smith, William D. 40
Smith, William L. 40, 172
Snapp, Charles Edward 188
Snapp, Hannah Elizabeth (Mrs. Samuel Harper) 187